STUDY GUIDE FOR
LIPSEY AND RAGAN

MICROECONOMICS

TENTH

William J. Furlong
University of Guelph

CANADIAN

E. Kenneth Grant
University of Guelph

EDITION

Addison
Wesley
Longman

Toronto

ISBN 0-201-66470-4

Acquisitions Editor: Dave Ward
Development Editor: Maurice Esses
Interior and Cover Design: Anthony Leung
Production Editor: Jennifer Therriault
Production Coordinator: Deborah Starks
Page Layout: Rena Potter

7 8 9   05 04 03

Printed and bound in Canada

CONTENTS

TO THE STUDENT

The content of this book tests and reinforces your understanding of the concepts and analytical techniques stressed in each chapter of *Economics*, 10th Canadian edition, by Professors Lipsey and Ragan. Our own teaching experience has led us to believe that students have the most trouble understanding technical information and applying theoretical concepts to particular situations. Consequently, most multiple choice questions and exercises in this *Study Guide* are technical and numerical in nature. We feel that policy issues and specific applications of theory to real-world examples are primarily the responsibility of the textbook. You will find excellent discussions of issues and policy applications in the body of the text, especially in the boxes titled Applying Economic Theory and Extensions in Theory.

Each chapter in this *Study Guide* corresponds to a text chapter and is divided into seven basic sections. The **LEARNING OBJECTIVES** restate the learning objectives from the textbook. The **CHAPTER OVERVIEW** provides a brief summary of the important concepts and issues addressed in the chapter. It serves to enable you to anticipate topics covered in the chapter.

The **CHAPTER REVIEW** section is divided into subsections corresponding to the main sections and topics covered in the text chapter. The introduction to each topic reminds you of study goals and also provides some suggestions and tips for effective study. The multiple choice questions in this section are primarily nontechnical in nature. They are intended to give you quick feedback on your understanding of the material in the chapter, and to identify any areas that might need further study.

In some ways the greatest reinforcement to learning economics comes from doing the questions in the **EXERCISES** section. Some of our colleagues have indicated that some students rarely attempt the questions in this section, since the format of many introductory economics examinations consists primarily of multiple choice questions. We urge you *not* to make this mistake. These questions often require you to demonstrate numerically and/or graphically the sense of what has been expressed verbally. You may wish to review the mathematical exercises in Chapter 2 before attempting the questions in subsequent chapters. In addition, you are often asked to explain your method of analysis and your results. The ability to solve problems and to communicate and interpret results are important goals in an introductory economics course. We firmly believe that these exercises will enhance your ability to do well on multiple choice questions! Do not be discouraged if you have difficulty with certain exercises. The most effective learning sometimes comes from struggling with a problem. The solutions to the exercises (given at the end of the chapter) provide answers as well as explanations and/or derivations. A full appreciation of the points involved can be achieved only after you have participated in lectures, carefully read the text, and thought your way through the concepts and issues. We have also provided some more challenging problems in the subsection entitled **EXTENSION EXERCISES**.

The **PRACTICE MULTIPLE CHOICE TEST** reviews your comprehension of the entire chapter. Unlike the Chapter Review section, the Practice Test focuses more on analytical concepts and numerical techniques. When you answer these, avoid the temptation to leap at the first answer that seems plausible. There is one best answer for each question. You should be able to explain why any other answer is not as satisfactory as the one you have chosen.

At the end of each chapter, we provide **SOLUTIONS** for all the questions and exercises. However, we caution that our answers are brief. Your instructors often require much fuller explanations on midterm and final examinations.

Acknowledgments

We would like to thank those individuals who provided invaluable assistance in the preparation of this tenth edition of the *Study Guide*: Mara Grant for her computing and research assistance, and Evi Adomait for her critical review of the manuscript. In addition, we would like to thank Professors Larry Smith of the University of Waterloo and Cheryl Jenkins of John Abbott College for their valuable input as reviewers of the manuscript.

Finally, we dedicate this edition of the *Study Guide* to our respective families: Sally, Dylan and Liam; and Baiba, Mark and Mara.

William J. Furlong

E. Kenneth Grant

PART ONE

WHAT IS ECONOMICS?

CHAPTER 1

ECONOMIC ISSUES AND CONCEPTS

 LEARNING OBJECTIVES

1. View the market economy as a self-organizing entity in which order emerges from a large number of decentralized decisions.

2. Understand the importance of scarcity, choice, and opportunity cost, and how all three concepts are illustrated by the production possibilities boundary.

3. Explain the circular flow of income and expenditure.

4. Recognize that there are several types of pure economic systems, but that all actual economies are mixed systems, having elements of free markets, tradition, and government intervention.

CHAPTER OVERVIEW

This introductory chapter discusses some of the major issues that confront all economies. An economy is endowed with scarce resources while human wants are unlimited. Choices must therefore be made regarding **production** and **consumption**. A central element of choice is the concept of **opportunity cost** which measures the benefit of the best foregone alternative when making a choice. An economy's opportunity cost in production is illustrated through its **production possibility boundary**. In addition to production and consumption choices, economies must also address how to avoid unemployment and how to ensure adequate growth over time. Different types of economic systems make these choices through different processes. This chapter reviews the main features of *command* and *market* economies.

Economists focus on three sets of decision makers in a market economy: individuals (consumers), firms (producers), and government. Consumers are assumed to have the objective of maximizing their well-being, while firms' decisions are made with the goal of maximizing their profits. (The objectives of government are discussed in later chapters). The interactions between households and firms through markets is best illustrated in a diagram depicting the circular flow of income and expenditure.

One of the great economic debates of the twentieth century concerns the relative merits of **centrally planned economies** (command economies) versus **free-market economies**. The pros and cons of each are reviewed. The central lesson from this chapter is that the market economy is a self-organizing entity that coordinates millions of decentralized, independent decisions made by self-interested consumers and producers.

CHAPTER REVIEW

The Complexity of the Modern Economy

Modern economies involve millions of economic decisions. The coordination of these decisions is the subject of this section. Coordination can occur through a centralized process—the command economy—or a decentralized process—the market economy. This section is intended to whet your appetite for study of "the economic problem."

1. One of the great insights of Adam Smith was that
    (a) modern economies require cental planning.
    (b) benevolence is the foundation of economic order.
    (c) the rich will get richer and the poor will get poorer in a market economy.
    (d) central coordination is required for any modern economy.
    (e) by acting in their own self-interest, people produce a spontaneous social order.

2. Which of the following is *not* one of the main characteristics of a market economy?
    (a) Individuals pursue their own self-interest.
    (b) Private property.
    (c) Sellers compete to sell their wares to potential buyers.
    (d) Firms seek to meet production quotas.
    (e) People respond to incentives.

3. The failure of central planning was caused by
    (a) production bottleneccks, shortages and gluts.
    (b) an incentive to produce goods of poor quality.
    (c) a failure to protect the environment.
    (d) poor incentives that didn't reward hard or efficient work.
    (e) all of the above.

Resources and Scarcity

After studying this section you should: understand the problem of scarcity, the need for choice and opportunity cost; be able to illustrate the relationship between scarcity, choice, and opportunity cost with a production possibility boundary (PPB); and, explain why growth in a country's productive capacity can be represented by an outward shift in its PPB and why unemployment of resources can be represented by points inside its PPB.

4. The fundamental problem of economics is, in short,
    (a) the existence of too many poor people.
    (b) the difficulty in finding jobs for all.
    (c) the scarcity of resources relative to wants.
    (d) constantly rising prices.
    (e) None of the above.

5. Scarcity is a problem that
    (a) more efficient production would eliminate.
    (b) is nonexistent in wealthy economies.
    (c) exists due to finite amounts of resources and unlimited human wants.
    (d) arises when productivity growth slows down.
    (e) exists in command economies but not market economies.

6. Which of the following is not an example of a factor of production?
    (a) a bulldozer.   (b) a mechanic.
    (c) a farm hand.   (d) a tractor.
    (e) a haircut.

7. Opportunity cost measures the
    (a) different opportunities for spending money.
    (b) the monetary cost of purchasing a commodity.
    (c) alternative means of producing output.
    (d) amount of one good forfeited to obtain a unit of another good.
    (e) market price of a good.

8. If a compact disc (CD) costs $10 and a cassette costs $5, then the opportunity cost of five CDs is
    (a) 50 cassettes.   (b) 10 cassettes.
    (c) 5 cassettes.   (d) 2 cassettes.
    (e) $25.

9. Assuming the alternative is employment, the opportunity cost of a university education is
    (a) tuition costs only.
    (b) tuition and book costs only.
    (c) the forgone salary only.
    (d) tuition costs plus book costs plus the forgone salary.
    (e) the direct costs of university such residence fees and books.

10. A downward-sloping production possibility boundary that is also a straight line implies
    (a) constant opportunity costs.   (b) zero opportunity costs.
    (c) only one good is produced.   (d) rising opportunity costs.
    (e) None of the above.

11. Which of the following causes an outward shift in the production possibility boundary?
    (a) A decrease in unemployment.
    (b) A loss in the productive capacity of agricultural acreage caused by a prolonged drought.
    (c) An increase in the productivity of all factors of production.
    (d) Shifting resources away from the production of one good towards another.
    (e) All of the above are correct.

12. Putting currently unemployed resources to work can be illustrated by
    (a) shifting the production possibility boundary outward.
    (b) a movement along a given production possibility boundary.
    (c) moving from a point on the boundary to a point outside it.
    (d) moving from a point inside the boundary to a point on it.
    (e) moving from a point on the boundary to a point inside it.

Who Makes the Choices and How?

This section will enable you to discuss the market interactions of consumers and producers through the circular flow of income and expenditure. You will also better understand how modern economies are based on the specialization and division of labour and appreciate the tendency towards economic globalization.

13. In economics, the term *market economy* refers to
    (a) institutions such as the Toronto Stock Exchange.
    (b) a place where buyers and sellers physically meet, such as at farmers' markets.
    (c) a society where individuals specialize in productive activities and enter voluntary trades.
    (d) a society where most economic decisions are made by marketing analysts.
    (e) an economy in which advertising is central to the marketing of goods and services.

14. In a barter economy, individuals
    (a) haggle over the price of each and every commodity.
    (b) trade goods directly for other goods.
    (c) use money to lubricate the flow of trades.
    (d) must each be a "jack of all trades."
    (e) All of the above.

15. The introduction of production lines where individuals specialize in performing specific tasks is known as
    (a) the division of labour.
    (b) the specialization of labour.
    (c) the market economy.
    (d) the advent of labour as a factor of production.
    (e) lean production.

16. Economic theory assumes that individuals
    (a) make choices to maximize their utility.
    (b) seek to maximize profits.
    (c) are the principal buyers of the factors of production.
    (d) specialize their labour.
    (e) are the sole buyers of goods and services in a market economy.

17. A central assumption in economic theory regarding firms is that they
    (a) are each owned by a single individual.
    (b) must be incorporated.
    (c) seek to maximize profits.
    (d) must all be making profits.
    (e) are the principal owners of the factors of production.

18. The two major types of markets in the circular flow of income are
    (a) public markets and private markets.
    (b) product markets and factor markets.
    (c) free markets and controlled markets.
    (d) markets for goods and markets for services.
    (e) regulated markets and open markets.

19. The circular flow of income and expenditure shows the flow of
    (a) goods and services from firms to consumers.
    (b) payments for goods and services from consumers to firms.
    (c) factor services from consumers to firms.
    (d) payments for factor services from firms to consumers.
    (e) All of the above.

20. The use of money when buying and selling makes
    (a) exchange easier.
    (b) barter more difficult.
    (c) specialization of labour more difficult.
    (d) opportunity cost lower.
    (e) the division of labour more difficult.

21. A barter economy
    (a) refers to the direct trading of goods.
    (b) does not require the use of money.
    (c) requires a double coincidence of wants.
    (d) involves costly searches for satisfactory exchanges.
    (e) All of the above.

22. Specialization of labour leads to a more efficient resource allocation because of
    (a) more self-sufficiency.
    (b) the use of barter.
    (c) the principle of comparative advantage.
    (d) a decrease in scarcity.
    (e) All of the above.

23. The market in which an individual sells his labour services is called a
    (a) product market.
    (b) factor market.
    (c) foreign-exchange market.
    (d) mixed market.
    (e) goods market.

Is There an Alternative to the Market Economy?

This section emphasizes the remarkable achievement of the market economy in providing order to millions of independent and decentralized decisions. After reading this section you will develop a better appreciation of the twentieth century's great economic debate on the relative merits of a market economy versus a command economy.

24. Which of the following would be a source of similarity among alternative types of economic systems?
    (a) Ownership of resources (private and public)
    (b) The process for making economic decisions.
    (c) The need to determine what is to be produced and how to produce it.
    (d) The role that tradition plays in determining production and employment.
    (e) Both (a) and (c).

25. In the Canadian economy, the majority of decisions on resource allocation are made by
    (a) consumers and firms through the price system.
    (b) the various levels of government.
    (c) negotiation between unions and firms.
    (d) business firms only.
    (e) legal contract.

26. Which countries are best characterized by public ownership of resources?
    (a) Canada and the United States.
    (b) Cuba and North Korea.
    (c) France and Germany.
    (d) Sweden and Norway.
    (e) (a), (c) and (d) are correct.

27. Complex economic plans for many sectors of the economy are most associated with
    (a) a market system.
    (b) the Canadian economy.
    (c) a command economy.
    (d) a feudal system.
    (e) a traditional economy.

EXERCISES

1. Four key economic problems are identified in Chapter 1:
   (1) What is produced and how? (resource allocation)
   (2) What is consumed and by whom? (distribution)
   (3) How much unemployment and inflation are there? (total employment and the price level)
   (4) How is productive capacity changing? (economic growth)

   After each of the following topics, identify which of the four types of economic problems applies. Use each classification only once.
   (a) Rises in oil prices during the 1970s encouraged a switch to alternative energy sources.
   (b) The standard of living in Canada, measured by real output per capita, has risen steadily over the past century.
   (c) Large harvests worldwide cause lower grain prices, thereby helping consumers but hurting farmers.
   (d) The unemployment rate has decreased in the late 1990s.

2. **The Production Possibility Boundary**

   The following exercise is designed to give you practice in constructing and interpreting a production possibility boundary.

   The economy of Islandia produces only two consumer goods, necklaces and fish. Only labour is required to produce both goods, and the economy's labour force is fixed at 100 workers. The table below indicates the daily outputs of *necklaces* and *fish* that can be produced with various quantities of labour.

Number of Workers	Daily Necklace Production	Number of Workers	Daily Fish Production (kilograms)
0	0	0	0
20	10.0	20	150
40	20.0	40	250
60	25.0	60	325
80	27.5	80	375
100	30.0	100	400

(a) Draw the production possibility curve for this economy, using the grid in Figure 1-1. (*Hint:* The labour force must always be fully employed along the production possibility boundary.)

Figure 1-1

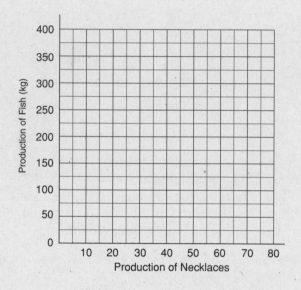

(b) What is the opportunity cost of producing the first 10 necklaces? What is the opportunity cost of producing the next 10 necklaces (i.e., from 10 to 20)? What happens to the opportunity cost of necklaces as their production is continuously increased?

(c) Suppose that actual production levels for a given period were 20 necklaces and 250 kilograms of fish. What can you infer from this information?

(d) Suppose a central planner in this economy were to call for an output combination of 35 necklaces and 150 kilograms of fish. Is this plan attainable? Explain.

(e) New technology is developed in necklace production, so that each worker can now produce double the daily amount indicated in the schedule. What happens to the production possibility curve? Draw the new curve on the grid. Can the planner's output combination in (d) now be met?

3. **Individual Choice and Opportunity Cost**

This exercise illustrates the concept of opportunity cost for an individual who faces fixed prices and has a fixed income.

Junior gets a weekly allowance of $10. He spends all of his allowance on only two commodities: video games at the arcade and chocolate bars. Assume that the price of a video game is 50 cents and the price of a chocolate bar is $1.

(a) Plot Junior's weekly attainable combinations of consumption.

Figure 1-2

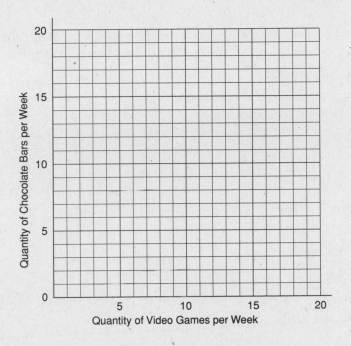

(b) Can Junior attain the following consumption combinations?
   (i)   15 video games and 2 chocolate bars
   (ii)   4 video games and 8 chocolate bars
   (iii) 7 video games and 7 chocolate bars

(c) What is the opportunity cost of Junior's first chocolate bar? his second? his third?

(d) By visual inspection of Junior's consumption possibility boundary, what could you say about his opportunity cost of consuming each of these commodities?

4. **The Opportunity Cost of University Education**

This question also explores opportunity cost but without diagrams.

Pamela, a first year student at Lakehead University, is considering whether or not to advance her studies by taking summer courses. Her monetary expenses would be: tuition, $1,000; books, $350; and living expenses, $1,500. Her alternative is to work as a lifeguard, which would earn her $3,500 for the summer. What is Pamela's opportunity cost of taking summer courses?

EXTENSION EXERCISES

E-1.   The following exercise addresses an economy's production possibilities algebraically. In the upcoming chapters you will be asked to make more use of algebra.

An economy's production possibility boundary is given by the mathematical expression $20 = 4A + B$, where A is the quantity of good A, and B is the quantity of good B.

(a)   If all resources in the economy were allocated to producing good A, what is the maximum level of production for this good? What is the maximum level of production for good B?

(b)   Suppose that the production of B is increased from 12 to 16 units and that the economy is producing at a point on the production possibility boundary. What is the opportunity cost per unit of good B? What is the opportunity cost per unit of good B if the production of this good was increased from 16 to 20?

(c)   In what way is this production possibility boundary different from that in Exercise 2 in terms of opportunity costs?

(d)   In what way does the combination of four units of good A and five units of good B represent the problem of scarcity?

E-2.   The following problem is conceptually challenging. The ability to solve it would reflect an excellent understanding of the production possibilities concept.

Consider the production possibilities for two totally dissimilar goods, such as apples and machine tools. Some resources are suitable for apple production and some for the production of machine tools. However, there is no possibility of shifting resources from one product to another. In this case, what does the production possibility boundary look like? Explain and show graphically.

PRACTICE MULTIPLE CHOICE TEST

1.   If the factors of production available to an economy were unlimited
   (a) the opportunity cost of producing more goods would be zero.
   (b) the price of cars would be infinitely high.
   (c) there would be no unemployment.
   (d) scarcity would become the most serious economic problem.
   (e) All of the above.

2. If a 12-month membership in a fitness club costs as much as tickets for 24 Montreal Expos baseball games, the opportunity cost of a one-month membership in the fitness club is
(a) 1/2 baseball game.   (b) 1 baseball game.
(c) 2 baseball games.   (d) 12 baseball games.
(e) 24 baseball games.

Questions 3 to 6 refer to Figure 1-3:

Figure 1-3

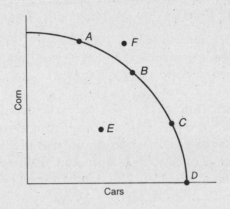

3. If a market economy is operating at point A,
(a) resources are fully employed.
(b) there is considerable unemployment.
(c) the central planner values corn more than cars.
(d) car producers are losing money due to low sales.
(e) the opportunity cost of producing cars is zero.

4. Point E represents a situation that
(a) is currently unattainable and can be expected to remain so.
(b) will be attainable only if there is economic growth.
(c) results from inefficient use of resources or failure to use all available resources.
(d) has a higher opportunity cost than points on the boundary itself.
(e) can never occur in a market economy.

5. With currently available resources, point F represents a situation that
(a) results if resources are not fully employed.
(b) can be achieved if consumers demand fewer cars than at point C.
(c) is currently attainable.
(d) can be achieved if all resources were allocated to the production of cars.
(e) None of the above.

6. Assuming the initial situation is point B, which one of the following represents a reallocation of resources away from car production to corn production?
(a) point A.   (b) point C.
(c) point E.   (d) point D.
(e) point F.

Questions 7 through 14 refer to the following schedule of production possibilities for combinations of corn and beef produced on a land tract of a given size and fertility.

Corn (bushels)	Beef (kilograms)
10,000	0
8,000	900
6,000	1,200
4,000	1,400
2,000	1,475
0	1,500

7. What would be the opportunity cost of producing 400 additional kilograms of beef if the current production were 8,000 bushels of corn and 500 kilograms of beef?
(a) 500 bushels of corn.
(b) 400 kilograms of beef.
(c) Zero.
(d) 900 kilograms of beef.
(e) None of the above.

8. What would be the opportunity cost of producing 2,000 additional bushels of corn if the current production were 6,000 bushels of corn and 1,200 kilograms of beef?
(a) 900 kilograms of beef.
(b) 1,200 kilograms of beef.
(c) 300 kilograms of beef.
(d) Zero.
(e) None of the above.

9. Which of the following combinations represent unattainable production levels with the current tract of land?
(a) 8,000 bushels of corn and 500 kilograms of beef.
(b) 8,000 bushels of corn and 1,200 kilograms of beef.
(c) 2,000 bushels of corn and 1,475 kilograms of beef.
(d) 6,000 bushels of corn and 1,300 kilograms of beef.
(e) Both (b) and (d).

10. What is the opportunity cost of increasing beef production from 1,475 kilograms to 1,500 kilograms?
(a) 2,000 bushels of corn.
(b) 50 bushels of corn.
(c) 25 kilograms of beef.
(d) 800 bushels of corn.
(e) None of the above.

11. The opportunity cost of increasing corn production from 4,000 to 6,000 bushels is
(a) the same as the opportunity cost of increasing corn production from 8,000 to 10,000.
(b) the same as the opportunity cost of increasing corn production from 2,000 to 4,000.
(c) 0.1 kilograms of beef per bushel of corn.
(d) 1,200 kilograms of beef.
(e) None of the above.

12. Which of the following events is likely to lead to an outward shift of the production possibility boundary?
(a) A reallocation of land use such that corn production increases from 6,000 bushels to 8,000 bushels while beef production decreases from 1,200 kilograms to 900 kilograms.
(b) Some of the land is lost due to a flood.
(c) Twenty of the existing acres are not used for either beef or corn production.
(d) Corn prices fall relative to beef prices.
(e) None of the above.

13. The opportunity cost per bushel of corn is 0.15 kilograms of beef when
    (a) corn production is increased from 8,000 to 10,000.
    (b) corn production is increased from 6,000 to 8,000.
    (c) corn production is increased from 4,000 to 6,000.
    (d) beef production is decreased from 1,500 to 1,475 kilograms.
    (e) None of the above.

14. Assuming that land is fully utilized and that corn production continually increases by 2,000 bushels, the opportunity cost in terms of beef production
    (a) increases.   (b) decreases.
    (c) is zero.   (d) remains constant.
    (e) is undefined.

15. In a command economy, where to produce on the production possibility boundary is determined by
    (a) the preferences of consumers, who spend their income accordingly.
    (b) a central plan established by the government.
    (c) traditional patterns of spending that change little from year to year.
    (d) the preferences of workers, who vote to indicate their preferences.
    (e) relative prices of goods.

16. Decisions on resource allocation are
    (a) necessary only in centrally planned economies.
    (b) made by central planners in traditional economies.
    (c) necessary only in economies that are not industrialized.
    (d) decentralized, but coordinated by the price system, in market economies.
    (e) primarily determined by traditional customs in market economies.

17. In a market economy, the allocation of resources is determined by
    (a) the government and its marketing boards.
    (b) the various stock exchanges in the country.
    (c) a central planning agency.
    (d) the millions of independent decisions made by individual consumers and firms.
    (e) the sobering discussions at the annual convention of the Canadian Economics Association.

18. The "invisible hand"
    (a) can only be seen by economists.
    (b) refers to excessive government taxation.
    (c) refers to a market economy's price system.
    (d) refers to the central planning agency of a command economy.
    (e) refers to hidden taxes.

SOLUTIONS

Chapter Review

1.(e) 2.(d) 3.(e) 4.(c) 5.(c) 6.(e) 7.(d) 8.(b) 9.(d) 10.(a) 11.(c) 12.(d) 13.(c) 14.(b) 15.(a) 16.(a) 17.(c) 18.(b) 19.(e) 20.(a) 21.(e) 22.(c) 23.(b) 24.(c) 25.(a) 26.(b) 27.(c)

Exercises

1. (a) 1 (b) 4 (c) 2 (d) 3

2. (a) **Figure 1-4**

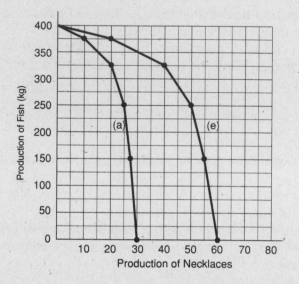

(b) 25 kilograms of fish (i.e., fish production decreases from 400 to 375). 50 kilograms of fish. The opportunity cost of producing necklaces is increasing — increasing necklace production by yet another 10 units from 20 to 30 would imply forgoing an additional 325 kilograms of fish.

(c) This production combination lies inside the production possibility boundary, so some workers are unemployed or inefficiently used.

(d) This combination is outside the production possibility boundary and is therefore unattainable with current resources and technology.

(e) The production possibility boundary shifts to the right as graphed in (a). The planner's output combination is now attainable but is inside the new boundary, implying that if it were indeed achieved, the economy would be inefficiently using its resources.

3. (a) **Figure 1-5**

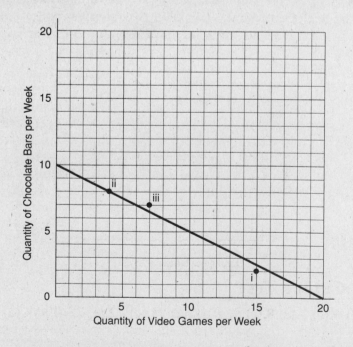

(b) (i) Yes, this combination lies inside his consumption possibility and is therefore affordable with $10.

(ii) Yes, this combination is on his consumption possibility boundary and therefore costs exactly $10.

(iii) No, this combination lies outside his consumption possibility boundary and therefore costs more than a $10 allowance permits.

(c) To purchase the first chocolate bar, Junior must pay $1, which could have been used to purchase two video games. Thus the opportunity cost of the first chocolate bar is two video games. The opportunity cost of the second and third bars is also two video games each.

(d) Since the consumption possibility boundary is linear (i.e., a straight line), the opportunity cost is constant.

4. $4,850. Living expenses would have to be incurred regardless of her decision.

Extension Exercises

E-1. (a) If all resources were allocated to the production of good A, there would be no production of good B. Hence, according to the mathematical expression, the maximum production of good A is five units. If all resources were used to produce good B, then B = 20, and the production of good A is zero.

(b) The increase from 12 to 16 units of B requires a loss in production of good A of one (from two to one). An increase in B from 16 to 20 requires a loss in production of good A of one (from one to zero). Therefore, the opportunity cost *per unit* of good B is 0.25 units of A in each case.

(c) The opportunity cost is constant, whereas it was increasing for Exercise 2 above.

(d) According to the equation, four units of A and four units of B are possible. The combination of four units of A and five units of B is not feasible and indicates that more resources are required than are currently available.

E-2. When all resources suitable to apple production are employed, the resulting apple output is A' in Figure 1-6. When all resources suitable to machine tool production are employed, the resulting quantity of machine tools is M'. Since there is no possibility of shifting resources between these two outputs, the production possibility boundary is simply the point corresponding to the coordinates (A', M'). Any combination of apples and machine tools either inside or on the dashed lines implies unemployed or inefficiently used resources.

Figure 1-6

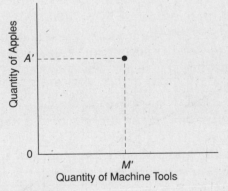

Practice Multiple Choice Test

1.(a) 2.(c) 3.(a) 4.(c) 5.(e) 6.(a) 7.(c) 8.(c) 9.(e) 10.(a) 11.(c) 12.(e) 13.(b) 14.(a) 15.(b) 16.(d) 17.(d) 18.(c)

CHAPTER 2

HOW ECONOMISTS WORK

LEARNING OBJECTIVES

1 Recognize the difference between positive and normative statements.

2 Understand how theorizing and model-building help economists think about the economy.

3 Explain the interaction between economic theories and empirical observations.

4 Understand why testing theories about human behaviour usually requires studying large numbers of individuals.

5 Recognize several types of economic data, including index numbers, time-series and cross-section data, and scatter diagrams.

6 Understand that economic theories involve relations between variables and that such relations can be expressed in words, equations, or graphs.

7 Recognize that the slope of a relation between X and Y is interpreted as the marginal response in Y to a unit change in X.

CHAPTER OVERVIEW

The previous chapter provided an overview of the types of issues economists consider. This chapter presents some important distinctions made by economists and discusses the approaches used to analyze economic questions.

Economists evaluate *hypotheses* that purport to explain economic behaviour. An important distinction is made between **positive statements** which concern what is, was or will be, and **normative statements** which are judgments of what should be done. Disagreements over positive statements are appropriately settled by an appeal to the facts (i.e., they are testable). Disagreements over normative statements cannot be settled in this way.

Theories are designed to give meaning to observed sequences of events. A theory typically consists of definitions of **variables** and assumptions about how things behave. Any theory has certain logical implications that must hold if the theory is not to be rejected. These are the theory's predictions or hypotheses. Theories are tested by checking their predictions against the evidence. In economics the evidence is most often comprised of data drawn from the real world.

The relationships among variables in economic theories are usually presented in tables, graphs or equations. These provide compact summaries of a large number of data observations, and play an important role in economic modelling.

CHAPTER REVIEW

Positive and Normative Advice

The objective of this section is to distinguish between positive and normative statements. Positive statements are assertions of fact that can, in principle, be tested. On the other hand, normative statements cannot be tested as they are value judgements.

1. Normative statements
   (a) concern an individual's beliefs in what ought to be.
   (b) are based on value judgments.
   (c) cannot be subjected to empirical scrutiny.
   (d) cannot be deduced from positive statements.
   (e) All of the above.

2. "Capital punishment deters crime" is an example of a
   (a) positive statement.   (b) value judgment.
   (c) normative statement.   (d) analytic statement.
   (e) untestable statement.

3. "Capital punishment should be reintroduced in Canada" is an example of a
   (a) positive statement.   (b) normative statement.
   (c) analytic statement.   (d) testable hypothesis.
   (e) None of the above.

Economic Theories and Models

This section contains a nontechnical discussion of the components of a theory and the role of models. After reading this section you should understand the basic structure of economic theories; the roles of variables, definitions, assumptions, and predictions in developing theories, and the purpose and usefulness of economic modelling.

4. Economic predictions are intended to
   (a) forecast the behaviour of each consumer.
   (b) forecast the behaviour of groups of individuals.
   (c) test normative statements.
   (d) anticipate the irrational behaviour of certain odd individuals.
   (e) Both (b) and (c) are correct.

5. If the assumptions imposed in an economic theory are unrealistic, then the theory
   (a) will always be refuted by the evidence.
   (b) is incorrect and should be rejected.
   (c) will not predict well and should be rejected.
   (d) will require more complex statistical techniques for testing.
   (e) may nonetheless predict better than any alternative theory.

6. The role of assumptions in theory is to
   (a) represent the world accurately.
   (b) abstract from reality.
   (c) avoid simplifications of the real world.
   (d) ensure that the theory considers all features of reality, no matter how minor.
   (e) None of the above.

7. A theory may contain all *but* which of the following?
   (a) Predictions about behaviour that are deduced from the assumptions.
   (b) A set of assumptions defining the conditions under which the theory is operative.
   (c) Hypotheses about how the world behaves.
   (d) A normative statement expressed as a functional relation.
   (e) Hypothesized relationships among variables.

Testing Theories

Economic theories are not intended to predict the behaviour of specific individuals. Rather, they attempt to predict "average" or "typical" behaviour in a group of individuals. The law of large numbers is essential to this objective; it suggests that random or erratic behaviours will tend to offset themselves. Although there tends to be broad agreement among economists on many issues, there are nonetheless some dissenting opinions and views. It is useful to recognize the causes of disagreement.

8. The "law" of large numbers basically says that
   (a) the greater the number of observations, the greater the sum of each variable.
   (b) measuring error increases with the number of observations.
   (c) a few observations are just as accurate as a large number of observations.
   (d) erratic behaviour by individuals tends to offset itself in a large group.
   (e) the greater the number of observations, the greater is the potential for prediction errors.

9. In measuring the area of a room, the "law" of large numbers implies that
   (a) more people will make small errors than large ones.
   (b) roughly the same number of people will understate the area as overstate it.
   (c) the average error of all individuals is approximately zero.
   (d) the more people taking the measurement, the smaller is the average error.
   (e) All of the above.

10. The statement that the quantity produced of a commodity and its price are positively related is
    (a) an assumption economists usually make.
    (b) a testable hypothesis.
    (c) a normative statement.
    (d) not testable as currently worded.
    (e) a value judgement.

11. The theory that extra-terrestrials exist and visit Earth in flying saucers
    (a) has been disproved by scientific evidence.
    (b) is inconsistent with scientific observation.
    (c) can never be disproved.
    (d) has been refuted.
    (e) Both (b) and (c).

12. Which of the following is not a possible source of disagreement among economists?
    (a) Use of different benchmarks.
    (b) Failure to distinguish between theories and models.
    (c) Failure to distinguish between short-term and long-term consequences. ×
    (d) Different values among economists.
    (e) Failure to acknowledge the extent of their ignorance. ×

Economic Data

Economists use data drawn from real world observations to test their theories. This section reviews two ways in which data can be examined: index numbers and graphs.

13. If a particular index number in 1999 is 159 and the base year is 1996, then the index shows an increase of
    (a) 5.9 percent between 1996 and 1999.
    (b) 59 percent between 1996 and 1999.
    (c) 159 percent between 1996 and 1999.
    (d) 0.59 percent between 1996 and 1999.
    (e) an indeterminable amount, since the value of the index in the base year is unknown.

14. Suppose the Consumer Price Index was 160 last month and rose by 2 percent over the base year during the current month. The price index for the current month is
    (a) 162.0.
    (b) 163.2
    (c) 160.02.
    (d) 160.2.
    (e) 80.0.

15. An unweighted index of prices for some group of goods
    (a) assigns all prices a weight of zero.
    (b) assigns all prices an equal weight.
    (c) merely calculates the sum of prices in the group.
    (d) assigns each price a weight according to its relative importance in the group.
    (e) adjusts each price based upon that good's weight in the group.

16. Which of the following is an example of cross-sectional data?
    (a) Annual unemployment rates for Canada.
    (b) Vancouver housing prices for the period 1950–1999.
    (c) Last year's crime rates for all Canadian cities.
    (d) A series of this year's daily interest rates.
    (e) None of the above.

17. Observations drawn repeatedly from successive months are
    (a) cross-sectional data.
    (b) time-series data.
    (c) unweighted data.
    (d) logarithmic data.
    (e) scattered data.

18. A scatter diagram can be used to plot
    (a) time-series data, but not cross-sectional data.
    (b) cross-sectional data, but not time-series data.
    (c) neither cross-sectional nor time-series data.
    (d) either cross-sectional or time-series data.
    (e) data in which time or location is a variable on one of the axis.

Graphing Economic Theories

Relationships between economic variables are often expressed algebraically and then displayed graphically. This is an important section that reviews the algebraic and graphical tools that are required for this course. After completing this section, you should be comfortable reading functional relationships, translating equations into graphs and interpreting graphs.

19. The slope of a straight line is
    (a) always positive.
    (b) calculated by dividing the variable measured on the horizontal axis by that measured on the vertical axis.
    (c) zero.
    (d) constant.
    (e) increasing or decreasing, depending upon whether the slope is positive or negative, respectively.

20. Suppose that economic analysis estimates the following relationship between imports (IM) and national income (Y): $IM = 100 + 0.15Y$. This means that
    (a) imports are negatively related to national income.
    (b) when national income is zero, imports are zero.
    (c) imports are 15 percent of national income.
    (d) imports are 15 times greater than national income.
    (e) other things remaining constant, for every increase of $1 in national income, imports will rise by 15 cents.

EXERCISES

1. **Positive and Normative Statements**

   After each phrase, write P or N to indicate whether a positive or a normative statement is being described.
   (a) A statement of fact that is actually wrong. _____
   (b) A value judgment. _____
   (c) A prediction that an event will happen. _____
   (d) A statement about what the author thinks ought to be. _____
   (e) A statement that can be tested by evidence. _____
   (f) A value judgment based on evidence known to be correct. _____
   (g) A hurricane forecast. _____
   (h) An opinion survey that indicates a majority of Canadians believe taxes ought to be reduced. _____

2. **Endogenous and Exogenous Variables**

In this exercise you are required to distinguish between cause and effect. In each of the following statements, classify the italicized variables as being endogenous (N) or exogenous (X).
(a) *Market price and equilibrium quantity* of a commodity are determined by demand and supply. _____
(b) The number of sailboats sold annually is a function of *national income*. _____
(c) The *condition of forest ecosystems* can be affected by regional air pollutants. _____
(d) The quantity of housing services purchased is determined by the *relative price of housing, income, and housing characteristics*. _____
(e) Other things being equal, *consumer expenditures* are negatively related to interest rates.
_____

3. **A University Price Index**

This exercise asks you to construct a price index for an item that is of concern to most students, the out-of-pocket cost of attending university. You may want to refer to Tables 2-2 and 2-3 of the text to review index numbers before attempting this exercise.

The following table presents data on three components of the out-of-pocket expenses for attending university: tuition, residence and meals. (Recall from the discussion in Applying Economic Concepts 1-1 of the text that these three do not represent the opportunity cost of a university education.) Tuition here refers to the annual fees for a B.A. degree; residence refers to the annual fee for a double occupancy room; and, food is the annual cost of a full meal plan in residence. The data are drawn from the University of Guelph for the years 1989–99, but are representative of all Ontario universities.

Year	Tuition	Residence	Food
1989–90	$1,374	$1,710	$1,660
1990–91	1,518	1,910	1,760
1991–92	1,638	2,050	2,000
1992–93	1,770	2,192	2,250
1993–94	1,894	2,352	2,400
1994–95	2,026	2,462	2,520
1995–96	2,228	2,462	2,600
1996–97	2,451	2,582	2,660
1997–98	2,930	2,672	2,670
1998–99	3,223	2,672	2,760

Source: University of Guelph Undergraduate Calendar (1989–1999).

(a) Using 1989–90 as the base year, construct a price index for each of the three expense items. (Note: Those students familiar with a spreadsheet software may wish to use it in answering this question).

(b) Which of these three items increased the most in percentage terms for the period 1989–90 to 1990–91? the period 1989–90 to 1998–99?

(c) Construct an unweighted (i.e., equal weight) index for all three fees.

(d) Use the proportion of each item's share of total cost in the base year, 1989–90, to construct a weighted index of all three fees.

(e) If you were president of the Student Council which index would you use when arguing against fee increases? If you were president of the university, which index would you use to support fee increases? Explain.

4. **Linear Relationships**

This exercise gives you practice in interpreting and graphing linear relationships.

Suppose that an economist hypothesizes that the annual quantity demanded of a specific manufacturer's personal computers (Q^D) is determined by the price of the computer (P) and the average income of consumers (Y). The specific functional relationship among these three variables is hypothesized to be the expression $Q^D = Y - 4P$.

(a) Which of these variables are endogenous and which are exogenous?

(b) What does the minus sign before the term $4P$ imply about the relationship between Q^D and P? What does the implicit positive sign before the term Y imply about the relationship between income and quantity demanded?

(c) Suppose for the moment that average income equals $8,000. Write a simplified expression for the demand relationship.

(d) Assuming that $Y = 8,000$, calculate the values of Q^D when $P = 0$, $P = \$500$, $P = \$1,000$, and $P = \$2,000$.

(e) Plot the relationship between P and Q^D (assuming $Y = \$8,000$) on the graph in Figure 2-1. Indicate the intercept value on each axis.

Figure 2-1

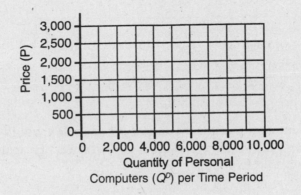

(f) Calculate the slope of this relationship.

(g) Assuming that $Y = \$8,000$, calculate the change in the quantity demanded when the price increases from $1,000 to $2,000. Do the same for a price increase from $500 to $2,000. Call the change in the quantity demanded ΔQ^D and the change in the price ΔP. Determine the ratio $\Delta Q^D / \Delta P$. Is this ratio constant?

(h) Now suppose that evidence indicates that in subsequent time periods, the average income of consumers changes to $9,000 per month. Plot the new relationship between P and Q^D. What are the intercept values and the slope?

EXTENSION EXERCISES

The following exercises review two methods for solving a system of linear equations. The techniques reviewed here are used throughout the course. Although they are not required until Chapter 3 of the text when the demand and supply model is presented, it is useful to review them now while we are covering linear relationships. The first exercise works through the diagrammatic solution method while the next uses the algebraic approach. Students should be competent in using both solution techniques.

E-1.   Consider the following two linear equations:

$$(1)\ N_1 = 5 + 0.5X$$

$$(2)\ N_2 = 55 - 0.5X$$

(a) Complete the following table using the N_1 column for equation 1 and the N_2 column for equation 2.

X	N_1	N_2	N_3
10	_____	_____	_____
20	_____	_____	_____
30	_____	_____	_____
40	_____	_____	_____
50	_____	_____	_____
60	_____	_____	_____

(b) Plot the relationships between X and N_1 and N_2 in the graph provided below.

Figure 2-2

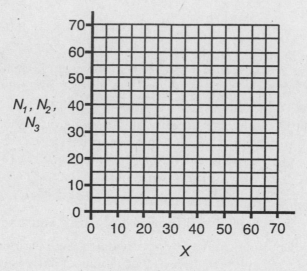

(i) The linear curve relating variables X and N_1 has a (positive/negative) _____ slope of _____.

(ii) The linear curve relating variables X and N_2 has a (positive/negative) _____ slope of _____.

(c) These equations are said to be solved when $N_1 = N_2$—call this the solution value N. At what value of X does $N_1 = N_2$? What are the corresponding values of N and X?

(d) Assume that the constant term in equation 1 increases from 5 to 25. Complete column N_3 in (a), and plot the new relationship on the graph in (b). The curve in equation (1) has shifted _____. The slope is _____.

(e) What is the new solution to this system of equations?

E-2. The following exercise reviews the procedure for solving a system of simultaneous equations by algebraic methods. This approach is extremely useful in both micro and macro chapters of this Study Guide. It is an alternative to diagrammatic solutions that were reviewed above in question E-1.

Consider two equations describing the relationships between two variables x and y

$$x_1 = a + by, \tag{1}$$

$$x_2 = c - dy. \tag{2}$$

where a, b, c and d are positive constants. The objective is to find values of x and y for which both equations are satisfied. First, note that there are two equations and three unknowns—the unknowns are the solution values to x_1, x_2 and y. Thus, if a unique solution exists, there is a missing equation. The missing equation to this system simply states that in the solution:

$$x_1 = x_2 \tag{3}$$

The solution procedure requires elimination of unknowns and equations by means of substitution. Each substitution must reduce the system by both an unknown and an equation, until all that remains is a single unknown in a single equation.

(a) Eliminate equation (1) and x_1 from the system. Count the remaining equations and unknowns.

(b) Now eliminate equation (2) and x_2 from the system. Count the remaining equations and unknowns.

(c) Solve for the solution value of y.

(d) Use the solution value of y to obtain solution values for x_1 and x_2.

(e) Often the constants in equations (1) and (2) are numerical. For example, suppose a = 200, b = 2, c = 400 and d = 3. Repeat questions (a) to (d) to solve for the numerical values of x and y.

PRACTICE MULTIPLE CHOICE TEST

1. Which of the following is the best example of a positive statement?
   (a) Equal distribution of national income is a desirable goal for society.
   (b) Foreign ownership is undesirable for Canada and should therefore be eliminated.
   (c) Although free trade may cause some Canadians to lose their jobs, it will significantly increase the income of the average Canadian.
   (d) Taxes should be lowered.
   (e) Deficit reduction should be the government's priority.

2. With respect to agriculture, weather is an example of
   (a) an exogenous factor of production.　(b) an endogenous input.
   (c) a dependent variable.　(d) an induced input variable.
   (e) a positive statement.

3. If annual per capita consumption expenditure decreases as average annual income decreases, these two variables are then said to be
   (a) negatively related.　(b) positively related.
   (c) randomly related.　(d) independent of each other.
   (e) None of the above.

4. Which of the following statements about economic theories is most appropriate?
   (a) The most reliable test of a theory is the realism of its assumptions.
   (b) The best kind of theory is worded so that it can pass any test to which it is applied.
   (c) The most important thing about the scientific approach is that it uses mathematics and diagrams.
   (d) We expect our theories to hold only with some margin of error.
   (e) Economic theories are based upon normative statements, and can therefore never be refuted.

5. A scientific prediction is a conditional statement because it
   (a) takes the form "if that occurs, then this will result."
   (b) is conditional on being correct.
   (c) is impossible to test.
   (d) is true in theory but not in practice.
   (e) is derived from normative statements.

6. The term "economic model" may refer to
   (a) an application of a general theory in a specific context.
   (b) a specific quantitative formulation of a theory.
   (c) a particular theory or subset of theories in economics.
   (d) an illustrative abstraction of some real world phenomenon.
   (e) All of the above.

7. Economic hypotheses are generally accepted only when
   (a) the evidence indicates that they are true with a high degree of probability.
   (b) they have been proved beyond a reasonable doubt.
   (c) they have been established with certainty.
   (d) the evidence supports the hypotheses in all cases.
   (e) Both (c) and (d) are correct.

8. Suppose that a scatter diagram indicates that imports are, on average, positively related to national income over time. If in one year imports fall when national income increases, the observation
   (a) disproves the positive relationship between the two variables.
   (b) suggests that other factors also influence the quantity of imports.
   (c) proves a negative relationship between the two variables.
   (d) suggests that a measurement error has necessarily been made.
   (e) suggests that the two variables are independent of each other.

9. Which of the following equations is consistent with the hypothesis that federal income tax payments (T) are positively related to family income (Y) and negatively related to family size (F)?
   (a) $T = -733 + 0.19Y + 344F.$ (b) $T = -733 - 0.19Y - 344F.$
   (c) $T = -733 + 0.19Y - 344F.$ (d) $T = +733 - 0.19Y + 344F.$
   (e) None of the above.

Use the following graph to answer questions 10 to 12:

Figure 2-3

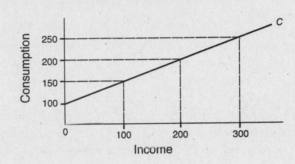

10. In the graph above, the slope of the line showing the relationship between consumption and income is
    (a) –2.   (b) 0.5.
    (c) 2.   (d) 2.5.
    (e) 150.

11. According to the graph above, when an individual has no income, consumption is
    (a) –200.   (b) –100.
    (c) 0.   (d) 100.
    (e) None of the above.

12. The line showing the relationship between consumption (C) and income (Y) can be represented mathematically as:
    (a) $C = 0.5Y.$ (b) $C = 2Y.$
    (c) $C = 100 + 0.5Y.$ (d) $C = 100 + 2Y.$
    (e) $C = -100 + Y.$

Questions 13 to 17 refer to the following graph which depicts the relationship between performance on an economics examination and hours spent studying late the night before the early morning exam!

Figure 2-4

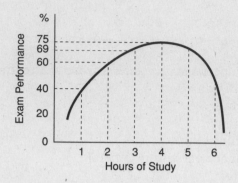

13. Exam performance is a(n) _____ variable and hours of study is a(n) _____ variable.
    (a) nonlinear; nonlinear.
    (b) marginal; contour.
    (c) exogenous; endogenous.
    (d) endogenous; exogenous.
    (e) slope; marginal.

14. The slope of this curve between 1 and 2 hours of study is calculated by
    (a) 60/2.
    (b) (60–30)/2.
    (c) (60–40)/2.
    (d) (60–40)/(2–1).
    (e) (60+40)/(2+1)

15. The marginal return to the third hour of study is
    (a) 69%.
    (b) 9%.
    (c) 23%.
    (d) 6%.
    (e) 3%.

16. As study time increases from 1 hour to 4 hours, the marginal return to study is _____ and the total return is _____.
    (a) diminishing; increasing.
    (b) increasing; increasing.
    (c) diminishing; diminishing.
    (d) increasing; diminishing.
    (e) diminishing; zero.

17. At four hours of study, the marginal return to a minute of study more or less is (approximately)
    (a) 75%.
    (b) increasing.
    (c) diminishing.
    (d) zero.
    (e) cannot be determined with information provided.

18. Due to a lack of sleep, exam performance suffers from a fifth and sixth hour of study. For this range of study hours, one can say
    (a) total returns are diminishing.
    (b) marginal returns are negative.
    (c) marginal returns are diminishing.
    (d) the slope of the performance curve is negative.
    (e) All of the above are correct.

SOLUTIONS

Multiple-Choice Questions

1.(e) 2.(a) 3.(b) 4.(b) 5.(e) 6.(b) 7.(d) 8.(d) 9.(e) 10.(b) 11.(e) 12.(b) 13.(b) 14.(a) 15.(b) 16.(c) 17.(b) 18.(d) 19.(d) 20.(e)

Exercises

1. (a) P (b) N (c) P (d) N (e) P (f) N (g) P (h) N.

2. (a) N (b) X (c) N (d) X (e) N

3.

Year	Tuition Index	Residence Index	Food Index
1989–90	100	100	100
1990–91	110	112	106
1991–92	119	120	120
1992–93	129	128	136
1993–94	138	138	145
1994–95	147	144	152
1995–96	162	144	157
1996–97	178	151	160
1997–98	213	156	161
1998–99	235	156	166

(b) The cost of residence increased by 12% for the period 1989–90, while that of tuition and food increased by 10% and 6%, respectively. During the decade 1989–1999, the fees for tuition, residence and food increased 135%, 56%, and 66%, respectively.

(c) The unweighted index is obtained by taking the average of the three indexes. For example, the unweighted index for 1998–99 is 186 = (235 + 156 + 166)/3.

Year	Unweighted Index	Weighted Index
1989–90	100	100
1990–91	109	109
1991–92	120	120
1992–93	131	131
1993–94	140	140
1994–95	148	148
1995–96	154	154
1996–97	163	162
1997–98	177	174
1998–99	186	182

(d) In 1989-90 the total fee was $4,744 = $1,374 + $1,710 + $1,660. Thus, the weights are: tuition, 0.29 = 1,374/4,744; residence, 0.36 = 1,710/4,744, and; food, 0.35 = 1,660/4,744. The weighted index is a weighted average of the indexes for each year. For example, in 1998–99, the weighted index is 182 = 0.29(235) + 0.36(156) + 0.35(166). See the table above for other years.

(e) The president of the Student Council would cite the tuition price index which shows a 135% increase over the decade to argue that fees have already increased enough. The university president would cite the weighted index to show that the cost of a university education has only increased 82% over the decade to justify higher fees. The difference is due to the small weight tuition has in the base year (0.29), relative to its weight in the most recent academic year (0.37). Note that tuition only became the most costly of the three items in 1997–98.

4. (a) Q^D and P are determined in the market for personal computers; they are endogenous variables. Average income, which is determined in many other markets, is not influenced to any significant extent by the computer market; it is exogenous to the market for computers.

(b) Q^D and P are negatively related; as P increases, Q^D falls. Q^D and Y are positively related; as Y increases, Q^D increases.

(c) The equation becomes $Q^D = 8,000 - 4P$.

(d) $Q^D = 8000;\ 6,000;\ 4,000;\ 0$.

(e) As shown in Figure 2-5, the intercept on the P axis is 2,000, and the intercept on the Q^D axis is 8,000.

Figure 2-5

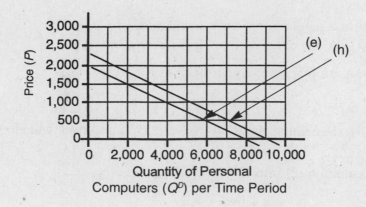

(f) The slope is calculated as $\Delta P/\Delta Q^D$; for example, –2,000/8,000 = –1/4.

(g) The change in quantity demanded is -4,000 when P increases from 1,000 to 2,000. When P increases from 500 to 2,000, quantity demanded falls by 6,000. In both cases the ratio $\Delta Q^D/\Delta P$ is equal to –4. It is the inverse of the slope.

(h) The intercept on the P axis is $2,250, and the intercept on the Q^D axis is 9,000. The slope remains –1/4. See Figure 2-5 above.

Extension Exercises

E-1.   (a)

X	N_1	N_2	N_3
10	10	50	30
20	15	45	35
30	20	40	40
40	25	35	45
50	30	30	50
60	35	25	55

(b)

Figure 2-6

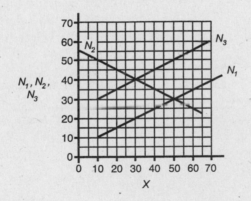

(i)   positive; +1/2
(ii)   negative; –1/2

(c) $N_1 = N_2$ when the two curves intersect. $N = 30$ and $X = 50$ solves this system of equations.

(d)   leftward (or equivalently, upward); unchanged at +1/2.

(e) $N = 40$ and $X = 30$.

E-2.   (a)   Substitute equation (1) into equation (3) for x_1. This yields

$$a + by = x_2. \tag{3'}$$

There are two remaining equations, (2) and (3'), and two remaining unknowns, x_2 and y.

(b)   Substitute equation (2) into (3') for x_2. This yields

$$a + by = c - dy. \tag{3''}$$

There is only one equation remaining (3′) and only one unknown y.

(c) Rearranging terms in (3″) yields: $by + dy = c - a$, or equivalently, $(b + d)y = c - a$. Division by $(b + d)$ yields $y^* = (c - a)/(b + d)$ which is the solution value for y.

(d) Substitute y^* into equation (1), which yields

$$x_1{}^* = a + b(c - a)/(b + d)$$

which simplifies to $x_1 = (ad + bc)/(b + d)$. In view of equation (3), this is also the solution value to $x_2{}^*$.

(e) $x_1 = x_2 = x = 280$ and $y = 40$.

Practice Multiple Choice Test

1.(c) 2.(a) 3.(b) 4:(d) 5.(a) 6.(e) 7.(a) 8.(b) 9.(c) 10.(b) 11.(d) 12.(c) 13.(d) 14.(d) 15.(b) 16.(a) 17.(d) 18.(e)

PART TWO

AN INTRODUCTION TO DEMAND AND SUPPLY

CHAPTER 3

DEMAND, SUPPLY,
AND PRICE

LO *LEARNING OBJECTIVES*

1   Understand what determines "quantity demanded," the amount of some product that households want to purchase.

2   Distinguish between a shift in a demand curve and a movement along a demand curve.

3   Understand what determines "quantity supplied," the amount of some product that firms want to sell.

4   Distinguish between a shift in a supply curve and a movement along a supply curve.

5   Recognize the forces that drive market price to equilibrium.

6   Understand the four "laws" of demand and supply.

CHAPTER OVERVIEW

This chapter introduces you to the economic model of **demand** and **supply**, which describes how the interactions of buyers and sellers determine the **equilibrium price** and quantity exchanged in the markets for goods and services.

A downward-sloping **demand curve** shows the relationship between price and **quantity demanded**. From a buyer's perspective, the lower the (relative) price of a product, the more attractive it is to purchase. A **supply curve** shows the relationship between price and **quantity supplied**. From a seller's perspective, higher relative prices for a product make it more attractive to sell. If quantity supplied does not equal quantity demanded, the model predicts changes in price until the plans of buyers and sellers are satisfied at the equilibrium price.

Using the method of **comparative statics**, the effects of a shift in either demand or supply can be determined. The equilibrium price and quantity exchanged respond to changes in the determinants of demand (income, tastes, population, and prices of substitutes or complements) or supply (prices of inputs, technology, and the number of firms). These responses are called the "laws" of demand and supply.

CHAPTER REVIEW

Demand

The ability to distinguish between the concepts of quantity demanded and demand is an important objective in this section. Remember that quantity demanded refers to the amount of a product consumers desire to purchase at a specific price, whereas demand refers to the entire relationship between price and quantity demanded. It is of central importance that the student understand when there is a *movement along* a demand curve and when there is a *shift* in the demand curve. An understanding of the causes of shifts in demand curves is crucial to this distinction.

1. The term quantity demanded refers to the
   (a) amount of a good that consumers are willing to purchase at some price during some given time period.
   (b) amount of some good that consumers would purchase if they only had the income to afford it.
   (c) amount of a good that is actually purchased during a given time period.
   (d) minimum amount of a good that consumers require and demand for survival.
   (e) amount of a good that consumers are willing to purchase regardless of price.

2. An increase in quantity demanded refers to
   (a) rightward shifts in the demand curve only.
   (b) a movement up along a demand curve.
   (c) a greater willingness to purchase at each price.
   (d) an increase in actual purchases.
   (e) a movement down along a demand curve.

3. The demand curve and the demand schedule
   (a) each reflect the relationship between quantity demanded and price, *ceteris paribus*.
   (b) are both incomplete in that neither can incorporate the impact of changes in income or tastes.
   (c) are constructed on the assumption that price is held constant.
   (d) illustrate that in economic analysis, only two variables are taken into account at any one time.
   (e) characterize the relationship between price and actual purchases.

4. An increase in demand means that
   (a) consumers actually buy more of the good.
   (b) at each price, consumers desire a greater quantity.
   (c) consumers' tastes have necessarily changed.
   (d) price has decreased.
   (e) All of the above are correct.

5. If goods A and B are complements, an increase in the price of good A will lead to
   (a) an increase in the price of good B.
   (b) a decrease in the quantity demanded of good B.
   (c) a decrease in demand for good B.
   (d) no change in demand for good B because A and B are not substitutes.
   (e) a rightward shift in the demand for good B.

6. Increased public awareness of the adverse health effects of smoking
   (a) is a noneconomic event that cannot be incorporated into the demand and supply model.
   (b) is characterized as a change in tastes that leads to a leftward shift in the demand curve for cigarettes.
   (c) will lead to an eventual increase in the price of cigarettes due to shifts in the demand curve for cigarettes.
   (d) induces a decrease in the supply of cigarettes.
   (e) decreases the quantity demanded of cigarettes.

Supply

Similar to demand, it is important that the student understand the difference between quantity supplied and supply, as well as a movement along a supply curve as opposed to a shift in the curve. A movement along a supply (demand) curve is referred to a change in quantity supplied (demanded) while a shift in the entire curve is referred to as a change in supply (demand). Make sure you know what causes a shift in the supply curve.

7. A shift in the supply curve may be caused by any of the following except
   (a) an improvement in technology.
   (b) an increase in the wage paid to labour.
   (c) an increase in average consumer income.
   (d) an increase in the number of firms in the industry.
   (e) Both (b) and (c).

8. A rightward shift in the supply curve indicates
   (a) a decrease in price.
   (b) an increase in demand.
   (c) an increase in quantity supplied.
   (d) that at each price quantity supplied has increased.
   (e) an increase in consumers desire for a product.

9. An increase in the price of an input will
   (a) decrease quantity supplied.
   (b) decrease quantity supplied at each price.
   (c) decrease supply.
   (d) cause the supply curve to shift to the left.
   (e) (b), (c) and (d) are correct.

10. A movement along a supply curve could be caused by
    (a) an improvement in technology.
    (b) a change in the prices of inputs.
    (c) a shift in the demand curve.
    (d) a change in the number of producers.
    (e) an decrease in production costs.

The Determination of Price

If, at a particular market price, quantity demanded is not equal to quantity supplied, pressures are exerted on price to change until the market clears—i.e., until quantity demanded is equal to quantity supplied. You should understand these pressures. Furthermore, you should be able to show how equilibrium price and quantity exchanged are affected by changes in demand and supply—these are the laws of demand and supply.

11. Excess demand exists whenever
    (a) price exceeds the equilibrium price.
    (b) quantity supplied is greater than quantity demanded.
    (c) the equilibrium price is above the existing price.
    (d) there is downward pressure on price.
    (e) there is surplus production.

12. The "laws of demand and supply" are
    (a) federal statutes and are therefore enforced by the RCMP.
    (b) enshrined in the Canadian Constitution.
    (c) irrefutable propositions concerning economic behaviour.
    (d) basic assumptions in economic theory.
    (e) predictions of economic behaviour that have tended to withstand much, but not all,
        empirical testing.

13. An increase in both equilibrium price and quantity exchanged is consistent with
    (a) an increase in supply.   (b) a decrease in supply.
    (c) a decrease in quantity supplied. (d) an increase in demand.
    (e) a decrease in demand.

14. Assuming a downward-sloping demand curve, an improvement in production technology for
    some good is predicted to lead to
    (a) a decrease in supply.
    (b) an increase in both equilibrium price and quantity exchanged.
    (c) a decrease in equilibrium price and an increase in equilibrium quantity exchanged.
    (d) a decrease in equilibrium price but no change in equilibrium quantity exchanged.
    (e) an increase in equilibrium price and a decrease in equilibrium quantity exchanged.

15. Comparative statics
    (a) is the analysis of market equilibria under different sets of conditions.
    (b) is the analysis of demand without reference to time.
    (c) refers to constant equilibrium prices and quantities.
    (d) describes the path by which equilibrium price changes.
    (e) refers to disequilibrium prices and quantities.

EXERCISES

1. This question asks you to solve for market equilibrium using demand and supply schedules.

    The demand and supply schedules for athletic shoes sold at Trendy Shoes Inc. at the local
    mall are hypothesized to be as follows (in pairs per week):

(1) Price	(2) Quantity Demanded		(3) Quantity Supplied	(4) Excess Demand (+) Excess Supply (−)
	D	D'		
$120	40	_____	130	_____
110	50	_____	110	_____
100	60	_____	90	_____
90	70	_____	70	_____
80	80	_____	50	_____
70	90	_____	30	_____
60	100	_____	10	_____

(a) Using the grid provided in Figure 3-1, plot the demand and supply curves (approximately). Indicate the equilibrium levels of price and quantity.

Figure 3-1

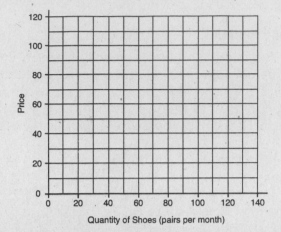

Quantity of Shoes (pairs per month)

(b) Fill in column 4 for values of excess demand and excess supply. What is the value of excess demand (supply) at equilibrium?_____

(c) Suppose there is a change in teenage fashion such that a substitute shoe, Doc Martens, becomes trendy. As a result, the quantity demanded of athletic shoes at Trendy Shoes Inc. decreases by 30 units per week at each and every price. Fill in the new quantity demanded in column (2) above, and draw the new demand curve D' on the grid.

(d) Supposing that price initially remains at the level you reported in answer (b). Explain the pressures that are exerted upon price by this change in tastes.

(e) After price has adjusted to the new equilibrium, what are the equilibrium price and quantity?

2. **Fair Pricing at Equality U?**

The executive of the Students' Association at the University of Equality has recently announced that "in the interests of fairness" all seats for on campus concerts will sell at the same price regardless of the popularity of the performer (clearly, there are no economics majors on the executive). The campus concert hall has a seating capacity of 5,000. Suppose that *average* demand for tickets for a *typical* concert or performer is as follows:

Price	Quantity Demanded
$6	8,000
8	5,000
10	2,500
12	1,500
14	1,000

(a) If the executive sets a price of $10 per seat, is there an excess demand or supply of concert tickets (on average)?

(b) What price would fill the concert hall without creating a shortage of seats at a typical concert?

(c) Suppose the quantity of tickets demanded at each price doubles when a particularly popular performer is booked. What would be the equilibrium ticket price for a popular performer?

(d) Do you think ticket scalping would be more profitable if the executive set price equal to, above or below equilibrium? Explain.

3. The Laws of Demand and Supply

Read the description of events in each of the following markets. Predict the economic impact of these events by drawing the appropriate shifts of curves in the accompanying diagram. Also, use + and − to indicate whether there will be an increase or decrease in demand (*D*), supply (*S*), equilibrium price (*P*), and equilibrium quantity (*Q*). If there is no change, use *0*. If the change cannot be deduced with the information provided, use *U* for uncertain.

Figure 3-2

Market	Event		D	S	P	Q
(a) Canadian wine	Early frost destroys a large percentage of the grape crop in British Columbia	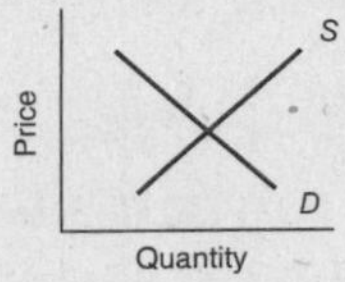				
(b) Wood-burning stoves	The price of heating oil and natural gas triples	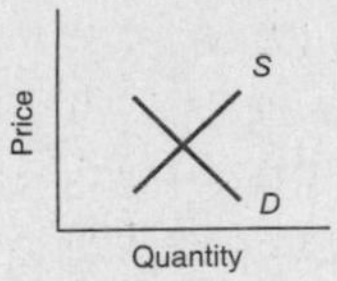				
(c) Laser printers	Technological advances reduce the costs of producing laser printers	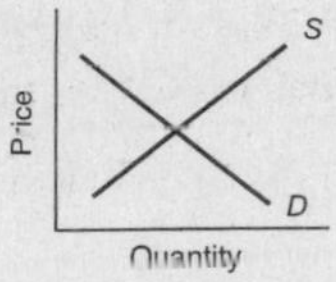				
(d) Gold	Large gold deposits are discovered in northern Ontario	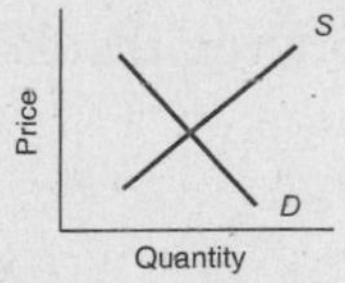				
(e) Fast foods	The public show greater concern over high sodium and cholesterol; also, there is an increase in the minimum wage	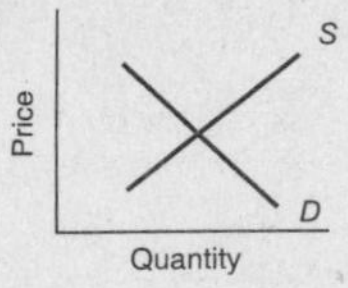				
(f) Bicycles	There is increasing concern about physical fitness; also the price of gasoline rises	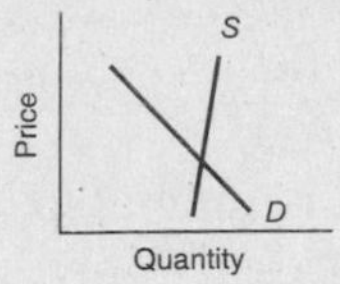				
(g) Beer	Population of drinking age increases; also, brewery unions negotiate a large increase in remuneration	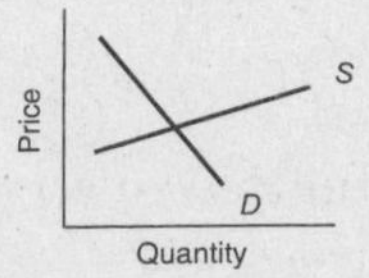				
(h) Candles	Ice storm knocks out electrical power for an extended period of time	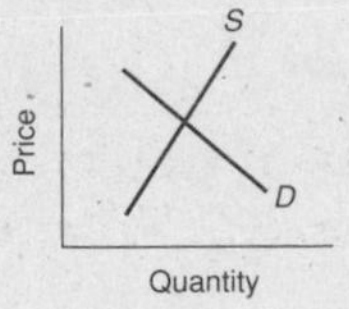				

4. Algebraic Solution of Equilibrium

The purpose of this question is to encourage you to obtain the market equilibrium by algebraically solving a system of simultaneous equations. The required algebra is reviewed in Exercise E-2 of Chapter 2.

The demand and supply of widgets are given by

$$Q^D = 30 - 1.0P, \text{ and}$$

$$Q^S = 1.0P, \text{ respectively.}$$

(a) Plot the demand and supply curves on the graph below, and label them D and S, respectively.

Figure 3-3

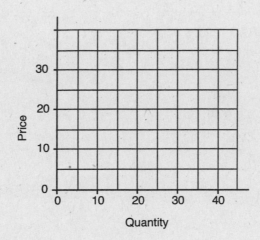

(b) Determine the equilibrium price and the equilibrium quantity by using two methods. First, solve by interpreting the diagram. Second, impose the equilibrium condition that

$$Q^D = Q^S$$

and solve algebraically.

(c) Now suppose that the demand curve changes to

$$Q^D = 30 - 1.5P$$

but the supply curve is unchanged. Before price adjusts from your answer in (b), is there excess demand or excess supply in the market? How much? Use algebra to solve for the new equilibrium.

(d) Confirm your answers in (c) by plotting the new demand curve and label it D'.

5. Equilibrium Again!

The following question demonstrates how changes in exogenous variables impact upon market equilibrium. This question walks you through both the algebraic and diagrammatic solution methods.

The quantity demanded of gadgets (Q^D) depends on the price of gadgets (P) and average household income (Y) according to the following relationship:

$$Q^D = 30 - 10P + 0.001Y$$

The quantity of gadgets supplied (Q^S) is positively related to the price of gadgets and negatively related to W, the price of some input (e.g., labour) according to

$$Q^S = 5 + 5P - 2W$$

(a) Assume initially that Y = \$40,000 and W = \$5. Substitute these values into the equations to obtain the demand and supply curves.

(b) Now use the equilibrium condition $Q^D = Q^S$ to solve the demand and supply curves simultaneously for the equilibrium price.

(c) Finally, substitute the equilibrium price into either the demand or supply curve to obtain the equilibrium quantity.

(d) Use the grid in Figure 3-4 to graph the demand and supply curves for gadgets in (a), and label them D_0 and S_0, respectively. Confirm that your answers in (b) and (c) are correct.

Figure 3-4

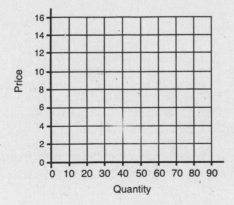

(e) Now, suppose that average household income increases to \$55,000 but W remains constant. What are the new levels of equilibrium price and quantity? Plot the new demand curve, label it D_1, and confirm your answer.

(f) Now assume that the input price W increases to $12.50. Using the demand curve you derived in (e), determine the new levels of equilibrium price and quantity. Plot the new supply curve, label it S_1, and again confirm your answer.

6. **Movements versus Shifts**

For each of the following statements, determine if the sentence is referring to a change in demand, a change in quantity demanded, a change in supply or a change in quantity supplied. If applicable, indicate the resulting change in equilibrium.

(a) Oil prices rise as OPEC members agree to new restrictions on output.

(b) Prices of personal computers fall despite a substantial increase in the number sold.

(c) Apartment rental prices rise as student enrolment swells.

(d) Lower air fares spark the busiest-ever air travel over a holiday period.

(e) Increases in the prices of Christmas trees spur tree planting on land previously used by dairy farmers.

(f) The moratorium on fishing east coast cod is linked to an increase in the price of west coast salmon.

EXTENSION EXERCISE

E-1. This extension exercise introduces government intervention in the market. Specifically, government is introduced as an additional demander of a product.

The diagram in Figure 3-5 illustrates a hypothetical market for farm machinery in Canada.

Figure 3-5

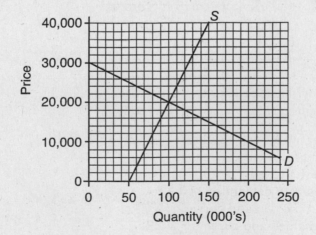

The federal government has decided that output in this industry should increase by 50 percent. Since current industry output is 100,000 units, it therefore plans to purchase 50,000 units of farm machinery *regardless of price*. The government intends to give away these units to less developed countries as part of Canada's foreign aid.

(a) Draw the new demand curve for farm machinery that takes into account government demand. What are the new levels of equilibrium price and quantity?

(b) By how much does industry output increase in percentage terms? Why does this increase fall short of the government's target of 50 percent?

(c) How many units would the government have to purchase in order to satisfy its objective of increasing industry output to 150,000 units? What is the associated quantity demanded by the private sector (i.e., by nongovernment consumers in Canada)?

(d) What erroneous assumption did the government make about the supply of farm machinery if they believed that buying 50,000 units would increase production by 50 percent?

PRACTICE MULTIPLE CHOICE TEST

1. When the Multiple Listing Service (MLS) reports that in the month of April at an average selling price of $250,000, total sales of homes in Toronto were 2,000 units, they are referring to
   (a) quantity demanded.
   (b) quantity supplied.
   (c) equilibrium quantity.
   (d) actual purchases, which may or may not equal quantity demanded or quantity supplied.
   (e) Both (a) and (c) are correct.

2. A decrease in the price of VCRs will result in
   (a) an increase in demand for VCRs.
   (b) a decrease in supply of VCRs.
   (c) an increase in the quantity demanded of VCRs.
   (d) a movement up along the demand curve for VCRs.
   (e) a rightward shift in the demand curve for VCRs.

3. A decrease in the price of compact disc (CD) players will induce
   (a) a leftward shift in the demand curve for cassette players (a substitute).
   (b) an increase in demand for cassette tapes.
   (c) a rightward shift in the demand curve for CDs (a complement).
   (d) a rise in demand for CD players.
   (e) Both (a) and (c) are correct.

4. A change in demand could be caused by *all but which* one of the following?
   (a) A decrease in average income.
   (b) An increase in the price of a substitute good.
   (c) A decrease in the cost of producing the good.
   (d) An increase in population.
   (e) A government program that redistributes income.

5. An increase in the supply of broccoli could be caused by *all but which* of the following?
   (a) A decrease in the price of broccoli.
   (b) A decrease in the price of labour employed in harvesting broccoli.
   (c) An improvement in pesticides, thereby decreasing the variability in broccoli output.
   (d) An increase in the number of producers.
   (e) An improvement in harvesting technology.

Questions 6 and 7 refer to the following diagram.

Figure 3-6

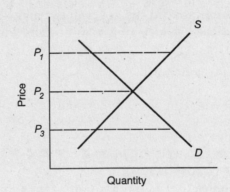

6. At a price of P_1,
   (a) there is upward pressure on price.
   (b) demand will rise to restore equilibrium.
   (c) quantity supplied is greater than quantity demanded.
   (d) the market has reached an equilibrium price.
   (e) a shortage exists.

7. When price equals P_3,
   (a) quantity exchanged equals quantity demanded.
   (b) there is excess supply.
   (c) there is a tendency for price to rise.
   (d) the market is in equilibrium.
   (e) a surplus exists.

8. Should polyester leisure suits become fashionable, economic theory predicts
   (a) a decrease in the price of these suits but an increase in the quantity exchanged.
   (b) an increase in both equilibrium price and quantity.
   (c) a shift in the supply curve to the right.
   (d) an increase in equilibrium price and a decrease in equilibrium quantity.
   (e) a leftward shift of the demand curve.

9. Simultaneous increases in both demand and supply are predicted to result in
   (a) increases in both equilibrium price and quantity.
   (b) a higher equilibrium price but a smaller equilibrium quantity.
   (c) a lower equilibrium price but a larger equilibrium quantity.
   (d) a larger equilibrium quantity but no predictable change in price.
   (e) a higher price, but no predicable change in equilibrium quantity.

10. A decrease in input prices as well as a simultaneous decrease in the price of a good that is substitutable in consumption will lead to
    (a) a lower equilibrium price and a larger equilibrium quantity.
    (b) a lower equilibrium price but no change in equilibrium quantity.
    (c) a lower equilibrium price and an uncertain change in quantity.
    (d) a lower equilibrium price and a smaller equilibrium quantity.
    (e) an unpredictable change in both price and quantity.

11. Which of the following is *not* a potential cause of an increase in the price of housing?
    (a) Construction workers' wages increase with no offsetting increase in productivity.
    (b) Cheaper methods of prefabricating homes are developed.
    (c) An increase in population.
    (d) An increase in consumer incomes.
    (e) The price of land (an input) increases.

12. Today the price of strawberries is 60 cents a quart, and raspberries are priced at 75 cents a quart. Yesterday strawberries were 80 cents and raspberries $1. Thus, for these two goods,
    (a) the relative price of raspberries has fallen.
    (b) the relative price of strawberries has fallen by 20 cents.
    (c) the relative prices of both goods have fallen.
    (d) relative prices have not changed.
    (e) the relative price of strawberries has risen.

13. In price theory, which of the following represents a relative price increase for strawberries, assuming that the average price level rises by 10 percent?
    (a) An increase in price from $1.00 to $1.05 per quart.
    (b) An increase in price from $1.00 to $1.10 per quart.
    (c) An increase in price from $1.00 to $1.15 per quart.
    (d) Both (a) and (c) are correct.
    (e) All of the above are correct.

Questions 14 to 20 refer to the following diagram which depicts the market for hamburgers in Collegeville, Ontario.

Figure 3-7

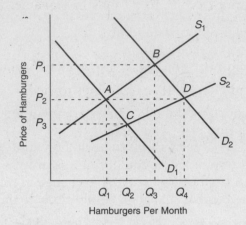

14. A change in Collegeville's market equilibrium from *A* to *B* may be caused by
    (a) a decrease in wages of part-time workers.
    (b) a decrease in the price of hot dogs.
    (c) an increase in the student population of Collegeville.
    (d) an increase in the price of hamburgers.
    (e) Both (c) and (d) are correct.

15. An increase in the price of hot dogs may be depicted in the hamburger market by a change in equilibrium from
    (a) *A* to *D*
    (b) *A* to *C*
    (c) *C* to *D*
    (d) *A* to *B*
    (e) Both (c) and (d) are correct.

16. A change in equilibrium from *A* to *D* may be explained by
    (a) an increase in Collegeville's student population.
    (b) a decrease in the price of beef patties.
    (c) an increase in the price of hot dogs coupled with an increase in the wages of restaurant employees.
    (d) a technological improvement in the production of hamburgers coupled with consumer concern about Mad Cow disease.
    (e) a decrease in the price of fries (a complement to hamburgers) coupled with a reduction in the wages of restaurant employees.

17. Which event would best explain a decrease in equilibrium quantity from Q_4 to Q_3?
    (a) An increase in the price of beef patties.
    (b) A decrease in Collegeville's student population.
    (c) A decrease in the price of fries (a complement to hamburgers).
    (d) An increase in the supply of hamburgers due to entry of new firms.
    (e) Consumer concern about Mad Cow disease.

18. If equilibrium changes from *A* to *B*, one could say
    (a) there has been an increase in demand.
    (b) quantity supplied has increased.
    (c) price has increased.
    (d) supply has not changed.
    (e) all of the above are correct.

19. A decrease in equilibrium price from P_1 to P_3, may be explained by
    (a) a decrease in supply.
    (b) a decrease in quantity supplied.
    (c) a decrease in demand and a decrease in supply.
    (d) a decrease in demand and an increase in supply.
    (e) an increase in supply and a decrease in quantity supplied.

20. An increase in average student incomes and an increase in the number of hamburger firms can be depicted by a change in equilibrium from
    (a) D to B.
    (b) C to D.
    (c) D to A.
    (d) C to B.
    (e) A to D or B to C, depending upon whether the demand for hamburgers is normal or inferior, respectively.

SOLUTIONS

Review Questions

1.(a) 2.(e) 3.(a) 4.(b) 5.(c) 6.(b) 7.(c) 8.(d) 9.(e) 10.(c) 11.(c) 12.(e) 13.(d) 14.(c) 15.(a)

Exercises

1. (a)

    Figure 3-8

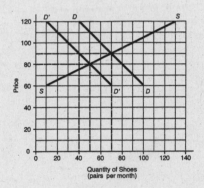

    Equilibrium price and quantity are $90 and 70 pairs per month, respectively.

(b)

Price	Excess demand (+) or excess supply (–)
$120	–90
110	–60
100	–30
90	0
80	+30
70	+60
60	+90

There is no excess demand or supply.

(c) See above diagram.

(d) With the change in tastes (i.e., along D') quantity demanded at the original price of $90 is now 40 units per week while quantity supplied remains at 70 units. Thus, 30 units remain unsold each week; this accumulating inventory exerts downward pressure on price.

(e) The new equilibrium is obtained at a price of $80 and quantity of 50 units per week.

2. (a) Excess supply of 2,500 seats.
    (b) At $8, quantity demanded and quantity supplied each equal 5,000 seats.
    (c) Since quantity demanded doubles at every price, 5,000 tickets would be demanded if price were $10.
    (d) Scalpers would do better if price were set below equilibrium which creates excess demand. For example, at a price of $6, the quantity demanded for an "average" concert is 8,000 but only 5,000 are sold. Thus, scalpers who are fortunate to purchase at $6 have a better chance of finding a buyer who is willing to pay more than $6.

3.

	D	S	P	Q
(a)	0	–	+	–
(b)	+	0	+	+
(c)	0	+	–	+
(d)	0	+	–	+
(e)	–	–	U	–
(f)	+	0	+	+
(g)	+	–	+	U
(h)	+	0	+	+

4. (a)

Figure 3-9

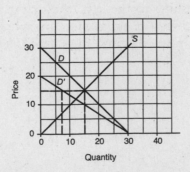

(b) $Q^D = Q^S$ is equivalent to: $30 - 1.0P = 1.0P$ which solves for $P = \$15$. Now substitute the equilibrium price into the equation for either Q^D or Q^S, and obtain the equilibrium quantity $Q = 15$. (e.g., $Q^S = 1.0(15) = 15$).

(c) When price is $15, $Q^S = 15$ and $Q^D = 7.5$; thus there is excess supply of 7.5 units. The new equilibrium now obtains where $30 - 1.5P = 1.0P$, which solves for $P = \$12$ and $Q = 12$.

(d) see Figure 3-9

5. (a) $Q^D = 30 - 10P + 0.001(40,000) = 70 - 10P$.
$Q^S = 5 + 5P - 2(5) = -5 + 5P$.

(b) For equilibrium, $Q^D = Q^S$, so that: $70 - 10P = -5 + 5P$, which solves for the equilibrium price of $5.

(c) Substituting this value into either Q^D or Q^S, one obtains the equilibrium quantity of 20 units.

(d)

Figure 3-10

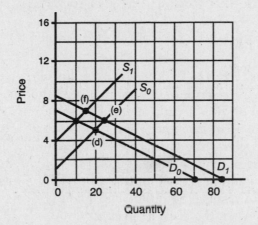

(e) Now $Q^D = 85 - 10P$. Setting $Q^D = Q^S$, or $85 - 10P = -5 + 5P$ yields $P = \$6$ and $Q = 25$.

(f) Now $Q^S = -20 + 5P$ and $Q^D = 85 - 10P$, so that $Q^D = Q^S$ solves for $P = \$7$ and $Q = 15$.

6. (a) The supply curve for oil shifts to the left, resulting in a higher equilibrium price.

(b) The supply curve for computers shifts to the right, resulting in a lower equilibrium price and a greater quantity exchanged. (Although, demand may have also shifted to the right, the effect of the supply shift dominates, resulting in a lower price.)

(c) The demand for apartments increased (i.e., demand curve shifts to the right), resulting in higher rents.

(d) Increase in quantity demanded. Lower air fares induce a movement down along the demand curve for air travel.

(e) Increase in quantity supplied. The higher price results in a movement up along the supply curve for Christmas trees.

(f) The supply of east coast cod shifts to the left, resulting in a higher price for cod. To the extent that east coast cod and west coast salmon are substitutes, the higher price for cod will induce a rightward shift in the demand for salmon, leading to a price increase in salmon.

Extension Exercise

E-1.　(a)

Figure 3-11

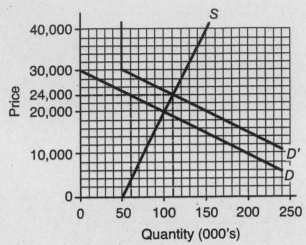

The equilibrium price is $24,000, and the equilibrium quantity is 110,000 units.

(b)　Industry output increases from 100,000 to 110,000 units, or by 10 percent. The additional demand of 50,000 units created by the government exerts upward pressure on the price of farm machinery and thereby decreases the quantity demanded by the private or nongovernment sector of the economy. These private-sector consumers reduce their purchases from 100,000 to 60,000 units.

(c)　The government would have to purchase all 150,000 units, which would be supplied only when the price reached $40,000. The quantity demanded by the private sector is reduced to zero when the price reaches $30,000.

(d)　They erroneously assumed the supply curve was horizontal.

Practice Multiple Choice Test

1.(d) 2.(c) 3.(e) 4.(c) 5.(a) 6.(c) 7.(c) 8.(b) 9.(d) 10.(c) 11.(b) 12.(d) 13.(c) 14.(c) 15.(e) 16. (e) 17.(a) 18.(e) 19.(d) 20.(e)

CHAPTER 4

ELASTICITY

LEARNING OBJECTIVES

1 Understand the measurement of price elasticity of demand, and know its determinants.

2 Understand the measurement of price elasticity of supply, and know its determinants.

3 Explain how an excise (or sales) tax affects the producer price and the consumer price.

4 Recognize that the incidence of a sales tax depends on relative demand and supply elasticities.

5 Understand the effect of income on quantity demanded, and how this elasticity defines normal and inferior goods.

6 Recognize the difference between substitute and complement goods, and how the degree of substitutability can be measured by the cross elasticity of demand.

CHAPTER OVERVIEW

The interaction of demand and supply was shown to determine equilibrium price and quantity in the previous chapter. The present chapter examines another important aspect of the interaction of demand and supply: the responsiveness of quantity demanded (or supplied) to changes in price (or other determinants of demand and supply).

Price elasticity of demand is measured as the percentage change in quantity demanded divided by the percentage change in price. When the percentage change in quantity demanded exceeds the percentage change in price (in absolute terms), demand is said to be **elastic** (as opposed to **inelastic** when the reverse holds, or unit elastic when the two percentage changes are of equal magnitude). If the price elasticity of demand for a product is known, one can predict the percentage change in quantity demanded that would result from a given percentage price change. The magnitude of a product's elasticity also allows us to predict whether an increase in its price will result in an increase or a decrease in total expenditure on the good. Whether demand (supply) is elastic or inelastic depends upon the availability of substitutes.

Tax incidence refers to the distribution of the *burden* of a tax between consumers and producers. This chapter shows that tax incidence is independent of who pays the tax. Rather, the distribution of the burden of a sales tax critically depends upon the relative magnitudes of the elasticities of demand and supply.

Additional elasticity measures are relevant when consumer income or the price of another good changes, which involves the **income elasticity** and **cross-price elasticity**, respectively. The sign of the income elasticity indicates whether the good is **normal** or **inferior**, while that of the cross-price elasticity indicates whether the goods are substitutes or complements.

CHAPTER REVIEW

Price Elasticity of Demand

In this section we focus on the responsiveness of quantity demanded to changes in price—the elasticity of demand. Pay particular attention to the formula for elasticity: there are several alternative ways of expressing the same thing. Sometimes elasticity is expressed in percentages, other times it is expressed in discrete changes. The nature of the information you are provided determines which form of the equation you should use. Depending upon its magnitude, elasticity is classified as elastic, inelastic or unit elastic. Make certain you understand the implications of this classification for the effect of a commodity's price change on its total expenditure.

1. The price elasticity of demand refers to a measure that shows the
    (a) responsiveness of quantity demanded of a good to changes in its price.
    (b) variation in prices due to a change in demand.
    (c) size of price changes caused by a shift in demand.
    (d) degree of substitutability across commodities.
    (e) magnitude of the shifts in a demand curve.

2. The price elasticity of demand is measured by the
    (a) change in quantity demanded divided by the change in price.
    (b) change in price divided by the change in quantity demanded.
    (c) slope of the demand curve.
    (d) percentage change in quantity demanded divided by the percentage change in price.
    (e) average quantity demanded divided by the average price.

3. If the percentage change in price is greater than the percentage change in quantity demanded, demand
    (a) is elastic.   (b) is inelastic.
    (c) is unit-elastic.   (d) shifts outward to the left.
    (e) shifts to the right.

4. An increase in the price of a good and a decrease in total expenditure on this good are associated with
    (a) inferior goods.   (b) substitute goods.
    (c) normal goods.   (d) elastic demand.
    (e) inelastic demand.

5. The price elasticity of demand for a good will be greater
    (a) the less available are suitable substitutes for this good.
    (b) the longer the time period considered.
    (c) for a group of related goods as opposed to an element of that group.
    (d) the greater is income.
    (e) All of the above are correct.

6. If a 10 percent increase in the price of ski lift tickets causes a 5 percent decrease in total expenditure on lift tickets, then demand is
   (a) elastic.   (b) inelastic.
   (c) perfectly inelastic.   (d) normal.
   (e) inferior.

7. Which of the following commodities is more likely to have an elastic demand?
   (a) Toothpicks.   (b) Cigarettes.
   (c) Heart pacemakers.   (d) Broccoli.
   (e) Vegetables.

Price Elasticity of Supply

The responsiveness of quantity supplied to a change in price can also be classified as elastic or inelastic. Make sure you understand the special case when the supply curve is linear and goes through the origin—if you are uncertain about it, review the discussion associated with Figure 4-6 of the text. Similar to demand, the magnitude of elasticity of supply depends upon the availability of substitutes.

8. A value of zero for the elasticity of supply of some product implies that
   (a) the supply curve is horizontal.
   (b) supply is highly responsive to price.
   (c) the supply curve is vertical.
   (d) the product will not be supplied at any price.
   (e) None of the above.

9. The elasticity of supply for a product will tend to be larger
   (a) the higher is the elasticity of demand for the product.
   (b) the lower is the elasticity of demand for the product.
   (c) the harder it is for firms to shift from the production of one product to another product.
   (d) the easier it is for firms to shift from the production of one product to another product.
   (e) the shorter the time period involved.

10. In the short run, a shift in demand will generally cause
    (a) the price to overshoot its long-run equilibrium value.
    (b) the price to undershoot its long-run equilibrium value.
    (c) the quantity exchanged to overshoot its long-run equilibrium values.
    (d) both price and quantity exchanged to overshoot their long-run equilibrium values.
    (e) None of the above.

11. Suppose that the short-run demand for a good is relatively more inelastic than its long-run demand. A given rightward shift in the supply curve will lead to a
    (a) smaller decrease in price in the long-run than in the short-run.
    (b) smaller increase in quantity in the long-run than in the short-run.
    (c) larger decrease in price in the long-run than in the short-run.
    (d) smaller decrease in both price and quantity in the long-run than in the short-run.
    (e) larger decreases in both price and quantity in the long-run than in the short-run.

An Important Example Where Elasticity Matters

Who bears the burden of a tax, consumers or producers? Surprisingly, the answer does not depend upon who pays the tax. Rather, it depends on the relative magnitudes of the elasticities of demand and supply. The more elastic is demand (supply), the smaller will be consumers' (producers') share of the burden of taxation. The distinction between consumer and seller prices is critical to understanding this section.

12. "Tax incidence" refers to
    (a) who is legally responsible for paying the tax revenue to the government.
    (b) the legislative process taxes must pass through.
    (c) the economic costs of avoiding taxes.
    (d) who ultimately bears the burden of the tax.
    (e) None of the above.

13. Suppose the market supply curve for some good is upward sloping. If the imposition of a sales tax causes no change in the equilibrium quantity sold in the market, the good's demand curve must be_____, meaning that the burden of the tax has fallen completely on the _____.
    (a) vertical, firms.
    (b) vertical, consumers.
    (c) horizontal, firms.
    (d) horizontal, consumers.
    (e) not enough information to answer this question.

14. Since the Goods and Services Tax (GST) is added to the price a consumer must pay for a commodity the
    (a) entire burden of the tax is borne by consumers.
    (b) consumer price increases by the amount of the tax.
    (c) seller price is unaffected.
    (d) burden is borne by producers who must collect the tax.
    (e) distribution of the burden depends upon the elasticities of demand and supply.

15. Consumers bear a greater share of the burden of the tax, the more
    (a) inelastic is supply.   (b) elastic is supply.
    (c) inelastic is demand.   (d) elastic is demand.
    (e) Both (b) and (c) are correct.

Other Demand Elasticities

Elasticity measures the responsiveness of one variable to another. It is an arithmetic measure and is not unique to economics (any more than the measurement "average" is). The income elasticity of demand and the cross-price elasticity of demand provide insights into the nature of the products being discussed. Are they luxuries or necessities, substitutes or complements, normal or inferior? Review the Terminology of Elasticity (see Extensions in Theory 4-1 in the text) to ensure a thorough understanding of the classification of the various elasticity measures.

16. Which of the following pairs of commodities is likely to have a cross-elasticity of demand that is positive?
    (a) Hockey sticks and pucks.   (b) Bread and cheese.
    (c) Cassettes and compact discs.   (d) Perfume and garden hoses.
    (e) Hamburgers and French fries.

17. Margarine and butter are predicted to have
    (a) the same income elasticities of demand.
    (b) very low price elasticities of demand.
    (c) negative cross-elasticities of demand with respect to each other.
    (d) positive cross-elasticities of demand with respect to each other.
    (e) elastic demands with respect to price.

18. Inferior commodities have
    (a) zero income elasticities of demand.
    (b) negative cross-elasticities of demand.
    (c) negative elasticities of supply.
    (d) highly elastic demands.
    (e) negative income elasticities of demand.

19. Which of the following goods is more likely to have an income elasticity of demand that is less than one?
    (a) Hot dogs.   (b) Microwave ovens.
    (c) Perfume.   (d) Winter vacations.
    (e) Sailboats.

Appendix to Chapter 4—More Details About Demand Elasticity

The material in this appendix examines the relationship between arc and point elasticity. It also discusses some diagrammatic features of linear demand curves that characterize the magnitude of elasticity.

Use the following figure to answer questions 20 to 23.

Figure 4-1

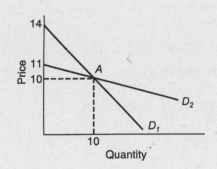

20. The point elasticity of D_1 at point A is [*Hint:* Multiply the ratio of price to quantity at point A by the reciprocal of the slope.]
    (a) 0.1   (b) 2.5
    (c) 1.0   (d) 10.0
    (e) 4.0

21. The point elasticity of demand for D_2 at point A is
    (a) 0.1   (b) 2.5
    (c) 1.0   (d) 10.0
    (e) 4.0

22. At a price of $10, demand curve D_1
    (a) has the same elasticity as any other point along D_1.
    (b) is more elastic than at any other price below $10.
    (c) is more elastic than D_2.
    (d) is inelastic.
    (e) None of the above.

23. Starting from point A, a 10 percent reduction in price along D_1 will result in an increase in quantity demanded of
    (a) 25 percent.   (b) 100 percent.
    (c) 10 percent   (d) 1 percent.
    (e) 2.5 percent.

EXERCISES

1. **Calculating and Classifying the Price Elasticity of Demand**

   This exercise reviews your ability to calculate and classify elasticity. Recall that there are alternative ways of expressing the elasticity formula; the data you are provided with determines which one you use.

   In each of the following scenarios, categorize the price elasticity of demand as *elastic, inelastic,* or *unit-elastic.* Where calculations are required, use average price and quantity. Note that categorization may not always be possible with the information provided.

   (a) The price of personal computers falls from $2,750 to $2,250, and the quantity demanded increases from 40,000 units to 60,000 units.

   (b) Canada Post increases the price of a stamp from 48 cents to 50 cents, but expenditure on postage stamps remains the same.

   (c) The price of matchbooks doubles from 1 cent to 2 cents, but the quantity purchased does not change.

   (d) An increase in the demand for blue jeans causes the price to increase from $45 to $55 and the amount purchased to increase from 1 million to 1.1 million.

   (e) A sudden decline in the supply of avocados leads to an increase in price by 10 percent and an accompanying reduction in quantity demanded by 20,000 units from the original level of 90,000 units.

(f) A 5 percent decrease in the price of gasoline results in a decrease in gasoline expenditure of 5 percent.

(g) A 10 percent increase in consumer income results in a 15 percent increase in the price of snowboards as well as a 15 percent increase in purchases.

2. **Elasticity and Total Expenditure**

This question reviews the relationship between the price elasticity of demand and total expenditure. Two alternative demand curves are depicted in the upper panels of Figure 4-2.

Figure 4-2

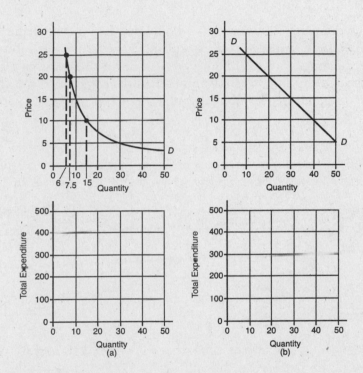

(a) Calculate the total expenditure associated with each demand curve at the following prices: $25, $20, $15, $10, and $5. Graph the respective total expenditure curves in the grids provided in the lower panels of Figure 4-2.

(b) By inspection of these expenditure curves, what can you say about the price elasticity of demand along each of the demand curves?

3. **Elasticity and Total Expenditure Again**

This exercise is designed to review your understanding of how the magnitude of elasticity determines the relationship between a price change and the resulting change in total expenditure. Fill in the following table:

	Price Elasticity	Change in Price	Change in Total Expenditure
(a)	2.0	up	_____
(b)	1.0	down	_____
(c)	_____	up	none
(d)	0.0	down	_____
(e)	0.6	_____	up

4. Linear Demand and Elasticity

Even though the magnitude of elasticity is related to the slope of a demand curve, a constant slope does not imply a constant elasticity for a downward sloping demand curve. This exercise establishes the point.

(a) Use the four price-quantity segments indicated by the dots on the demand curve (i.e., the arcs A to B, B to C, C to D and D to E) to calculate the numerical values of price elasticity along the linear demand curve in Figure 4-3. Confirm that elasticity declines as price decreases even though the slope is constant.

Figure 4-3

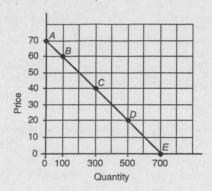

(b) What is the elasticity of demand when the price falls from $40 to $30? What would happen to total expenditure if the price falls further?

5. The Revenue-Maximizing Price

Policy makers sometimes erroneously presume that a price increase will always raise total expenditure. The following provides an vivid demonstration of this fallacy.

Suppose that you are hired as a consultant for the Guelph Transportation Commission. Its statisticians inform you that at the current fare of $1.30, the system carries 20,000 riders per day. They also indicate that for each $0.05 increase (decrease) in the fare, ridership decreases (increases) by 1,000 passengers.

(a) What is the arc price elasticity of demand at the current fare? (Hint: Consider a change in fare from 5 cents below the current fare to 5 cents above.)

(b) The commission has an objective of raising its total fare revenue (i.e., total expenditure by bus riders), and has asked you to determine by how much it should increase the fare. What do you advise? Why?

(c) What fare will maximize total revenue for the transit system? What is the associated ridership?

6. The Honourable Member from Clearair

The Honourable Mr. Camel, MP from the riding of Clearair, Ontario, has introduced a private member's bill in Parliament that will significantly increase taxes on cigarettes. He has argued this represents good social policy because it would reduce consumption of cigarettes, thereby increasing the amount of money families of low-income smokers would have leftover to spend on items such as food and shelter. Comment on Mr. Camel's reasoning using the concept of elasticity.

7. Predicting Responses to Price Changes

Elasticity measures are critical to the success of many policies. Consider the following example from the market for wheat:

(a) If the price of wheat falls 10 percent and farmers produce 15 percent less, what is the elasticity of supply for wheat?

(b) Suppose the government's goal is to raise wheat production by 30 percent to help fight famine. Based upon the elasticity calculated above, by what percentage must price increase to reach this goal?

(c) If the price of wheat falls by 5 percent, by what percentage will wheat production decline, given the elasticity you calculated above?

8. The Elasticity of Supply

This exercise reviews the calculation of the elasticity of supply.

(a) Given the supply curves in Figure 4-4, demonstrate that the elasticity of supply equals 1 along S_1 but falls as price increases along S. (Compute arc elasticities between the points indicated.)

Figure 4-4

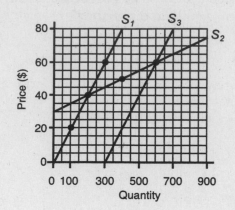

(b) How is the result for S_1 related to the fact that this supply curve passes through the origin?

(c) What does a supply curve such as S_3 imply when price equals zero?

9. **Tax Incidence**

Tax incidence depends upon the elasticities of demand and supply. This exercise emphasizes the relationship.

The following diagrams depict the demand and supply curves for the beer and orange juice markets in Ontario. Suppose a sale tax of $\$t$ per litre is imposed in each of these markets.

Figure 4-5

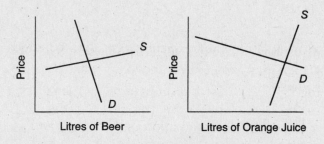

(a) Shift the appropriate curve to show the impact of the tax in each market. Label the new consumer price and seller price in the beer market P_{cb} and P_{sb}, respectively. In the market for orange juice, label them P_{cj} and P_{sj}, respectively.

(b) In which market is most of the burden of the tax borne by consumers? How would you characterize the elasticities of demand and supply in this market?

(c) In which market is most of the tax borne by producers? How would you characterize the elasticities of demand and supply in this market?

(d) In which market is the difference between the consumer price and the seller price greater?

EXTENSION EXERCISES

E-1.   Calculation of the elasticity of one variable in response to changes in another requires that all other variables are held constant. The following exercise establishes the point. WARNING: This exercise is *tough*! Successful completion of it would certainly indicate a thorough understanding of elasticity.

The following table provides data on income as well as prices and quantity demanded of goods x and y for five different periods (or observations):

Period	Income	P_x	Q_x^D	P_y	Q_y^D
(1)	$10,000	$25	10	$10	42
(2)	10,000	28	9	10	40
(3)	10,000	28	8	15	35
(4)	11,000	28	9	15	36
(5)	11,500	34	7	20	32

(a)   Why should no elasticities be calculated between periods 4 and 5?

(b)   Calculate the following elasticities, selecting appropriate periods and using arc formulas:

price elasticity for x _____, based upon periods ____ and ____;
price elasticity for y _____, based upon periods ____ and ____;
income elasticity for x _____, based upon periods ____ and ____;
income elasticity for y _____, based upon periods ____ and ____;
cross-elasticity of demand for y with respect to the price of x _____, based upon
     periods ____ and ____;
cross-elasticity of demand for x with respect to the price of y _____, based upon
     the periods ____ and ____.

E-2.   The classification of elasticity can often be determined by diagrammatic features of the relevant curves. This exercise explores the idea. The six diagrams in Figure 4-7 represent different combinations of elasticities of demand and supply at the equilibrium price P_E. Indicate which diagrams correspond to each of the following statements. (η_d refers to elasticity of demand, and η_s refers to elasticity of supply).

(a) η_d is greater than one and η_s is unity _____
(b) η_d is unity and η_s is infinity _____
(c) η_d is unity and η_s is unity _____
(d) η_d is greater than one and η_s is zero _____
(e) η_d is zero and η_s is unity _____
(f) η_d is infinity and η_s is unity _____

Figure 4-6

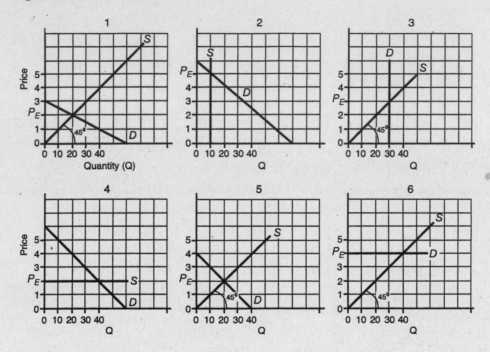

APPENDIX EXERCISE

The following exercise is based on the material in the appendix to this chapter. Read the appendix before attempting this exercise.

A-1.   The appendix discusses the distinction between *point* and *arc* elasticity. Point elasticity measures elasticity at a particular point on the demand curve rather than over an interval (arc elasticity). This exercise requires you to calculate point and arc elasticities for the demand curve drawn in the following diagram. Note that the demand curve is linear with a constant slope of $\Delta P/\Delta Q = -1/2$ so that $\Delta Q/\Delta P = -2$ (the slope of the demand curve is $\Delta P/\Delta Q$ because price is measured on the vertical axis and quantity on the horizontal).

Figure 4-7

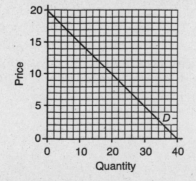

(a) Calculate the *point* elasticity of demand at a price of $10.

(b) Calculate the *arc* elasticity of demand for the following price changes (calculations should be to two decimal places).

Price Change	Arc Elasticity
$18 to $10	_____
$14 to $10	_____
$12 to $10	_____
$11 to $10	_____

(c) What happens to the difference between arc elasticity and point elasticity as the price change gets smaller? When is arc elasticity likely to be a good approximation of point elasticity?

PRACTICE MULTIPLE CHOICE TEST

1. If the price elasticity of demand for a good is 2 and price increases by 2 percent, the quantity demanded
    (a) decreases by 4 percent.   (b) decreases by 1 percent.
    (c) decreases by 2 percent.   (d) does not change.
    (e) is indeterminable with data provided.

Questions 2 through 5 refer to the four diagrams in Figure 4-8.

Figure 4-8

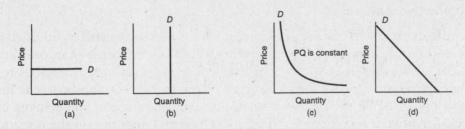

2. The demand curve with an elasticity of zero is
    (a) a.   (b) b.
    (c) c.   (d) d.
    (e) None of the above.

3. The demand curve with an elasticity of unity is
    (a) a.   (b) b.
    (c) c.   (d) d.
    (e) None of the above.

4. The demand curve with an elasticity of infinity is
   (a) a.   (b) b.
   (c) c.   (d) d.
   (e) None of the above.

5. The demand curve with an elasticity that is variable is
   (a) a.   (b) b.
   (c) c.   (d) d.
   (e) Both (c) and (d).

6. The price elasticity of demand for snowmobiles is estimated to be 1.2; thus an increase in price
   (a) always decreases quantity demanded by 12 percent.
   (b) always decreases quantity demanded by 1.2 percent.
   (c) increases total expenditure.
   (d) decreases total expenditure.
   (e) decreases total expenditure by 1.2 percent.

7. If the demand for some commodity has an elasticity of unity, a decrease in price
   (a) causes a 1 percent decrease in quantity demanded.
   (b) induces no change in quantity demanded.
   (c) results in no change in total expenditure.
   (d) is matched by a unit increase in quantity demanded.
   (e) Both (a) and (c) are correct.

Questions 8 to 10 refer to the following schedule. (Use average prices and quantities in your calculations.)

Price per Unit	Quantity Offered for Sale
$10	400
8	350
6	300
4	200
2	50

8. As price increases from $4 to $6, the elasticity of supply is
   (a) 1.0.   (b) 50.
   (c) 0.5.   (d) 5.0.
   (e) 2.0.

9. As price rises from $6 to $10 per unit, the supply response is
   (a) elastic.   (b) of unit elasticity.
   (c) of zero elasticity.   (d) inelastic.
   (e) infinitely elastic.

10. The supply curve implied by the schedule is
    (a) elastic for all price ranges.
    (b) inelastic for all price ranges.
    (c) of zero elasticity for all price ranges.

(d) of variable elasticity, depending on the initial price chosen.

(e) of constant elasticity.

11. A perfectly inelastic demand curve means that

(a) a percentage decrease in price exactly increases quantity demanded by the same percentage.

(b) an increase in price reduces quantity demanded.

(c) the price elasticity of demand is infinity.

(d) any change in price is perfectly matched by a change in quantity demanded.

(e) quantity demanded does not change in response to any price change.

12. A decrease in income by 10 percent leads to a decrease in quantity demanded by 5 percent; the income elasticity of demand is therefore

(a) -0.5.   (b) 2.0.

(c) 0.5.   (d) 50.0.

(e) 15.0.

13. A commodity is classified as a normal good if

(a) a decrease in consumer income results in a decrease in demand.

(b) it is consumed by a majority of the population.

(c) its price and quantity demanded are negatively related, ceteris paribus.

(d) an increase in its price leads to an increase in quantity supplied.

(e) a decrease in consumer income results in an increase in demand.

14. If an individual allocates $200 as monthly expenditure on compact discs and decides to spend no more and no less regardless of price, this individual's demand for compact discs is

(a) perfectly inelastic.   (b) perfectly elastic.

(c) of unit elasticity.   (d) less than one but greater than zero.

(e) of zero elasticity.

15. A shift in demand would not affect price when supply is

(a) perfectly inelastic.

(b) perfectly elastic.

(c) of unit elasticity.

(d) a straight line through the origin.

(e) of zero elasticity.

16. The producers' share of the burden of a sales tax will be greatest

(a) the more elastic is supply.

(b) the more inelastic is supply.

(c) the more elastic is demand.

(d) the more inelastic is demand.

(e) both (b) and (c) are correct.

17. Suppose the market supply curve is upward sloping. If the imposition of a sales tax causes no change in the price consumers pay, the good's demand curve must be _____, implying that the burden of the tax is _____.

(a) vertical; entirely borne by producers.

(b) horizontal; entirely borne by consumers.

(c) perfectly inelastic; shared equally by consumers and producers.

(d) perfectly elastic; entirely borne by producers.

(e) downward sloping; shared by consumers and producers.

18. If two goods have a negative cross price elasticity of demand, we know that
    (a) they are both inferior goods.
    (b) they are substitutes.
    (c) they are both normal goods.
    (d) they are complementary goods.
    (e) one is inferior and the other is normal, but we can't determine which is which.

19. Pizza and hamburgers are likely to have
    (a) a positive cross elasticity of demand.
    (b) positive income elasticities of demand.
    (c) a negative cross elasticity of demand.
    (d) price elasticities of demand greater than one.
    (e) a cross elasticity of demand equal to zero.

20. A commodity with an income elasticity equal to −0.5
    (a) is said to have an inelastic demand.
    (b) is an inferior good.
    (c) is a complementary good.
    (d) has a downward sloping demand curve.
    (e) has a demand curve with a constant slope of 0.5 in absolute terms.

SOLUTIONS

Chapter Review

1.(a) 2.(d) 3.(b) 4.(d) 5.(b) 6.(a) 7.(d) 8.(c) 9.(d) 10.(a) 11.(a) 12.(d) 13.(b) 14.(e) 15.(e) 16.(c) 17.(d) 18.(e) 19.(a) 20.(b) 21.(d) 22.(b) 23.(a).

Exercises

1. (a) $\eta = 2.0 = (20{,}000/500 \times 2{,}500/50{,}000)$; elastic demand.
    (b) Elasticity of unity.
    (c) Perfectly inelastic demand.
    (d) η cannot be determined because the demand curve has shifted.
    (e) $\eta = 2.5 = ((20{,}000/80{,}000) \times 100)$ percent ÷ 10 percent; elastic demand.
    (f) Perfectly inelastic demand.
    (g) η cannot be determined because the demand curve shifts.

2. (a)

    Figure 4-9

    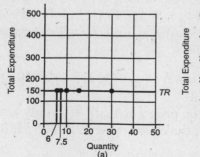 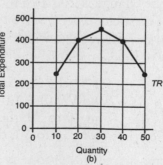

(b) Panel (a): Since total expenditure does not change along the demand curve, the price elasticity of demand is equal to unity at every point along this demand curve.

Panel (b): Since total expenditure increases as price falls from $25 to $20 to $15, demand is elastic over this range. Total expenditure is at its maximum value of $450 when price equals $15; this corresponds to unit elasticity. For further price decreases from $15 to $10 to $5, total revenue decreases, and hence demand is inelastic along this portion of the demand curve.

3. (a) down; (b) none; (c) 1; (d) down; (e) up.

4. (a) The following measures express elasticity as: $(\Delta Q/\Delta P)(P_A/Q_A)$, where Q_A and P_A are the average quantity and price, respectively.

A – B, $\eta = (100/10)(65/50) = 13.0$;
B – C, $\eta = (200/20)(50/200) = 2.5$;
C – D, $\eta = (200/20)(30/400) = 0.75$;
D – E, $\eta = (200/20)(10/600) = 0.167$.

(b) $\eta = (\Delta Q/\Delta P)(P_A/Q_A) = (100/10)(35/350) = 1.0$. Over this interval, total expenditure is constant. With further declines in price, total expenditure will decline as we move into the inelastic portion of the demand curve.

5. (a) Calculate arc elasticity from $1.25 to $1.35 so that the average price corresponds to the current fare of $1.30.

$$\eta = \frac{2{,}000}{0.10} \times \frac{1.30}{20{,}000} = 1.3$$

(b) Since demand is elastic, any increase in price only serves to decrease total revenue. Thus you should recommend that the price be decreased in order to increase total revenue.

(c) Try successively lower fares until total revenue begins to decrease. The maximum total revenue is found to be $26,450, which obtains at a fare of $1.15 and a ridership of 23,000 passengers per day.

6. The Honourable Mr. Camel assumes a downward-sloping demand curve for cigarettes—as price increases, its consumption will fall. However, he also assumes that total expenditure on cigarettes will decrease. This would only be correct if demand were elastic; in the case of cigarettes, demand is more likely to be inelastic so that total expenditure on cigarettes would increase in response to higher taxes. The impact of this bill would be the exact opposite of what the MP intended.

7. (a) $\eta_s = 15/10 = 1.5$.
   (b) The necessary price change is 20 percent. It is obtained by dividing the output increase of 30 percent by the elasticity of 1.5. Since $\eta_s = \%\Delta Q/\%\Delta P$, it follows that $\%\Delta P = \%\Delta Q/\eta_s$.
   (c) The fall in output is 7.5%, which is calculated by multiplying the price decrease of 5 percent by the elasticity of 1.5.

8. (a) Starting from the origin for S_1, the elasticities of supply are: $(100/20)(10/50) = (100/20)(30/50) = (100/20)(50/250) = 1.0$.
   For S_2 when price rises from 40 to 50, the price elasticity of supply is: $(200/10)(45/300) = 3.0$, but when price rises from 50 to 60, the elasticity is $(200/10)(55/500) = 2.2$.

(b) Because S_1 passes through the origin, P and Q always change in the same proportion, which gives an elasticity value of 1.

(c) S_3 implies that firms are willing to supply the good (300 units) even when the price they receive is zero.

9. (a)

Figure 4-10

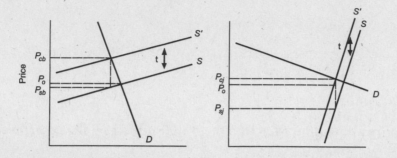

(b) The tax on beer is borne primarily by consumers. The relative slopes of the demand and supply curves in these markets suggest that the demand for beer is relatively inelastic, while its supply is relatively elastic.

(c) The tax on orange juice is borne primarily by producers. Demand in this market is relatively elastic, while supply is inelastic.

(d) The difference between consumer and seller prices are the same in each market. Specifically, the vertical distance by which each supply curve shifts is t in each market.

Extension Exercises

E-1. (a) Elasticity measures are calculated under the *ceteris paribus* assumption that other factors affecting demand are unchanged. Between periods 4 and 5, not only has income changed, but so have the prices of x and y.

(b) periods (1) to (2), price elasticity for

$$x = \frac{9 - 10}{28 - 25} \times \frac{(28 + 25)/2}{(9 + 10)/2} = 0.93$$

periods (2) to (3), price elasticity for

$$y = \frac{35 - 40}{15 - 10} \times \frac{(15 + 10)/2}{(35 + 40)/2} = 0.33$$

periods (3) to (4), income elasticity for

$$x = -\frac{9 - 8}{11,000 - 10,000} \times \frac{(11,000 + 10,000)/2}{(9 + 8)/2} = 1.24$$

periods (3) to (4), income elasticity for

$$y = -\frac{36 - 35}{11,000 - 10,000} \times \frac{(11,000 + 10,000)/2}{(36 + 35)/2} = 0.30$$

periods (1) to (2), cross-elasticity of demand for y with respect to the price of

$$x = \frac{40 - 42}{28 - 25} \times \frac{(28 + 25)/2}{(40 + 42)/2} = -0.43$$

periods (2) to (3), cross-elasticity of demand for x with respect to the price of

$$x = \frac{8 - 9}{15 - 10} \times \frac{(15 + 10)/2}{(8 + 9)/2} = 0.29$$

E-2.   (a) 1 and 6.   (b) 4.
       (c) 5.   (d) 2.
       (e) 3.   (f) 6.

Appendix Exercise

A-1.   (a) Point elasticity = -1.00 = $(-2)(10/20)$, or 1.00 neglecting the negative sign.

       (b)

Price Change	Arc Elasticity
$18 to $10	2.33
$14 to $10	1.50
$12 to $10	1.22
$11 to $10	1.11

       (c) As the change in price gets smaller, the values of arc elasticity and point elasticity converge. Thus arc elasticity serves as a good approximation of point elasticity for small changes in price.

Practice Multiple Choice Test

1.(a) 2.(b) 3.(c) 4.(a) 5.(d) 6.(d) 7.(c) 8.(a) 9.(d) 10.(d) 11.(e) 12.(c) 13.(a) 14.(c) 15.(b). 16.(e) 17.(d) 18.(d) 19.(a) 20.(b)

CHAPTER 5

MARKETS IN ACTION

LEARNING OBJECTIVES

1 Understand that individual markets do not exist in isolation, and that changes in one market typically have repercussions in other markets.

2 Understand the operation of a market that is subject to price ceilings or price floors.

3 Recognize who benefits and who loses from price controls.

4 Recognize legislated rent controls as an example of a price ceiling.

5 Understand the different short-run and long-run effects of such controls.

6 Examine various ways that governments intervene in agricultural markets in an effort to both stabilize and raise farmers' incomes.

CHAPTER OVERVIEW

This chapter gives you practice in applying the basic principles of supply and demand that were developed in Chapters 3 and 4. The chapter begins with a discussion of the interactions among markets that may result from three possible sources of market linkages. Supply and demand analysis is then used to evaluate the effects of government-imposed price controls.

Analysis of one market in isolation is called **partial-equilibrium** analysis. This simplified analytical approach provides many important insights and is widely used in introductory economics courses. Markets cannot always be treated as though they exist in isolation of each other. Events in one market can impact demand or supply in other markets. Consideration of the linkages across all markets is called **general-equilibrium analysis.** *Regional, input-output* and *resource constrained* linkages are three reasons markets may be connected.

Government *price controls* are policies that attempt to hold prices at some disequilibrium value. A *price floor* is a minimum permissible price; when *binding*, price floors result in excess supply. A *price ceiling* is a maximum permissible price; when *effective*, price ceilings result in excess demand. Price ceilings may also lead to **black markets**.

Rent controls are a vivid example of a price control. The effects of rent controls (especially, a discussion of who gains and who loses) are best understood by distinguishing between the short-term and the long-term. While it can be argued that rent controls may work in addressing a short-term housing shortage, they are not an effective solution to long-term shortages.

Several examples of government intervention in agricultural markets are also analysed. Unplanned and uncontrollable fluctuations in supply or price in many agricultural markets cause significant *instability* in farm income. Relatively large increases in productivity coupled with smaller gains in demand for agricultural products explain the long-term trend of declining relative incomes for farmers. Government programs to stabilize and increase farm income are often inefficient because the stated goals could be met by alternative, less costly policies.

CHAPTER REVIEW

The Interaction Among Markets

Events in one market are often linked to events in other markets. When examining the linkage between markets, first identify the nature of the linkage (i.e., whether it is regional, input-output or resource constrained), and then determine whether the demand or supply curve in the linked market is impacted.

1. The market for public transportation in Winnipeg is likely to be linked to which of the following markets?
   (a) Mass transit in Toronto.
   (b) Winnipeg Stock Exchange.
   (c) Mortgage rates in Canada.
   (d) Parking in downtown Winnipeg.
   (e) World market for wheat.

2. Partial equilibrium analysis refers to
   (a) shifts in the demand curve only.
   (b) shifts in the supply curve only.
   (c) short-run changes in equilibrium.
   (d) the study of all markets together.
   (e) the study of a single market in isolation.

3. The impact on Quebec's market for portable generators caused by the ice storm of 1998 is an example of which type of linkage?
   (a) Regional, with mobile supply.
   (b) Regional, with mobile demand.
   (c) Input-output.
   (d) Demand-side resource constraint.
   (e) Supply-side resource constraint.

4. Suppose Vancouver gets a professional baseball team. One would predict that the market for _____ would be impacted through a _____ linkage.
   (a) housing; input-output.
   (b) restaurant meals; supply-side resource constraint.
   (c) Vancouver Grizzlies basketball tickets; regional mobile demand.
   (d) Vancouver Canucks hockey tickets; demand-side resource constraint.
   (e) movies; regional mobile supply.

Government-Controlled Prices

This section considers two generic forms of price controls: ceilings and floors. Remember that ceilings refer to maximum prices while floors are minimum prices. When examining a price control you should first determine whether or not it is effective or binding and then consider which groups benefit or lose. After reading this section, you should be able to discuss the implications of excess supply or demand resulting from price controls.

5. When controls set price at some disequilibrium value, the quantity exchanged
    (a) is determined by quantity demanded.
    (b) is determined by quantity supplied.
    (c) is determined by the greater of quantity demanded and quantity supplied.
    (d) is determined by the lesser of quantity demanded and quantity supplied.
    (e) cannot be determined.

6. Holding a product's price below its equilibrium level will
    (a) ensure that everyone obtains the quantity they desire to purchase.
    (b) encourage an increased production of the good.
    (c) result in less of the good being consumed.
    (d) eliminate the incentive for black-market profiteering.
    (e) result in an excess supply of the good.

7. At a disequilibrium price,
    (a) profits of sellers are eliminated.
    (b) changes in demand must be matched by changes in supply.
    (c) there are always unsold goods.
    (d) there is always excess demand.
    (e) quantity demanded may be greater than or less than quantity supplied.

8. Price ceilings below the equilibrium price and price floors above the equilibrium price will both lead to
    (a) production controls.   (b) rationing.
    (c) a drop in quality.   (d) a reduction in quantity exchanged.
    (e) surplus output.

9. A black market may occur whenever
    (a) producers' prices cannot be controlled but retailers' prices can be controlled.
    (b) there is an excess supply of a commodity at the controlled price.
    (c) consumers are prepared to pay more than the ceiling price and exchange cannot be enforced at the ceiling price.
    (d) a ceiling price is maintained above the equilibrium price.
    (e) there is an effective price floor.

10. In a free market economy, the rationing of scarce goods is done primarily by
    (a) the price mechanism.   (b) the government.
    (c) business firms.   (d) consumers.
    (e) marketing boards

11. Allocation by sellers' preferences is feasible when
    (a) there is a disequilibrium price.
    (b) quantity supplied is less than quantity demanded.
    (c) there is a binding price floor.
    (d) there is excess supply.
    (e) the controlled price is set above the equilibrium price.

12. A price control that leads to the formation of a black market may nonetheless be consistent with government policy if the government's objective is to
    (a) keep the price low.
    (b) encourage output in this industry.
    (c) help producers obtain a more reasonable price for their output.
    (d) restrict output for conservation reasons.
    (e) All of the above.

Rent Controls: A Case Study of Price Ceilings

Although rent controls are introduced by well-intentioned governments, they often result in dire consequences for some of the very people they were intended to benefit (i.e., tenants). In any discussion of rent controls, it is important to distinguish between short- and long-term effects, and whether the increase in demand is permanent or temporary.

13. Rent controls are likely to produce all but which one of the following effects?
    (a) Rental housing shortage in the long-run.
    (b) Development of a black market.
    (c) Short-run increases in the supply of rental housing.
    (d) Resource allocation away from the rental housing industry.
    (e) Less expenditure by landlords on upkeep and maintenance.

14. The rental housing market is characterized by
    (a) long- and short-run supply elasticities of equal magnitude.
    (b) inelastic demand.
    (c) short-run inelastic supply and long-run elastic supply.
    (d) short-run elastic supply and long-run inelastic supply.
    (e) elastic supply in both the short- and long-run.

15. Which of the following groups is likely to benefit from rent controls?
    (a) Current tenants.
    (b) Future tenants.
    (c) Landlords.
    (d) Owner-occupiers.
    (e) Developers of rental housing.

16. Rent controls may be an effective policy in the market for rental accommodation when
    (a) increases in supply are temporary.
    (b) increases in demand are temporary.
    (c) demand is elastic.
    (d) supply is elastic.
    (e) increases in supply are permanent.

Agriculture and the Farm Problem

The historical problems that have confronted Canadian agriculture are reviewed in this section. The "farm problem" is attributable to short-term fluctuations in output or price, as well as to the long-term trend of declining relative income in the agricultural sector. Make certain that you fully understand both causes of the problem. In discussing short-term fluctuations, it is critically important that you identify whether the market under discussion is domestic or export and, in the latter instance, whether it is output or price that fluctuates. Each has different implications for policy. Make sure you fully appreciate the difference by rereading the subsections entitled

Production for Export Markets and Production for Domestic Markets in the text. After reading this section, you should be able to distinguish the roles of agricultural supply management schemes and marketing agencies in Canada, and to discuss the current system of income supplements in Canada. *TIP:* When analysing fluctuations in output or price, first determine whether demand is elastic or inelastic—this gives you the relationship between price changes and total revenue.

17. One of the long-term trends in Canadian agriculture has been
    (a) an increase in farm incomes relative to urban incomes.
    (b) an increasing proportion of the Canadian labour force working in the agricultural sector.
    (c) a relatively high income elasticity of demand for agricultural output by Canadians.
    (d) a decreasing demand for agricultural output.
    (e) growth in agricultural productivity that has been above the economy's average.

18. The main reason for agricultural price supports is to
    (a) attempt to stabilize farm incomes.
    (b) make certain that there are always extra stocks of goods on hand.
    (c) give the government control over agriculture.
    (d) reduce competition.
    (e) provide assistance to needy consumers.

19. Unplanned changes in output lead to greater fluctuations in price
    (a) the more inelastic is demand.
    (b) the flatter is the demand curve.
    (c) the more elastic is demand.
    (d) the more inelastic is the planned supply curve.
    (e) the greater the availability of close substitutes.

20. Farm receipts vary inversely with output levels
    (a) whenever buyers' preferences change.
    (b) when farm products have inelastic demands.
    (c) because lower outputs mean higher total costs.
    (d) as long as supply is elastic.
    (e) because world demand is perfectly elastic.

21. A low-yield crop would not alter total farm receipts if demand were
    (a) elastic.   (b) perfectly elastic.
    (c) perfectly inelastic.   (d) of unit elasticity.
    (e) of zero elasticity.

22. A price completely stabilized at the equilibrium level by a government buying surpluses and selling its stocks when there are shortages means that
    (a) poor farmers will benefit the most.
    (b) government has imposed a perfectly inelastic demand curve on farms.
    (c) farmers' revenues will be proportional to output.
    (d) all farms will have satisfactory incomes and farm receipts will be stabilized.
    (e) total farm receipts will increase.

23. When domestic farmers sell on world markets at a price that is unaffected by domestic output, they in effect face
    (a) perfectly elastic demand.   (b) perfectly inelastic demand.
    (c) inelastic demand.   (d) unit-elastic demand.
    (e) demand of zero elasticity.

24. An unplanned increase in output
    (a) will allow producers to sell more and thereby increase their income.
    (b) will always result in lower total receipts for producers.
    (c) may increase or decrease total income, depending on whether the output is sold on domestic or world markets.
    (d) may increase or decrease total income, depending on whether demand is inelastic or elastic.
    (e) may increase or decrease total income, depending on whether price rises or falls.

25. The Canadian Wheat Board is a good example of a marketing board that
    (a) acts as a selling agency for Canadian wheat in the international market.
    (b) actively engages in supply management schemes in order to influence price.
    (c) supports a market price that is well above the equilibrium price.
    (d) administers an effective price ceiling.
    (e) actively enforces production quotas.

EXERCISES

1. **The Oakton-Burlingville Housing Market Linkage**

    This question considers the issue of linkages across markets. Oakton and Burlingville are two suburban municipalities that are reasonably similar and adjacent to each other. City Council in Oakton has decided to substantially raise property taxes (perhaps to cover an unforeseen lawsuit). Use what you have learned about economic linkages across markets to discuss the impacts on the markets for housing in both Oakton and Burlingville. Accompany your discussion with diagrams depicting the housing markets in these two communities. How would you classify the linkage between these markets?

    Figure 5-1

    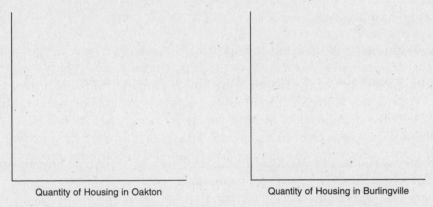

    Quantity of Housing in Oakton   Quantity of Housing in Burlingville

2. The purpose of this exercise is to demonstrate that the impact of a given shift in supply depends upon the elasticity of demand. Given the two markets depicted in the graphs of Figure 5-2, answer the following questions.

Figure 5-2

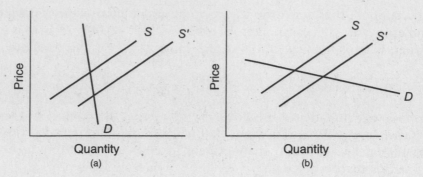

Quantity
(a)

Quantity
(b)

(a) If *S* and *D* denote the original supply and demand curves, indicate the total receipts (i.e., revenue) in each market by shading in the appropriate area.

(b) If the supply curve were to shift to *S'* in each market, indicate the new receipts with diagonal hatching.

(c) Which market shows the larger loss in total receipts? What is the nature of the demand curve in that market?

(d) Suppose a price floor equal to the original equilibrium price (before the shift in supply) existed and that the government was committed to purchasing unsold stocks at this price. Given the shift in supply in both markets, would there be any difference in the quantity the government would have to purchase in the two cases? Explain.

3. **Who Turned Out the Lights?**

During the ice storm of 1998, demand for many items such as firewood, propane, flashlights, and candles rose dramatically. Just as theory predicts, so did prices. Many businesses were accused of taking advantage of the situation by "price gouging." The *Montreal Gazette*, January 14, 1998, quoted a lawyer from the Quebec Consumers Association: "It's not illegal to increase prices when demand goes up, but we are in a crisis situation here ... and businesses should be helping people, not abusing them." The association set up a hotline for consumers to report instances of price gouging. The following exercise examines the implications of holding prices constant during the crisis.

Assume that prior to the ice storm, each of 100 households in the small town of Ville de Glace has an identical weekly demand for candles, and that the entire town's market demand curve is

$$Q^D = 200 - 100P.$$

Assume further that the supply of candles in Ville de Glace is perfectly inelastic at 100 candles per week.

(a) Find the equilibrium price and quantity. How many candles does each household consume per week?

(b) Now, suppose that when the Ice Storm knocks out the electrical supply, the demand for candles in Ville de Glace increases to $Q^D = 1100 - 100P$. If there is no intervention in the market, what is the new equilibrium? How many candles does each household consume?

(c) Suppose that public pressure or price controls are introduced to keep prices at their pre-ice storm levels. What is the equilibrium and how many candles does each household consume?

(d) Is there potential for a black market in candles? Explain.

4. Rent Controls

Two situations in the rental housing market are illustrated in the Figure 5-3. The first is the short-run in which supply is relatively inelastic, and the second depicts the long-run when supply is more elastic (S_{SR} and S_{LR}, respectively).

Figure 5-3

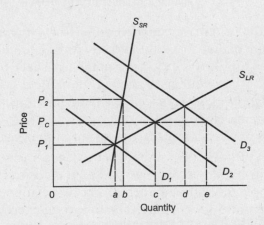

(a) Suppose that demand for rental housing shifts from D_1 to D_2. In the short-run, price would be expected to increase from _____ to _____, and the equilibrium quantity from _____ to _____.

(b) (i)   Assume that the predicted sharp increase in price alarms the public, so the government controls the price at P_c. Is this rent control an effective price ceiling? Explain.

(ii) In the long-run, quantity supplied will increase to _____, and P_c will be the _____ price. The main effects of the price control will be a short-run shift of income from (landlords/tenants) to (landlords/tenants). The long-run allocation of resources will be (efficient/inefficient), given P_c, because of short-run (overshooting/undershooting) of price.

(c) If P_c is maintained in the face of a further shift of the demand curve to D_3, P_c becomes a price (floor/ceiling), and the excess quantity demanded in the long-run will be _____.

5. Fluctuating Output—Domestic Markets

Agricultural output often differs from planned production due to erratic and uncontrollable weather conditions. This question illustrates the implications of these fluctuations, as well as the effects of selected attempts to address the implications.

Figure 5-4

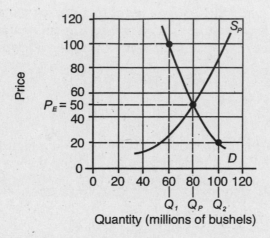

Assume all output is sold in a domestic market where the demand curve is denoted D in the above graph. S_P represents planned supply, so the expected equilibrium price is P_E, or $50, and the planned quantity supplied is Q_P, or 80 million bushels. Suppose that actual output is either Q_1 (a crop failure, 60 million bushels) or Q_2 (a bumper crop, 100 million bushels), and that each is equally likely. (For convenience, you should assume that good and bad crop years always occur consecutively.)

(a) Are producers in this market better off as a group in the year with a crop failure or the one with a bumper crop? Explain.

(b) What is average annual farm income in this market?

(c) Suppose that producers organize and operate a scheme whereby any year's output exceeding average annual output is added to storage and withdrawn in those years with below average outputs. Thus Q_P is offered for sale in each and every year. What are annual farm receipts?

(d) Now consider government intervention in this market in the form of a quota equal to Q_P. That is to say, any output in excess of Q_P must be destroyed. What would average annual receipts of producers be now?

(e) Which of these schemes do you think producers would prefer? Which do you think consumers of this product would prefer least? Why?

6. Fluctuating Output—Export Markets

The previous question investigated fluctuating output in a domestic market characterized by an inelastic demand. The present exercise addresses the problem of stabilizing domestic annual farm receipts in the presence of a fluctuating output that is sold entirely in export markets at some given world price.

Figure 5-5

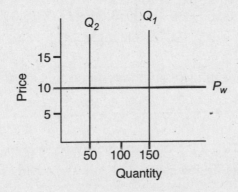

As illustrated in Figure 5-4, the world price is $10 and is expected to remain constant. Annual output, however, varies between 50 and 150 units, with each being equally likely so that average output is 100 units. Assume that the cost of storing a unit of output is $5 and that any excess revenue can be deposited in a savings account that pays a rate of return equal to 10 percent.

Suppose that current output is 150 units and it is certain that next period's output will be 50 units. Should the producers' association stabilize annual receipts by ensuring that exactly 100 units are offered for sale each year, or should it sell all 150 units now?

EXTENSION EXERCISES

E-1. The Cost to Taxpayers of Government Intervention

Governments often attempt to assist producers through various schemes that are designed to support prices above their equilibrium levels. This question investigates two such schemes and identifies the cost to taxpayers.

A small town in Saskatchewan has the following monthly demand and supply curves for kumquats:

$$Q^D = 4,600 - 2,000P \quad \text{and} \quad Q^S = -800 + 4,000P$$

(a) Graph the demand and supply curves for kumquats and label them D_1 and S_1, respectively.

Figure 5-6

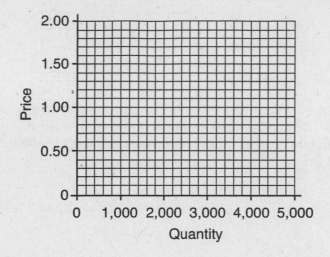

(b) What are the equilibrium price and quantity in this market?

The local government plans to assist kumquat producers by increasing the price of kumquats. It is studying the following two alternative schemes as a means of increasing price.

(c) In this first scheme, the government offers to purchase, at a price of $1.10 each, any amount of kumquats that are produced but not sold to consumers (it then intends simply to destroy its purchases). Producers therefore face a new demand that is the sum of consumer and government demand.

  (i) Draw this new demand curve (on the above grid), label it D_2, and determine the new equilibrium price and quantity in this market.

  (ii) How many kumquats are consumers purchasing, and how many is the government destroying?

  (iii) How much does this scheme cost the government (i.e., taxpayers)? Shade in the area on your graph that represents the cost to the government. (*Note:* Ignore all administrative and disposal costs.)

(d) In the alternative scheme, the government would purchase, at a price of $1.10 each, all of the kumquats produced. It would then put all of its purchases on the market for resale to consumers at whatever price consumers are willing to pay for that quantity.

(i) Draw the demand curve facing producers under this scheme (on the grid below), label it D_3, and determine the equilibrium price and quantity.

Figure 5-7

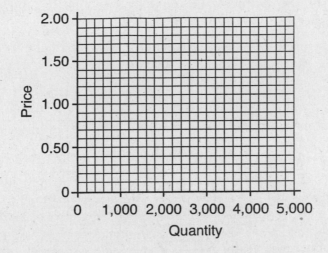

(ii) What price will the government receive when it resells all of its purchases?

(iii) What is the cost to the government of this scheme? Shade in with hatched lines the appropriate area on your graph to illustrate this cost (again, ignore administrative costs).

(e) What do you think are the relative merits of these two alternative policies?

E-2. **Fluctuating Price—Export Markets**

Exercise 5 examined the case where a fluctuating output is sold entirely in export markets at a stable world price. This question looks at the case where a stable output is sold in export markets at a world price that fluctuates. As the following graph illustrates, the constant level of annual output is 100 units. Assume, the world price is currently $5 per unit but is expected to be $15 next period.

Figure 5-8

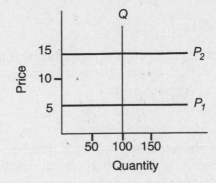

Suppose that the producers' association is committed to paying producers $1,000 each year even if it has to borrow in the first year to meet this obligation. Assume that storage costs are $5 per unit and that the association can borrow money at a 10 percent interest rate. Should the association attempt to stabilize annual receipts at $1,000 by putting all 100 units into storage in order to sell next year when price is high, or should it sell everything now and thereby avoid storage and large borrowing costs?

The following itemized statement of receipts and payments under each scheme will help you do this exercise.

	Receipts	Payments
If first year's output is stored:	$	$
Proceeds from loan		
Payment to producers in year 1		
Borrowing costs: (0.10 × $1000)		
Storage Costs: ($5 × 100)		
Crop revenue in year 2: ($15 × 200)		
Loan Repayment		
Payment to producers in year 2		
Total	$_____	$_____
If first year's output is sold:		
Crop revenue in year 1:($5 × 100)		
Proceeds from loan		
Payment to producers in year 1		
Borrowing costs: (0.10 × $500)		
Crop revenue in year 2:($15 × 100)		
Loan repayment		
Payment to producers in year 2		
Total	$_____	$_____

PRACTICE MULTIPLE CHOICE TEST

1. Partial-equilibrium analysis would look at
   (a) regional linkages with mobile supply or demand, but not both.
   (b) input or output linkages, but not both.
   (c) demand or supply constrained linkages, but not both.
   (d) Any of the above.
   (e) None of the above.

2. The strength of the linkage between regional markets depends upon
   (a) the degree of substitutability in demand and supply.
   (b) whether demand and supply are constrained.
   (c) the input-output relationships in their respective markets.
   (d) whether one is using partial or general equilibrium analysis.
   (e) the extent of government intervention in the regional markets.

3. When the supply of a product is mobile between two regions, we would expect
   (a) regional prices to move in opposite directions.
   (b) regional prices to move together.
   (c) an excess demand in one region to be matched by an excess supply in the other.
   (d) an increase in supply in one region to be offset by a decrease in demand in the other.
   (e) regional supply curves to shift in the same direction.

Questions 4 to 7 refer to the following graph.

Figure 5-9

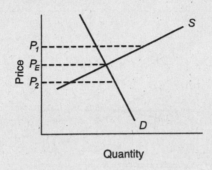

4. A price ceiling equal to P_1
   (a) results in excess supply.
   (b) results in excess demand.
   (c) results in neither excess demand nor excess supply.
   (d) can lead to a black market.
   (e) None of the above.

5. A price ceiling equal to P_2
   (a) leads to a level of consumption that is greater than quantity supplied.
   (b) results in a greater quantity produced than is actually sold.
   (c) is often justified as a means of helping producers.
   (d) may result in allocation by sellers' preferences.
   (e) results in unsold inventories.

6. A price floor equal to P_E would result in excess supply if
   (a) demand decreases due to a change in tastes.
   (b) supply falls due to an increase in labour costs.
   (c) the demand curve shifts to the right.
   (d) either curve shifts in a direction that causes upward pressure on price.
   (e) None of the above.

7. Suppose that the government decides that P_E is too high and therefore imposes a price ceiling equal to P_2. Further suppose that a black market develops that is able to sell all output at the highest attainable price. The black market price is
   (a) equal to P_E.   (b) greater than P_E.
   (c) greater than P_2, but less than P_E (d) equal to P_2.
   (e) None of the above.

8. Line-ups (or queues) are one possible allocative mechanism when there is
   (a) excess supply.
   (b) a binding price floor.
   (c) government intervention in the market that controls price above equilibrium level.
   (d) an effective price ceiling.
   (e) Both (b) and (d) are correct.

Questions 9 and 10 refer to Figure 5-10, in which the demand for rental housing increases from D_0 to D_1 (SR and LR refer to the short-run and the long-run, respectively).

Figure 5-10

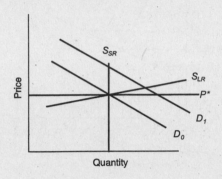

Quantity

9. If demand increases from D_0 to D_1 and there are no rent controls,
   (a) there will be a greater quantity increase in the short-run than in the long-run.
   (b) the short-run price overshoots its long-run equilibrium level.
   (c) the amount of rental housing will not be affected in the long-run.
   (d) rents will rise more in the long-run than in the short-run.
   (e) price will always equal P^*.

10. Assume that rents are controlled at price P^*. Which of the following best describes the likely events if demand increases from D_0 to D_1?
    (a) There will be no shortage of rental units in either the short-run or the long-run.
    (b) Landlords will have less opportunity to discriminate among prospective tenants.
    (c) The apartment shortage will be eliminated in the long-run.
    (d) Landlords will spend less on maintenance as well as new construction.
    (e) All consumers will have access to more affordable housing.

11. If domestic output is sold at a *given world price*, the incomes of domestic producers
    (a) are independent of domestic output.
    (b) vary in the direction opposite that of domestic output.
    (c) fluctuate in the same direction as fluctuations in domestic output.
    (d) increase during domestic crop failures and decrease during domestic bumper crops.
    (e) are constant.

12. When domestic output is sold at a *given world price*, the most desirable means of stabilizing total farm receipts due to fluctuations in annual output is
    (a) for the government to introduce a price support at the world price.
    (b) for farmers to stabilize the annual quantity sold by adding to storage in years with above average crops and depleting stocks in years with below average outputs.
    (c) to sell each year's output and save the above average revenue from the good years until it is needed in a bad year and in the meantime earn interest.
    (d) for the government to establish quotas at the average annual output.
    (e) for government to make the demand curve farmers face unit elastic.

13. Suppose that annual *domestic output is constant* but is sold at a *world price that fluctuates* from year to year. Suppose further that the current year's price is unusually low and is expected to rise. The most desirable policy for maximizing average annual receipts is to
    (a) sell all output at an average world price.
    (b) store output in order to sell at a higher future price.
    (c) sell output and invest the revenue to earn interest.
    (d) sell each year's output at the current price.
    (e) either store or sell the output, depending on storage costs, the future price, and the interest rate.

14. When there are fluctuations in output in a market with inelastic demand, quotas equal to the average annual output have the effect of
    (a) stabilizing annual output.
    (b) stabilizing annual receipts.
    (c) increasing average annual receipts.
    (d) increasing average annual output.
    (e) Both (a) and (b) are correct.

15. Quotas that lead to higher profits in some industry will in the long-run
    (a) result in more producers in the industry.
    (b) make it more costly to enter this industry.
    (c) result in a larger output for each producer.
    (d) help individuals who are just entering this industry.
    (e) All of the above are correct.

16. The size of a shortage of rental accommodation under rent controls depends upon
    (a) the elasticity of demand for rental accommodation.
    (b) the elasticity of supply for rental accommodation.
    (c) the length of time rent controls are in effect.
    (d) the amount by which the controlled price falls short of the equilibrium price.
    (e) all of the above are correct.

17. Unexpected crop failures will lead to increases in farm receipts when
    (a) when demand is inelastic.
    (b) when demand is perfectly elastic.
    (c) when government supports the price at its equilibrium level.
    (d) producers add to and deplete from storage so as to maintain constant sales.
    (e) government establishes a price above the equilibrium level.

18. If the government wishes to stabilize farm receipts, it must make the demand curve facing producers
    (a) perfectly elastic.
    (b) perfectly inelastic.
    (c) unit elastic.
    (d) horizontal.
    (e) vertical.

19. The Canadian Wheat Board
    (a) is an example of supply management.
    (b) has a primary goal of influencing the world price of wheat.
    (c) sets quotas for Canadian wheat producers.
    (d) competes with other purchasers for buying wheat from Canadian producers.
    (e) is a marketing agency that also helps secure farmers' incomes against intrayear fluctuations.

20. Supply management schemes use quotas to
    (a) help export Canadian agricultural products.
    (b) reduce the cost of becoming a producer.
    (c) provide producers with a unit elastic demand curve.
    (d) increase the price of output and stabilize annual farm receipts.
    (e) compete with imports.

SOLUTIONS

Chapter Review

1.(d) 2.(e) 3.(a) 4.(d) 5.(d) 6.(c) 7.(e) 8.(d) 9.(c) 10.(a) 11.(b) 12.(d) 13.(c) 14.(c) 15.(a) 16.(b) 17.(e) 18.(a) 19.(a) 20.(b) 21.(d) 22.(c) 23.(a) 24.(d) 25.(a)

Exercises

1. The initial equilibria are P_0 and Q_0 for Oakton and P_B and Q_B for Burlingville as depicted in Figure 5-11. For simplicity assume that the property tax is constant at $t per housing unit. The supply curve in Oakton then shifts up by $t, and the new consumer price in Oakton is P'_0 and the equilibrium quantity is Q'_0. Thus, the quantity demanded of housing in Oakton has been reduced by $Q_0 - Q'_0$. Some of these households will seek accommodation in Burlingville, thereby shifting its demand for housing to D'_B. The new equilibrium in Burlingville is P'_B and Q'_B. Notice that the consumer prices in these two municipalities tend to move together. This is an example of a regional linkage with mobile demand.

Figure 5-11

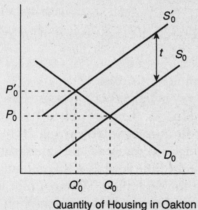
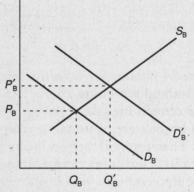

Quantity of Housing in Oakton

Quantity of Housing in Burlingville

2. (a) and (b) **Figure 5-12**

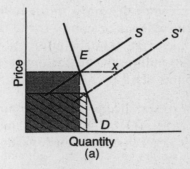
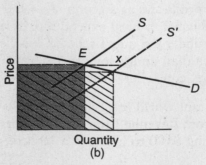

(c) Market **A**. The demand is inelastic compared to market **B**.

(d) No. The shift in supply is identical, and at a price equal to original equilibrium price, the quantity of unsold goods (*EX* in both markets) is the same.

3. (a) $Q^S = 100$, and setting $Q^D = Q^S$ and solving yields $P_E = 1$ and $Q_E = 100$. Total consumption is 100 candles per week and each of 100 households are assumed to have an identical demand, so each household consumes one candle per week.

(b) Setting $Q^D = Q^S$ now yields $100 = 1100 - 100P$, which solves for $P_E = 10$ and $Q_E = 100$. Again, each of 100 households consumes 1 candle per week but now pays $10 instead of $1.

(c) If price is kept at $1 during the Ice Storm, the quantity demanded is $Q^D = 1100 - 100P = 1000$. But there are only 100 candles available, thus there is excess demand of 900 candles per week. Since all households are assumed to have identical demand, each would like to purchase 10 candles. Thus, the first 10 households that get to the store purchase all 100 candles, thereby leaving 90 households without any candles.

(d) Yes, the first household that gets to the store can buy all 100 candles at $1 each and then sell them to other households that are willing to pay up to $10 for a single candle.

4. (a) P_1 to P_2; a to b.

(b) (i) Yes, in the short-run, since it is below the equilibrium price. (It would not be effective in the long-run since it equals the equilibrium price as the quantity supplied expands (along S_{LR}) to meet the demand—c on D_2.)

(ii) c; equilibrium; landlords to tenants; efficient; overshooting.

(c) Ceiling; quantity $e - c$.

5. (a) In a crop failure year, output is 60 million bushels and price per bushel is $100; therefore, total receipts are 100×60 million = $6 billion. In a bumper crop year, total harvest is 100 bushels, and price is $20, so total revenue is $2 billion. Therefore, in terms of total income, these producers as a group are better off in years with crop failures. The reason for the negative relationship between total output and total receipts is that demand for this product is inelastic.

(b) Since large and small harvests are equally likely, average annual farm receipts for this crop are $4 billion: ($6 billion + $2 billion)/2.

(c) When 100 million bushels are actually produced, 20 million are stored and only 80 million are offered for sale. In a year with a production level of only 60 million bushels, 80 million bushels are again put on the market for sale by withdrawing 20 million from stocks. Therefore, 80 million bushels are sold each year, and the equilibrium price each year is $50. Thus total receipts each year are $4 billion: 50×80 million.

(d) When output is 60 million bushels, it is sold for $6 billion. When output is 100 million, only the quota of 80 million bushels is sold, and the remaining 20 million bushels are destroyed. The 80 million bushels sell at a price of $50 so that total revenue is $4 billion. Average annual receipts are therefore $5 billion: ($6 billion + $4 billion)/2.

(e) Average annual revenue of producers is greatest with the quota. Therefore, in terms of income, producers as a group are better off with the quota. Since total revenue of producers is equal to total expenditure by consumers, consumers spend the most for this product under the quota scheme. Further, average annual consumption is lowest under the quota than under any other scheme: 70 million bushels as opposed to 80 million. Therefore, consumers would prefer the quota scheme the least.

6. With a constant world price, it is always best to stabilize producers' annual income by selling the entire crop. Revenue from the 150 units is $1,500. Of this, $1,000 must be paid to producers, leaving $500 to invest at a 10 percent rate of return, which yields another $50 rev-

enue. Next period, when output is below average, the $500 savings is added to the second year's crop revenue of $500 ($10 × 50) to keep total farm receipts at $1,000. Thus the association has stabilized incomes at the annual average of $1,000 and has a surplus revenue of $50 for further distribution. Had the association stored the 50 units exceeding average annual output in the first year, it would have incurred a storagecost of $250 ($5 × 50) and would not have the additional interest revenue from the investment. It would therefore be $250 short in its attempt to stabilize income at $1,000.

Extension Exercises

E-1. (a) **Figure 5-13**

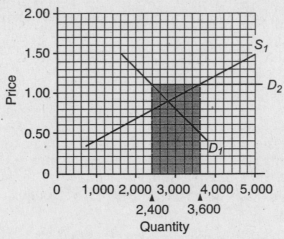

(b) At the intersection of D_1 and S_1 in the graph, the equilibrium price is 90 cents and the equilibrium quantity is 2,800 units per month.

(c) (i) As shown in the graph, the new demand curve is perfectly elastic at a price of $1.10. For prices greater than $1.10, the demand curve is D_1. The equilibrium now obtains at the intersection of D_2 and S_1, where $P = \$1.10$ and $Q = 3,600$ per month.

(ii) At a price of $1.10, quantity demanded by consumers is 2,400, so the remaining 1,200 units are purchased and destroyed by the government.

(iii) The government is purchasing 1,200 units at $1.10 each, so total cost (to taxpayers) is $1,320 per month.

(d) (i) In effect, producers face a perfectly elastic demand at a price of $1.10. As shown in the following graph, the new equilibrium occurs at the intersection of D_3 and S_1 with the same equilibrium price of $1.10 and equilibrium quantity of 3,600 per month.

Figure 5-14

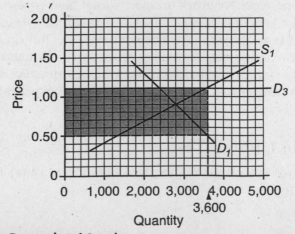

(ii) Consumers are willing to purchase 3,600 units when price is 50 cents.

(iii) The government pays $1.10 for each of its 3,600 units purchased and receives only 50 cents for each resale. Therefore, the cost to the government is 3,600 × ($1.10 − $0.50) = $2,160 per month.

(e) Although the second scheme costs the government more, it may be less costly for society as a whole in that everything that is produced is actually consumed, thereby yielding some benefits for consumers as well. The destroyed output in the first scheme is a net cost to society, since resources (which have an alternative use) are used up without any resulting benefits.

E-2. Regardless of whether the association stores or sells the first year's output, it must under these circumstances borrow in order to meet its obligation of paying producers $1,000 in the first year. If it stores the crop, it has no crop revenue and must therefore borrow all $1,000. If it sells at the current price, it receives revenue of $500, implying that an additional $500 must be borrowed. The following is an itemized account of the receipts and payments associated with each scheme:

	Receipts	Payments
If first year's output is stored:		
Proceeds from loan	$1,000	
Payment to producers in year 1		$1,000
Borrowing costs: (0.10 × $1,000)		100
Storage Costs: ($5 × 100)		
Crop revenue in year 2: ($15 × 200)	3,000	500
Loan Repayment		1,000
Payment to producers in year 2		1,000
Total	$4,000	$3,600
If first year's output is sold:		
Crop revenue in year 1:($5 × 100)	$500	
Proceeds from loan	500	
Payment to producers in year 1		$1,000
Borrowing costs: (0.10 × $500)		50
Crop revenue in year 2:($15 × 100)	1,500	
Loan repayment		500
Payment to producers in year 2		1,000
Total	$2,500	$2,550

Therefore, storing year l's output in order to sell next period when the price is high yields a net revenue (i.e., receipts less payments) of $400. Conversely, selling immediately so as to avoid storage costs yields a net revenue of −$50. Thus, in this particular numerical example, the association maximizes net revenues for producers by storing output. Unlike Exercise 6, there is no single best strategy when world price fluctuates. Rather, the decision whether to store or sell depends on prices in each period, storage costs, and the interest rate.

Practice Multiple Choice Test

1.(e) 2.(a) 3.(b) 4.(c) 5.(d) 6.(a) 7.(b) 8.(d) 9.(b) 10.(d) 11.(c) 12.(c) 13.(e) 14.(c) 15.(b) 16.(e) 17.(a) 18.(c) 19.(e) 20.(d)

PART THREE

CONSUMERS AND PRODUCERS

CHAPTER 6

CONSUMER BEHAVIOUR

LO *LEARNING OBJECTIVES*

1 Understand why marginal utility falls as the consumption of a product rises.

2 Recognize that maximizing utility requires consumers to adjust expenditure until the marginal utility per dollar spent is equalized across all products.

3 View consumer surplus as the "bargain" the consumer gets by paying less for the product than he or she was willing to pay.

4 Understand the distinction between total value, marginal value, and market value.

5 Explain how any change in price generates both an income and a substitution effect on quantity demanded.

CHAPTER OVERVIEW

This chapter develops a model that explains how individuals make consumption choices and how demand curves can be derived from the model. Economic theory assumes that consumers choose among products so as to maximize the **total utility** (i.e., satisfaction) that they receive from the goods and services they consume.

A central assumption of utility theory is diminishing **marginal utility**: the utility a consumer derives from additional units of a product diminishes as more of that product is consumed. Consumers maximize utility when the utility derived from the last dollar spent on each product is the same. As a product's price changes, consumers adjust the quantity demanded so as to again maximize their total utility; this behaviour results in a downward-sloping demand curve.

The amount that consumers actually have to pay to purchase a commodity is usually less than the maximum amount they would be willing to pay. The difference is called **consumer surplus**. This concept will prove to be very useful in later chapters when we evaluate the performance of the market system.

Any price change induces a consumer response that can be decomposed into the **substitution effect** and the **income effect**. The substitution effect is caused by a change in *relative prices* which disturbs the equilibrium condition that the marginal utility per dollar spent is equalized across goods. The income effect arises because a price change induces a change in the consumer's *purchasing power* or *real income*. The substitution effect always works to increase (decrease) consumption of a good whose price has decreased (increased). The income effect may increase or decrease consumption of a good whose price has decreased depending upon whether the good is normal or inferior, respectively. The appendix to this chapter analyses income and substitutuion effects using a more formal model of consumer behaviour—indifference curves.

CHAPTER REVIEW

Marginal Utility and Consumer Choice

It is important that you understand the difference between total and marginal utility. Total utility may be rising while marginal utility is falling—this can be a source of confusion for some students. The condition for utility maximization for any pair of goods can be interpreted in two ways. Be certain that you can discuss each by reviewing equations 6-1 and 6-2 (as well as the relevant discussions) in the text. The condition for utility maximization and the law of diminishing marginal utility together result in a negatively sloped demand curve. An understanding of this derivation is central to this section.

1. If the marginal utility from consuming a good is zero, total utility is
   (a) also zero.
   (b) constant.
   (c) negative.
   (d) decreasing.
   (e) increasing.

2. Sally is allocating her expenditure between movies and cappuccinos in such a way that she maximizes her utility. If the price of admission to the movies increases, Sally will reallocate her expenditure such that
   (a) the marginal utility of a movie increases.
   (b) her movie attendance will increase.
   (c) her cappuccino consumption will decrease.
   (d) the marginal utility of cappuccino increases.
   (e) the marginal utility per dollar spent on movies will exceed that for cappuccinos.

3. The hypothesis of diminishing marginal utility states that
   (a) the less of a commodity one is consuming, the less the additional utility obtained by an increase in its consumption.
   (b) the more of a commodity one is consuming, the more the additional utility obtained by an increase in its consumption.
   (c) the more of a commodity one is consuming, the less the additional utility obtained by an increase in its consumption.
   (d) the more of a commodity one is consuming, the less will be total utility.
   (e) marginal utility cannot be measured, but total utility can.

4. According to utility theory, a consumer will maximize total utility when goods A and B are consumed in quantities such that MU_A/MU_B
   (a) equals the ratio of the price of A to the price of B.
   (b) equals the ratio of total utility of A to that of B.
   (c) equals the ratio of the price of B to the price of A.
   (d) equals the ratio of the quantities demanded.
   (e) always equals unity.

5. If Monique's marginal utility is positive but decreases as more of a commodity is consumed, her total utility
   (a) is increasing.
   (b) is also decreasing.
   (c) is constant.
   (d) may be increasing, decreasing, or constant.
   (e) increases at the same rate.

Consumer Surplus

After completing this section you should be able to explain the concept of consumer surplus and the distinction between total and marginal valuations. Know how to measure what consumers are willing to pay for a given quantity of a commodity and what they actually have to pay—that's the ticket to a good understanding of this section! You should also be able to use these concepts to resolve the so-called Paradox of Value and inconsistencies in certain attitude surveys.

6. The consumer surplus derived from consumption of a commodity
   (a) is the difference between the total value placed on a certain amount of consumption and the total payment made for it.
   (b) will always be less than the total amount actually paid for the commodity.
   (c) will always be more than the total amount consumers are willing to pay for the commodity.
   (d) equals the total value of that commodity to consumers.
   (e) All of the above could be correct.

7. If an individual is prepared to pay $3 for the first unit of a commodity, $2 for the second, and $1 for the third unit, and the market price is $1,
   (a) consumer surplus is $3.
   (b) the individual will purchase three units of the commodity.
   (c) the individual's demand curve for this commodity is downward-sloping.
   (d) consumer surplus on the last unit purchased is zero.
   (e) All of the above.

8. The total value Mr. Wimpy places on his consumption of hamburgers equals
   (a) the amount he pays for them.
   (b) price times marginal value.
   (c) marginal value multiplied by quantity demanded.
   (d) price multiplied by quantity demanded.
   (e) his total expenditure on hamburgers plus his consumer surplus.

9. Consumer surplus can be measured by the area between the demand curve and the
   (a) quantity axis.
   (b) supply curve.
   (c) horizontal line at the market price.
   (d) vertical line at the quantity demanded.
   (e) price axis.

10. The "paradox of value" arises from the fact that
    (a) total and marginal utilities may move in opposite directions as consumption increases.
    (b) some goods are essential for life.
    (c) there is no necessary positive relationship between households' marginal and total values of consumption.
    (d) the higher the price of a good, the greater is the total value of consumption.
    (e) not all households behave as assumed in economic theory.

Income and Substitution Effects of Price Changes

The change in quantity demanded resulting from a price change can be divided into substitution and income effects. A price change affects consumer equilibrium in two ways. First, relative prices change—this induces a substitution effect on the quantity demanded. Second, the consumer's real income or purchasing power changes—this induces an income effect on the quantity demanded. The key to understanding this section is the ability to isolate each effect. This is achieved by conceptually holding purchasing power constant to isolate the substitution effect, and by then allowing purchasing power to change while holding relative prices constant at their new value to identify the income effect. Be alert to the possibility of an inferior good—this may result in a positively sloped demand curve! Reread Extensions in Theory 6-2 of the text if you are uncertain about the circumstances that give rise to this unusual but rarely observed demand curve.

11. The substitution effect refers to the change in quantity demanded that results from a change in
    (a) income.
    (b) total utility.
    (c) relative prices.
    (d) availability of substitute goods.
    (e) marginal utility.

12. The income effect refers to the change in quantity demanded that results from a change in
    (a) money income.
    (b) purchasing power.
    (c) total utility.
    (d) marginal utility.
    (e) wages.

13. If the price of good B increases, the substitution effect
    (a) decreases consumption of B.
    (b) increases consumption of B.
    (c) increases consumption of B if it is a normal good.
    (d) increases consumption of B if it is an inferior good.
    (e) decreases consumption of B only if it is an inferior good.

14. An increase in the absolute price of one good increases
    (a) money income.
    (b) real income.
    (c) purchasing power.
    (d) the opportunity cost of buying that good.
    (e) the relative price of other goods.

15. A change in the relative price of a good currently being consumed by a household, implies
    (a) a change in the household's real income.
    (b) a change in the household's purchasing power.
    (c) a change in the opportunity cost of buying goods.
    (d) that the current consumption bundle no longer maximizes utility at the new prices.
    (e) All of the above.

Appendix to Chapter 6—Indifference Curves

Indifference curve analysis assumes that the amount of good A a consumer is prepared to trade in return for more of good B diminishes as more of B is obtained. This assumption causes indifference curves to be negatively-sloped and of a particular curvature (i.e., bowed in towards the origin). Satisfaction is maximized by choosing a consumption bundle on the highest attainable indifference curve on the consumer's budget line. A change in quantity demanded induced by a price change can be graphically decomposed into the income and substitution effects.

16. An indifference curve indicates
    (a) constant quantities of one good with varying quantities of another.
    (b) the prices and quantities of two goods that can be purchased for a given sum of money.
    (c) all combinations of two goods that will give the same level of utility to the household.
    (d) combinations of goods whose marginal utilities are always equal.
    (e) all combinations of goods that can be purchased with a given income and constant prices.

17. The marginal rate of substitution between goods A and B
    (a) shows the amount of good A an individual would be willing to trade for one more unit of good B.
    (b) depends upon the amount of goods A and B consumed.
    (c) equals relative prices at the consumer's utility maximizing choice.
    (d) always has a negative algebraic value.
    (e) All of the above.

18. A budget line
    (a) describes the demand for two goods.
    (b) describes the quantity demanded at each and every price.
    (c) ranks bundles of goods according to a household's preferences.
    (d) separates bundles of goods that a household can afford to purchase at current income and prices from those that it cannot afford.
    (e) slopes upwards as income increases.

19. At the point where the budget line is tangent to an indifference curve,
    (a) equal amounts of goods give equal satisfaction.
    (b) the ratio of prices of the goods must equal the marginal rate of substitution.
    (c) the prices of the goods are equal.
    (d) a household cannot be maximizing its satisfaction.
    (e) the marginal rate of substitution is zero.

20. A household's demand curve can be derived from
    (a) a single indifference curve.   (b) a single budget line.
    (c) a price-consumption line.   (d) an income-consumption line.
    (e) the indifference map.

EXERCISES

1. **Calculating Consumer Surplus**

   Consumer surplus can be calculated in two ways—the following exercise guides you through both.

   The table that follows provides data on the total value that a certain student places upon the consumption of different quantities of personal pan pizzas per week.

Pizzas per Week	Total Value	Marginal Value
1	$14	_____
2	24	_____
3	31	_____
4	36	_____
5	40	_____

   (a) Calculate the marginal value the student places on each successive pizza consumed.

   (b) If the price of a pizza is $5, how many will this student purchase per week?

   (c) Calculate the associated consumer surplus at a market price of $5 by subtracting total expenditure from total consumption value.

   (d) Calculate consumer surplus by summing the incremental consumer surplus derived from each successive unit purchased.

2. **Utility Maximization and the Demand Curve**

   This exercise asks you to apply the condition for utility maximization to determine a consumer's consumption bundle, and then to derive a demand curve from the consumer's utility maximizing behaviour.

   A certain consumer spends recreation time and income on only two leisure activities: tennis and fishing. Assume the consumer has the basic equipment to pursue both activities. The price associated with these activities are ball replacement costs for tennis and the cost of bait for fishing. The marginal utility schedules for hours spent on these activities are shown in the table below.

Hours per Week	Marginal Utility Schedule	
	Fishing	Tennis
1	20	20
2	18	19
3	16	18
4	14	17
5	12	16
6	10	15
7	8	14
8	6	13

(a) For simplicity, assume the cost per hour of each activity is $1 (i.e., balls and bait used per hour). Further, assume that a $1 expenditure on other goods yields a marginal utility of 18. How many hours would this consumer spend on each leisure activity in order to maximize total utility?

(b) Suppose that the cost of fishing decreases to $0.55 per hour. What change in the "mix" of tennis and fishing would be required to maximize utility? Explain, using marginal utility to price ratios, why this is the case.

(c) Sketch the demand curve for fishing from the above information. (Assume it is linear.)

3. The differences among total value, total expenditure and consumer surplus are the focus of this exercise.

A household's demand for widgets is depicted in Figure 6-1.

Figure 6-1

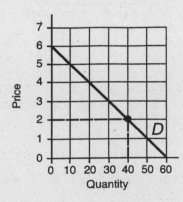

If widgets have a current price of $2 per unit, the total value this household places on its consumption of widgets is _____. However, the household's total expenditure on widgets is _____, so it receives consumer surplus of _____. If the market price drops to $1, this household's total valuation of widgets would (increase/decrease) by _____ and its consumer surplus would (increase/decrease) by _____. The value this household places on consumption of the twentieth widget is _____, and it is willing to pay _____ for 20 widgets.

4. *"Get Me Tickets for the Playoffs!"*

A certain chief executive officer (CEO) with a large corporation instructs her personal secretary (a recent graduate of a prestigious M.B.A. program) to purchase tickets to the Stanley Cup playoffs. Specifically, she tells him, "If the tickets are $150 each, buy one ticket for me; at $100 each, buy two; and, if the price is $50 each, buy me three." The young secretary (eager to make an impression) responds, "Madame, your instructions appear to be inconsistent. You are saying that you are *willing to pay* more in total for two tickets than for three!" Is the secretary correct? Explain. (*Hint:* Sketch the CEO's demand curve for tickets.)

EXTENSION EXERCISE

E-1. *Are You a Member?*

The concept of consumer surplus can be used to explain many observed pricing schemes. The following exercise addresses membership fees.

An individual's weekly demand for playing squash is given by:

$$Q^D = 10 - 2P$$

where Q^D is hours of squash time demanded per week and P is the price per hour (for each player) of court time (assume that this person can always find a partner).

(a) Plot the individual's demand curve for squash.

Figure 6-2

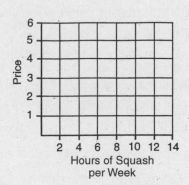

(b) The only squash courts available are at The Racquet Club, Inc., where each player is charged $2 per hour. How much squash does this person play per week?

(c) What is this individual's total valuation of the games consumed per week?

(d)   How much does this person actually spend on squash each week?

(e)   What is this individual's consumer surplus?

(f)   The Racquet Club, Inc., is considering a pricing scheme whereby individuals still pay $2 per hour of court time, but in addition they must also pay a mandatory membership fee. What is the largest fee The Racquet Club, Inc., could charge for a weekly membership without losing this individual as a customer? Explain.

(g)   As an alternative pricing scheme, suppose that The Racquet Club, Inc., introduces a membership fee but does not charge members for court time (i.e., members are entitled to unlimited use of the facility). What is the maximum amount this individual is willing to pay for a weekly membership under these circumstances?

APPENDIX EXERCISES

The following exercises are based on material in the appendix to this chapter. This should be read before attempting these exercises.

A-1.   **Budget Lines**

The purpose of this exercise is to review your understanding of budget lines.

Suppose an individual has an annual budget of $600 to spend on two recreation activities: skiing (at $20 per day) and golf (at $12 per 18-hole round).

(a)   Draw the budget line for recreation expenditures on the graph below. Label the budget line BLA.

(b)   Is a combination of 20 units of skiing and 20 rounds of golf attainable? Explain.

(c)   Suppose an increase in income allowed a 50 percent increase in the recreation budget. Graph the new budget line and label it BL_C—assume prices are unchanged.

Figure 6-3

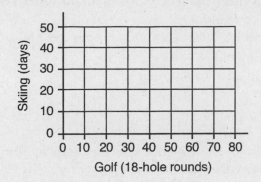

(d) Suppose now that the price of skiing increases to $30 per day, *ceteris paribus*. Draw the new budget line and label it BL_D.

(e) Finally, suppose that the price of a round of golf increases to $18. Graph the new budget line (BL_E). Compare BL_E and BL_A. Explain your findings.

A-2. **Indifference Curves and Equilibrium**

The exercise that follows uses indifference curve analysis to solve for the consumer's equilibrium and to derive a demand curve.

(a) The following table provides information on the combinations of food and clothing that are contained on indifference curves I, II, and III. For example, indifference curve I includes a combination containing 45 units of food and zero units of clothing, as well as a combination containing 30 units of food and 5 units of clothing.

Units of Food			Units of Clothing		
I	II	III	I	II	III
45	50	55	0	10	20
30	35	40	5	15	25
20	25	30	10	20	30
15	20	25	15	25	35
10	15	20	25	35	45

(i) Graph indifference curves I, II, and III on the grid provided below.

Figure 6-4

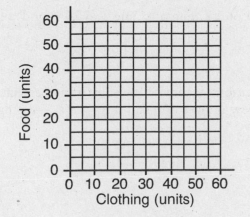

(ii) Draw a budget line on the graph that represents a budget constraint of $350 and food and clothing prices of $10 and $15, respectively.

(iii) Given (i) and (ii), what combination of food and clothing will maximize consumer satisfaction? Explain.

(b) Extend the analysis and use the same graph to show the derivation of a demand curve for clothing by proceeding as follows (assume that "food" stands for "everything consumed except clothing").

(i) Change the price of clothing so that a budget line with the same food intercept (35) is tangent to each of the indifference curves I, II, and III. Extend the X axis as necessary.
The X intercepts for budget lines tangent to indifference curves I, II, and III are approximately _____, _____, and _____, respectively.
The prices of clothing represented by the budget lines are approximately _____, _____, and, respectively.

(ii) Draw the price-consumption line on the graph.

(iii) Describe how the information on the price-consumption line can be used to derive a demand curve for clothing.

A-3. **Income and Substitution Effects**

This exercise uses indifference curve analysis to decompose the effect of a price change into income and substitution effects.

On the graph in Figure 6-5, an individual is shown to move from equilibrium E_0 to a new equilibrium E_1 in response to a decline in the price of commodity X.

Figure 6-5

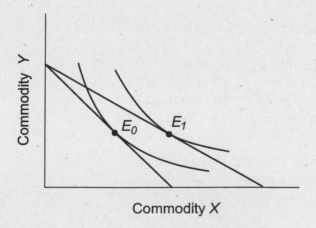

Commodity Y

Commodity X

(a) Illustrate on the graph the size of the substitution effect.

(b) Illustrate on the graph the size of the income effect.

(c) Is commodity X an inferior good? Explain.

A-4.   *"Turn out the lights!"*

This example develops a practical application of income and substitution effects.

During the 1970s the government of Ontario decided to promote conservation of electrical consumption. At the same time, it did not want to adversely affect the real incomes of households. The following example illustrates how a tax-and-rebate scheme which takes advantage of income and substitution effects can achieve these twin objectives. The student should note how relevant this policy remains today.

Assume a typical household in Ontario has $300 per month to spend on consumption of electricity and entertainment. Suppose the price of a kilowatt hour (kWh) of electricity is $0.10 while a unit of entertainment is $1.00. In its initial equilibrium, the household is consuming 2,000 kWh of electricity and 100 units of entertainment.

(a)   Draw the household's initial budget line on the following graph, and label its initial equilibrium E_A. Draw a representative indifference curve through E_A and label it I_A.

Figure 6-6

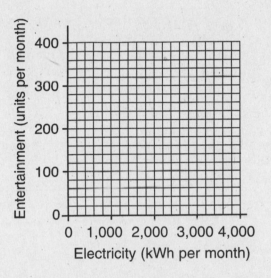

(b)   Now suppose a tax of 50 percent is imposed on electricity so that the consumer price of a kWh is now $0.15. This typical Ontario household responds by changing its consumption bundle to 90 units of entertainment and 1,400 kWh of electricity. Draw the new budget line and a possible indifference curve. Label the new equilibrium point E_B and the new indifference curve I_B.

(c)   The government now decides to compensate households for the electricity tax by using the resulting revenue to send each household a monthly rebate that restores its real income. Draw the new budget line and label the new equilibrium E_C. Explain.

(d)   Could the government of Ontario have achieved its twin objectives with this tax-and-rebate scheme? Explain.

PRACTICE MULTIPLE CHOICE TEST

1. If total utility is increasing, marginal utility is
   (a) increasing.
   (b) decreasing.
   (c) positive.
   (d) negative.
   (e) constant.

2. If marginal utility is negative, total utility is
   (a) negative.
   (b) positive.
   (c) increasing.
   (d) decreasing.
   (e) constant.

3. The idea that a consumer derives less additional satisfaction from consuming successive units of a good is called
   (a) the paradox of value.
   (b) diminishing marginal utility.
   (c) diminishing total utility.
   (d) diminishing consumer surplus.
   (e) diminishing total value of consumption.

4. Given any pair of goods X and Y, utility is maximized when
   (a) $MU_X/P_X = MU_Y/P_Y$.
   (b) $MU_X/MU_Y = P_X/P_Y$.
   (c) $MU_X = MU_Y$.
   (d) $P_X = P_Y$.
   (e) Both (a) and (b) are correct.

5. If all utility-maximizing consumers face identical prices, they will have identical
   (a) marginal utilities for each good.
   (b) total utilities for each good.
   (c) ratios of marginal utilities for each good.
   (d) ratios of total utilities for each good.
   (e) both (c) and (d) are correct.

6. Suppose Liam is maximizing utility by allocating his expenditure between CDs and movies. If the price of movies increases, Liam's
   (a) marginal utility of movies will increase and his marginal utility of CDs will decrease.
   (b) marginal utility of movies will decrease and his marginal utility of CDs will increase
   (c) marginal utility of both movies and CDs will decrease.
   (d) total utility of both goods increases.
   (e) consumption of both goods decreases.

Questions 7 to 9 refer to the following schedule which depicts the total value a student places on weekly restaurant meals.

Quantity of Restaurant Meals per Week	Total Value of Consumption
0	$0
1	30
2	50
3	66
4	74
5	80

7. The marginal value of the 3rd restaurant meal is
   (a) $22.
   (b) $16.
   (c) $146.
   (c) $8.
   (e) $66.

8. If the price of a restaurant meal were $8, how often would this student eat out per week?
   (a) 0.
   (b) 1.
   (c) 2.
   (d) 3.
   (e) 4.

9. If the price were $8, this student's consumer surplus would be
   (a) zero.
   (b) $66.
   (c) $18.50.
   (d) $42.
   (e) Cannot be determined with information provided.

10. If I am willing to pay $50 for a particular pair of blue jeans, but when I arrive at the store they are on sale for $30,
    (a) I should buy all the blue jeans in the store.
    (b) the value I place on the consumption of these blue jeans is lowered by $20.
    (c) I receive consumer surplus of $20 if I purchase the pair of blue jeans.
    (d) my valuation of consuming these blue jeans is now $70.
    (e) my consumer surplus decreases by $20.

11. Diamonds have a higher price than water because
    (a) the total value placed on the consumption of diamonds is greater than that of water.
    (b) the total consumption value of water is greater than that of diamonds.
    (c) the marginal consumption value of diamonds is greater than that of water.
    (d) households are willing to pay more in total for diamonds than for water.
    (e) all necessities of life have a high marginal value in consumption.

12. A law requiring that water (in finite supply) be provided free to everyone
    (a) ensures that only households with the highest marginal values will consume water.
    (b) ensures that all households will consume equal quantities of water.
    (c) is likely to result in some households with a low marginal value of water getting water while others with a higher marginal value do without.
    (d) ensures that all households can always consume water until the marginal value of water is zero.
    (e) would reduce the total consumption value of water.

13. When the price of a good declines, the income effect
    (a) will be greater for products that account for a large share of the consumer's budget.
    (b) implies that consumers' real income has also declined.
    (c) is predicted to increase consumption of inferior goods.
    (d) is predicted to decrease consumption of normal goods.
    (e) Both (c) and (d) are correct.

14. The substitution effect
    (a) is always dominated by the income effect for normal goods.
    (b) is caused by a change in real income.
    (c) may cause demand curves to be upward sloping.
    (d) is opposite in sign to the income effect for all normal goods.
    (e) always increases quantity demanded of a good whose price has fallen.

15. Demand curves for normal goods slope downward because
    (a) the substitution effect of a price change is greater than the income effect.
    (b) substitution and income effects work in the same direction.
    (c) the income effect is always greater than the substitution effect.
    (d) the income effect is always less than the substitution effect.
    (e) None of the above; demand curves for normal goods slope upward.

Appendix

The following questions are based on material in the appendix to this chapter. Read it before answering these questions.

Questions 16 to 20 refer to the four diagrams in Figure 6-7, which depict an initial budget line labelled *ab* and a new budget line *a'b'*. The new budget line results from a change in income, prices, or both.

Figure 6-7

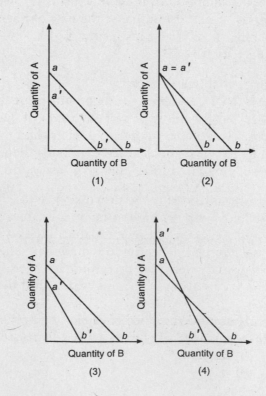

16. Which graph (or graphs) depicts the shift in a budget line that results from a decrease in income, *ceteris paribus*?
    (a) 1 only.   (b) 2 only.
    (c) 3 only.   (d) 4 only.
    (e) 1 and 3.

17. Which shift (or shifts) in the budget line could be explained by an increase in the price of good B, *ceteris paribus*?
    (a) 1 only.   (b) 2 only.
    (c) 3 only.   (d) 4 only.
    (e) 2 and 3.

18. Which shift (or shifts) could be explained by increases in the prices of both goods?
    (a) 1 only.   (b) 3 only.
    (c) 1 and 3.   (d) 3 and 4.
    (e) 1 and 4.

19. Which shift (or shifts) are consistent with a decrease in the price of good A and an increase in the price of good B?
    (a) 2 only.   (b) 3 only.
    (c) 4 only.   (d) 3 and 4.
    (e) 2 and 3.

20. Which graphs describe the shift in a budget line that results from decreases in both the price of good A and income?
    (a) 2 only.   (b) 2 and 4.
    (c) 2 and 3.   (d) 3 and 4.
    (e) 2, 3 and 4.

Questions 21 to 24 refer to Figure 6-8 which shows an individual's indifference curves and budget constraints between compact discs and all other goods.

Figure 6-8

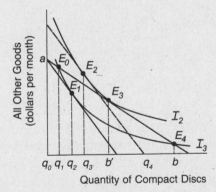

21. Starting from budget line *ab*, which consumption bundle maximizes utility?
    (a) E_0.   (b) E_1.
    (c) E_2.   (d) E_3.
    (e) E_4.

22. Starting from budget line *ab*, assume the price of compact discs increases such that the new budget line is ab'. Quantity demanded of compact discs decreases by
    (a) $q_3 q_0$.   (b) $q_3 q_1$.
    (c) $q_3 q_2$.   (d) $q_2 q_0$.
    (e) $q_3 q_4$.

23. The substitution effect of the price change is equal to the
    (a) increase from q_0 to q_2.   (b) increase from q_2 to q_3.
    (c) decrease from q_3 to q_2.   (d) decrease from q_2 to q_1.
    (e) decrease from q_3 to q_1.

24. The income effect of the price change is equal to the
    (a) increase from q_0 to q_2.   (b) increase from q_2 to q_3.
    (c) decrease from q_3 to q_2.   (d) decrease from q_2 to q_1.
    (e) decrease from q_1 to q_0.

25. From the information in Figure 6-8, one can say that CDs are
    (a) normal goods.
    (b) inferior goods.
    (c) Giffen goods.
    (d) snob goods.
    (e) Both (b) and (c) are correct.

SOLUTIONS

Chapter Review

1.(b) 2.(a) 3.(c) 4.(a) 5.(a) 6.(a) 7.(e) 8.(e) 9.(c) 10.(c) 11.(c) 12.(b) 13.(a) 14.(d) 15.(e) 16.(c) 17.(e) 18.(d) 19.(b) 20.(c)

Exercises

1. (a)

Pizzas per Week	Total Value	Marginal Value
1	$14	14
2	24	10
3	31	7
4	36	5
5	40	4

    (b) 4.
    (c) consumer surplus = total value – total expenditure = $36 – ($5 × 4) = $16.
    (d) Consumer surplus from each unit consumed equals the marginal value minus market price. Thus consumer surplus on the first unit is $9, on the second $5, on the third $2, and zero on the last unit consumed. Summing these yields $16.

2. (a) Utility maximization requires that $MU_T/P_T = MU_F/P_F = MU_o/P_o$. Since $MU_o/P_o = 18/1$, utility maximization implies three hours on tennis and two hours on fishing, for a total of five hours leisure time.
    (b) With the price of fishing reduced to $0.55, the condition that the marginal utility per dollar or expenditure is equalized across all goods is satisfied when 6 hours are allocated to fishing and three to tennis (approximately).

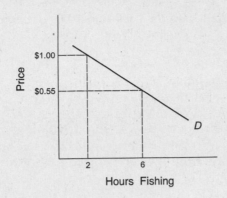

3. $160; $80; $80; increase; $15; increase; $45; $4; $100.

4. No, the secretary is not correct. The CEO's demand curve is sketched in the following diagram. The CEO is willing to pay $150 for the first ticket, $100 for the second, and $50 for the third. Thus for two tickets she is willing to pay $250:($150 + $100), and for three she is willing to pay $300:($150 + $100 + $50). If the price is $100 per ticket, she has only to pay $200 for two, and if the price is $50, she has only to pay $150 for three. What she is willing to pay is determined by the value she places on the consumption of these goods, not on the cost of purchasing them.

Figure 6-10

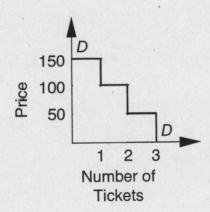

EXTENSION EXERCISE

E-1.   (a) **Figure 6-11**

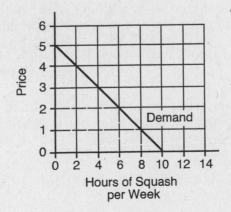

(b) Six hours per week.

(c) $21 (obtained by calculating the area under the demand curve up to a quantity of 6).

(d) $12 (i.e., $2 × 6).

(e) $9 (obtained by calculating the area below the demand curve and above the price line).

(f) For consumption of six hours, this person is willing to pay the total valuation of $21. At a price of $2, current payment is $12 for six hours. Therefore, this individual is willing to pay an additional $9 to play six hours of squash, which may be collected as a membership fee.

(g) By joining the club, the price per hour is zero, so as a member this person would now play 10 hours of squash each week. The value this individual places on 10 hours of squash is $25. Thus $25 could now be charged for a membership in The Racquet Club, Inc., without losing this person as a member.

APPENDIX EXERCISES

A-1. (a) Intercepts on the graph are 30 days of skiing and 50 rounds of golf.

(b) The combination of 20 units of each activity lies outside the budget line. It is therefore unattainable (unaffordable) at these prices with a total expenditure of $600.

(c) Intercepts are now 45 days of skiing and 75 rounds of golf.

(d) The intercept for golf would remain at 75 rounds; the skiing intercept changes to 30 days.

(e) The skiing intercept is 30 units and the golf intercept is now 50 rounds. BL_E and BL_A are identical because absolute prices and money income have changed in exactly the same proportions (i.e., by 50 percent).

A-2. (a) (i) and (ii) The indifference curves and budget line are shown on the following graph.

Figure 6-12

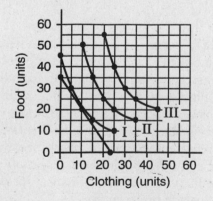

(iii) F = 20; C = 10. Given the budget constraint, curve I is the highest indifference curve attainable.

(b) (i) Approximate intercept quantities: 23.3; 58; 105. Approximate prices: $15; $6; $3.33.

(ii) Connect points of tangency.

(iii) Plot the corresponding price-quantity combinations on a graph with price on the Y axis and quantity demanded on the X axis.

A-3. (a) The substitution effect is *AB* in the graph.

(b) The income effect is *BC* in the graph.

(c) No. If X were an inferior good, there would have to be a negative income effect.

Figure 6-13

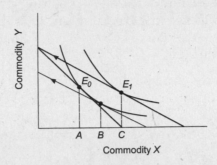

A-4. (a) The initial budget line is *ab* in the following graph.

Figure 6-14

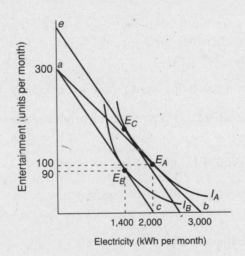

(b) The resulting budget line is *ac* in the above graph.

(c) If the household's real income (i.e., purchasing power) were restored, it would be able to re-purchase its initial level of utility represented by I_A at the new prices. Thus, the budget constraint would be parallel to budget line *ac* and just tangent to I_A. Budget line *ef* in Figure 6-14 is the new budget line. (N.B. The size of the rebate will vary for each answer since it depends upon the curvature of I_A which has been arbitrarily drawn by each student). In the above diagram, the rebate will be a sum that is sufficient increase entertainment purchases by *ae*, *ceteris paribus*.

(d) Yes, the government could have realized its twin objectives because bundle E_C necessarily represents a reduction in electrical consumption relative to that at E_A, but the same real income as before intervention.

Practice Multiple Choice Test

1.(c) 2.(d) 3.(b) 4.(e) 5.(c) 6.(a) 7.(b) 8.(e) 9.(d) 10.(c) 11.(c) 12.(c) 13.(a) 14.(e) 15.(b) Appendix: 16.(a) 17.(b) 18.(c) 19.(c) 20.(e) 21.(d) 22.(b) 23.(c) 24.(d) 25.(a)

CHAPTER 7

PRODUCERS IN THE SHORT RUN

LEARNING OBJECTIVES

1 Know the different forms of business organization and understand the various ways that firms can be financed.

2 Explain why firms sometimes make goods or services "in house" but other times purchase them from other firms.

3 Distinguish between accounting profits and economic profits.

4 Understand the relationships between total product, average product, and marginal product.

5 Explain the law of diminishing marginal returns.

6 Recognize that short-run production relationships have their counterparts in terms of short-run costs.

7 Understand the differences between fixed and variable costs, and know the relationships between total costs, average costs, and marginal costs.

CHAPTER OVERVIEW

This chapter opens with a discussion of several issues related to the nature of firms. The **proprietorship**, the **partnership** and the **corporation** are the major forms of business organization in Canada today. Further, each has subcategories. For example, partnerships can be **ordinary** or **limited,** while corporations may be private, public or **state-owned** (**Crown**). Firms have several methods of raising financial capital which is comprised of *equity* and *debt*.

Transaction costs help determine the boundaries of a firm—for example, whether the firm is to supply some good or service "in-house" or to "contract out." The *neoclassical* theory of the firm assumes that each firm behaves as a single, consistent decision-making unit whose goal is to maximize profit.

Profit is the difference between revenue and costs. In economics, costs to the firm are defined to include the full opportunity cost of resource use which includes *variable* and *fixed* costs as well as the opportunity cost of capital. It is this last item that distinguishes **economic profit** from the conventional accounting definition.

Production decisions are classified into three time horizons: the **short run**, the **long run**, and the **very long run**. In the short run, one or more factors of production are fixed (e.g., plant and equipment), whereas in the long run all factors are variable. The very long run allows for technological changes to occur. An important short run production phenomenon is the **law of diminishing returns**: as additional units of a variable factor of production are used with a given quantity of a fixed factor, the **marginal** and **average products** of the variable factor will eventually decrease.

The relationship between a firm's costs and output is depicted by its cost curves. **Total cost** is the sum of **total fixed cost** and **total variable cost.** These three "total" cost curves can be used to generate the associated "unit" cost curves: **average total cost, average fixed cost, average variable cost** and **marginal cost.** The hypothesis of diminishing returns implies that marginal and average costs eventually rise.

The material in the appendix re-examines the two assumptions in the neoclassical theory of the firm: profit maximization and behaviour as a single, consistent decision maker. First, the implications of separation of ownership from control are discussed. This is an example of a broader theory in economics known as the *principal-agent* problem which suggests that firms may pursue goals other than profit maximization. Pursuit of goals other than profit maximization makes a firm vulnerable to a **takeover** or **merger.**

CHAPTER REVIEW

Firms as Agents of Production

After reading this section you should be able to identify the various forms of business organizations and to understand equity and debt financing. You will also be able to discuss how transactions costs influence the "in house" versus "contracting out" decision. This section also states an important assumption in economics: the goal of the firm is to maximize profits. (The appendix considers some alternatives.)

1. One of the major differences between an ordinary partnership and a corporation is that
    (a) the owners of a corporation always outnumber the owners of a partnership.
    (b) a corporation always has more assets.
    (c) the owners of a corporation have limited liability, whereas partners have unlimited liability.
    (d) corporations are always more profitable.
    (e) all corporations are listed on a stock market such as the Toronto Stock Exchange.

2. Corporations can finance their operations by
    (a) reinvesting profits.   (b) issuing bonds.
    (c) issuing new equity.   (d) issuance of bills or notes.
    (e) All of the above.

3. The boundaries of a firm refer to
    (a) its market share.
    (b) which goods and services it provides internally and which externally.
    (c) which goods and services are produced in competitive markets.
    (d) the geographical regions in which the firm operates.
    (e) the distance at which transportation costs make the firm's goods noncompetitive.

4. The assumptions of profit maximization and consistent decision making
   (a) apply to single proprietorships only.
   (b) apply to all forms of business organizations except Crown corporations.
   (c) have been observed to be always true.
   (d) imply that profits are the only factor that influence business decisions.
   (e) allow theory to ignore the firm's internal and financial structures.

5. Debt financing by firms may involve any of the following except
   (a) "on demand" loans from banks.
   (b) selling bonds to the public.
   (c) issuance of bills.
   (d) retention of undistributed profits.
   (e) issuance of notes.

6. A firm's real capital refers to
   (a) money borrowed from banks.
   (b) the value of the firm's stocks.
   (c) its start-up financing provided by the original owners.
   (d) its plant and equipment.
   (e) its undistributed profits.

Production, Costs, and Profits

The important and fundamental concept of economic profit is introduced in this section. A full appreciation of the difference between economic and accounting profit is essential to understanding the economic theory of the firm. The distinction is based upon the opportunity cost of capital, which can sometimes be subtle. A careful rereading of the subsection entitled **Costs and Profits** in the text will prove to be a good investment for most students. You should know what is being held fixed and what is variable in each of the three time horizons faced by the firm. Lastly, this section discusses how profits provide important signals for the allocation of resources in the economy.

7. An example of an intermediate product is
   (a) asparagus.
   (b) bricks.
   (c) a middle manager.
   (d) the output of a clothing manufacturer.
   (e) unskilled labour.

8. Economic profits are defined as the difference between
   (a) accounting profits and normal profits.
   (b) total revenue and opportunity costs.
   (c) total revenue and the monetary costs of hiring resources for current use.
   (d) net income before and after taxes.
   (e) total revenue and imputed costs.

9. Opportunity cost refers to
   (a) what must be given up to secure the next best alternative.
   (b) unexpected costs to the firm.
   (c) the best rate of return possible on an investment.
   (d) the return to using something in the most profitable way.
   (e) the cost of hiring labour or renting equipment.

10. Applying the concept of opportunity cost to the firm is difficult because
    (a) it requires imputing certain costs.
    (b) most of a firm's costs are monetary costs.
    (c) many labour contracts include fringe benefits.
    (d) the firm uses many different tyes of inputs.
    (e) revenues are sometimes unknown.

11. Accounting profits are
    (a) always positive.
    (b) usually greater than economic profits.
    (c) the same as normal profits.
    (d) the result of technologically inefficient production.
    (e) less than normal profits.

12. Normal profits refer to
    (a) what all firms, on average, obtain as a return on investment.
    (b) the base used by Revenue Canada to levy business taxes.
    (c) the imputed return to capital and risk-taking required to keep firms in the industry.
    (d) the level of profits necessary to ensure that the firm covers its day-to-day operating expenses.
    (e) a return to capital that is comparable to rates of return earned on bank deposits.

13. If economic profits are zero for all firms in an industry, then
    (a) firms are earning less than normal profits and will shift resources toward alternative investments.
    (b) revenues equal the monetary costs of operation.
    (c) resources are earning a return in this industry at least equal to that available elsewhere.
    (d) firms will cease production immediately.
    (e) firms will exit the industry.

14. The short run is defined as a period
    (a) of less than a month.
    (b) during which there is insufficient time to change the employment level of *any* factor.
    (c) during which some factors are fixed and others are variable.
    (d) during which new firms can enter an industry and old firms can exit.
    (e) during which there is insufficient time to change output.

15. The long run time horizon
    (a) is the same for all firms.
    (b) allows the impact of new inventions to be felt.
    (c) is defined as the minimum length of time it takes to vary output.
    (d) is a length of time that is sufficient for all factors to be variable.
    (e) allows for changes in only labour employment levels.

16. The production function relates
    (a) outputs to inputs.
    (b) outputs to labour inputs only.
    (c) outputs to costs.
    (d) costs to inputs.
    (e) an economy's attainable combinations of output to alternative resource allocations.

Production in the Short Run

The relationship between output and the variable factor labour is developed in this section. This input-output relationship can be presented in three ways: total product, average product and marginal product. Make sure that you understand how all three are related to each other. The average-marginal relationship is of particular importance and shall be repeated in other contexts throughout the text. It is also important that you understand the role of diminishing returns in determining the shape of the product curves.

17. The law of diminishing returns refers to
    (a) the effects of increases in factor costs.
    (b) the division of labour.
    (c) the range of output over which average product is rising.
    (d) the effect of applying more and more labour to a fixed amount of capital.
    (e) the effect of transactions costs on "in house" production.

18. Assuming that capital is a fixed input and that labour is variable, the total product curve relates
    (a) output to various levels of capital and labour employment.
    (b) output to various levels of labour employment with capital held constant.
    (c) labour cost to the level of output.
    (d) total cost to various levels of labour employment.
    (e) output to the cost of labour.

19. When a firm increases employment of a variable input, it
    (a) shifts the production possibility curve.
    (b) shifts its total product curve upward.
    (c) alters its production function.
    (d) is making a long run decision.
    (e) moves along its total product curve.

20. If labour is the variable factor, average product is defined as
    (a) total product divided by total output.
    (b) the quantity of labour divided by total product.
    (c) the additional output produced by the last unit of labour.
    (d) output per unit of labour.
    (e) total product divided by capital.

21. The change in output that results when another unit of the variable factor is employed is referred to as
    (a) marginal product.   (b) average product.
    (c) average fixed product.   (d) total product.
    (e) average total product.

22. If average product is falling, marginal product
    (a) is less than average product.
    (b) is equal to average product.
    (c) is greater than average product.
    (d) can be greater than, equal to, or less than average product.
    (e) is negative.

23. The law of diminishing returns states that
    (a) as output increases, the rate of increase in costs will eventually decrease.
    (b) as output increases, profits will eventually decline.
    (c) the incremental output achieved by increases in a variable factor will eventually decrease.
    (d) as more labour is employed, the wage rate will increase and thereby increase costs.
    (e) as more labour is employed, the total product curve eventually has a negative slope.

Costs in the Short Run

This section develops three total cost curves (*TC, TFC* and *TVC*) and four unit cost curves (*ATC, AFC, AVC* and *MC*). It is important that you understand how these curves relate to the product curves in the previous section and to each other. There is a lot of technical information to learn in this section, and it will be used repeatedly throughout the course. Most students should invest in more than one careful reading of this section.

24. "Spreading one's overhead" is equivalent to
    (a) increasing capital to spread total costs.
    (b) decreasing average fixed costs.
    (c) increasing output to decrease average total costs.
    (d) any decrease in total costs.
    (e) increasing employment of the variable factor.

25. Using the notation in the text, AFC equals
    (a) *ATC – AVC.*　　　　　　(b) *AVC + MC.*
    (c) *ATC* at its minimum point.　(d) *TC – TVC.*
    (e) *ATC + AVC.*

26. AVC equals
    (a) *MC + AFC.*　　　　　　(b) *TVC* per unit of labour.
    (c) *ATC + AFC.*　　　　　　(d) *MC* at the minimum point of *AVC.*
    (e) *ATC + MC.*

27. If the difference between average total cost (*ATC*) and average variable cost (*AVC*) at 100 units of output is $1, at 200 units of output the difference between *ATC* and *AVC* must be
    (a) $2.　　　　　　　　　　(b) $1.
    (c) 50 cents.　　　　　　　　(d) $1.50
    (e) zero.

28. A firm's capacity
    (a) continuously declines as output increases.
    (b) is the output level corresponding to minimum average total cost.
    (c) is the size of its plant.
    (d) varies with its labour employment.
    (e) is the maximum output that can physically be produced with a given amount of capital.

29. A change in the wage rate paid to the variable factor labour will shift
    (a) only the *ATC* curve.　(b) only the *AVC* curve.
    (c) only the *MC* curve.　　(d) only the *AFC* curve.
    (e) the *ATC, AVC* and *MC* curves.

Appendix to Chapter 7—Do Firms Really Maximize Profits?

After studying this appendix, you should be able to: explain how the separation of ownership from control creates divergent interests in operating a firm; apply principal-agent analysis to indicate why managers may not pursue stockholders' interests; understand that if a firm does not realize its profit potential, it is vulnerable to a takeover bid; and, distinguish the key predictions of firm behaviour based on theories of profit maximization, sales maximization, and non-maximization.

30. Most economists believe that the threat of a takeover
    (a) induces an inefficient resource allocation.
    (b) will eventually drive the economy into another recession.
    (c) restricts managers from pursuing objectives other than profit maximization.
    (d) has no effect on the current managers of firms.
    (e) is disruptive to the efficient operation of a firm.

31. The theory of sales maximization subject to a minimum profit constraint is based on the premise that
    (a) a controlling management derives personal benefits from the size of a firm as well as its profit level.
    (b) the firm's objectives are always decided at the annual shareholders' meeting.
    (c) a minority of shareholders, who have goals different from those of the majority of shareholders, can form a majority of actual votes.
    (d) firms only desire a normal return to their investments.
    (e) All of the above.

32. Satisficing theory argues that
    (a) the majority of shareholders are satisfied with their management.
    (b) the firm's objective is not profit maximization but simply to attain some minimally acceptable profit level.
    (c) the firm will produce the output corresponding to maximum market share.
    (d) the most successful firms are those that produce goods that best satisfy consumers.
    (e) firms deliberately keep profits low to satisfy governments.

33. A basic difference between satisficing theory and the theories of profit maximization and sales maximization is that
    (a) satisficing is based on the goals of management, whereas the others are based on the goals of shareholders.
    (b) satisficing predicts the largest level of output among the three theories.
    (c) satisficing predicts that the firm will never produce the output level corresponding to either maximum profits or maximum sales.
    (d) satisficing predicts a range of outputs; the others predict unique output levels.
    (e) shareholders are satisfied with management so long as profits are positive.

EXERCISES

1. Opportunity Cost

This question addresses the opportunity costs involved in operating a business.

After five years of working, Sally Micmac left a $25,000 job to start her own business with the use of $20,000 she had saved. She charged the business $15,000 a year for her services but made no allowance for the 10 percent she might have earned on her savings in an investment of equal risk. In 1993 her accounting profits were $10,000. Had the business been economically profitable to that point? What needs to be known to decide whether it is economically profitable to continue the business?

2. Profits: Accounting versus Economic

The difference between accounting and economic profits is the emphasis of this exercise.

The following table presents last year's annual income statement for Harry's Hardware Store. Harry worked full-time at the store. He also used $25,000 of his savings to furnish and stock the store (included in costs). At the beginning of last year, he had been offered a $20,000 annual salary to work in another hardware store.

Annual Income Statement

Revenues		Costs	
Sales of merchandise	$90,000	Wholesale purchases	$60,000
Service revenues	5,000	Store supplies	2,000
		Labour costs (hired)	10,000
		Utilities	1,000
		Rent	5,000
		Depreciation on fixtures	2,000
Total revenues	$95,000	Total costs	$80,000

(a) Calculate last year's accounting profits for Harry's Hardware Store.

(b) What are some imputed costs that Harry should include in estimating the total costs of owning his business?

(c) Assume an interest rate of 10 percent. What are the total costs of Harry's business?

(d) Calculate his economic profits.

3. The following exercise addresses the imputed cost of depreciation.

   (a) For $10,000 a firm purchases a machine with an estimated 10 years of economic life and zero salvage value. What is the straight-line depreciation per year?

   (b) At the end of five years, this firm finds that the machine has a market value of only $1,000, which is expected to decline to zero after the five remaining years. What is the economically relevant depreciation per year now?

4. **Accounting and Economic Profits, Again**

   The following case is designed to highlight the tax implications of the important difference between accounting and economic profits

   Monique, a third-year honours economics student at Laurentian University, is considering the possibility of setting up her own business for the summer. Specifically, Monique plans to provide door-to-door delivery of the *Financial Post*, the *Wall Street Journal*, and the *New York Times* to cottagers in the Muskoka and Haliburton regions of Ontario. Because she will be graduating and seeking permanent employment next year, this enterprise is for one summer only and is an alternative to earning $3,000 after-tax income as a lifeguard.

   The following list itemizes the particulars:

   - Monique expects total revenues of $24,000 for the season.
   - To deliver the papers, she must purchase a van for $6,000, which she is certain to sell at season's end for $4,000.
   - The licence for distributing newspapers in these regions costs $3,000 and lasts for three years. However, it is nontransferable (i.e., it cannot be sold or used by anyone else).
   - To finance the purchase of the van and the licence, Monique will withdraw $9,000 from her savings account for a period of six months. This account pays an annual interest rate of 10 percent.
   - It will cost $8,000 to purchase the newspapers in bulk. To get this special price, Monique agrees to pay the $8,000 up front (i.e., at the beginning of the season). She borrows this amount from a bank for six months at an annual interest rate of 15 percent.
   - Costs of promotion, gas, and other incidentals come to $2,500.
   - Although Monique expects $24,000 in revenues, it may actually be less. Thus there is some risk involved. She feels that $1,000 would compensate her for taking the risk.
   - The tax rate on this business is 50 percent of net income.

   (a) What are Monique's direct and indirect costs for hired and purchased factors?
       (*Note:* Include any depreciation of assets.)

   (b) What are Monique's imputed costs?

(c) What is Monique's net profit before taxes and after taxes?

(d) What are her economic profits after taxes?

(e) If the business tax rate were applied to economic profits rather than to net income, would Monique be more or less likely to undertake this enterprise?

5. The Product Curves

The following exercise develops the relationships among the three product curves.

The data in the following table relate employment levels of a variable factor to the resulting output.

Variable Factor	Total Product	Average Product	Marginal Product
1	10	_____	
			_____
2	160	_____	
			_____
3	330	_____	
			_____
4	480	_____	
			_____
5	600	_____	
			_____
6	670	_____	
			_____
7	680	_____	

(a) Fill in the blanks. (Recall that marginal product refers to a change in output from one level of labour input to another. It is therefore shown between the lines referring to input levels.)

(b) Graph the total product curve in panel (i) of Figure 7-1, and the average product and marginal product curves in panel (ii). (Remember that marginal product is plotted at the midpoint on the horizontal axis—See Table 7-2 and its associated discussion in the text.)

Figure 7-1

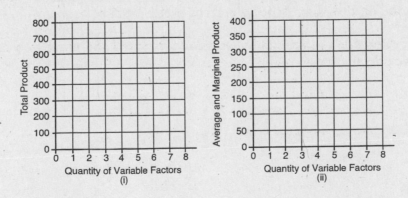

(c) At what output do diminishing returns begin?

6. The Relationship Between Productivity and Cost

This exercise is designed to illustrate the relationship between productivity and cost with a minimum of figures.

Assume the cost associated with the fixed factors is $30 and the cost of each variable unit is $10.

(a) Complete the following table.

Units of Variable Factor	Total Product	Marginal Product	Average Product	Total Cost	Marginal Cost	Total Cost
0	0		0	$30		
		2			$5.00	
1	2		2	40		$20.00
		3			___	
2	5		___	___	___	___
		___			___	
3	7		___	___	___	___
		___			___	
4	8		___	___	___	___
		___			___	
5	8		___	___		___

(b) Graph the total, average, and marginal product curves in panel (a) of Figure 7-2, and the three cost curves in panel (b). Remember that these "marginal" points are plotted at the midpoints of the intervals on the horizontal axis.

Figure 7-2

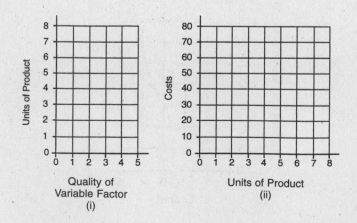

(i) Quality of Variable Factor

(ii) Units of Product

7. The Firm's Cost Structure

This exercise gives you practice reading information from a firm's cost structure. Given the family of cost curves in Figure 7-3, answer the following questions.

(a) The capacity of this firm occurs at an output of _____.

(b) The effect of diminishing marginal returns occurs after an output level of _____.

(c) The effect of diminishing average returns occurs after an output level of _____.

Figure 7-3

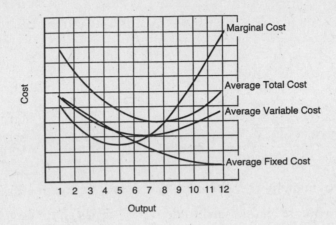

EXTENSION EXERCISES

The following two exercises ask you to derive a firm's cost structure by using different sets of information as the starting point.

E-1.   In this exercise you are given only the firm's total fixed costs and its marginal cost curve (in diagrammatic form). From these, you are asked to derive the firm's entire cost structure.

The marginal cost curve for a particular firm is presented in Figure 7-4. Because marginal cost is plotted at the midpoint, the marginal cost of producing (for example) the first unit of output is $50. In addition, suppose that the firm's fixed costs are $100.

Figure 7-4

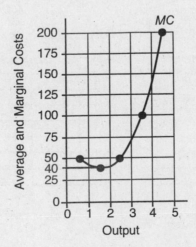

(a) Use the firm's MC curve together with the level of fixed costs to determine total variable costs (TVC), total costs (TC), average variable costs (AVC), and average total costs (ATC).

Output	MC	TVC	TC	AVC	ATC
0		___	___	___	___
	$50				
1		___	___	___	___
	___				
2		___	___	___	___
	___				
3		___	___	___	___
	___				
4		___	___	___	___
	___				
5		___	___	___	___

(b) Plot (approximately) the AVC and ATC curves on the graph.

E-2. In this exercise you are again asked to derive the firm's entire cost structure. However, in this case, you are provided only with the firm's total cost curve in algebraic form.

Assume that you are in the business of producing a commodity for which short run total cost is represented by the following equation:

$$TC = 30 + 3Q + Q^2$$

where Q is output of the commodity and TC is total costs.

(a) What are total fixed costs equal to?

(b) What is the equation that represents total variable costs?

(c) Derive the equation for average total costs (ATC).

(d) Fill in the blanks in the following table.

Q	TVC	TFC	TC	ATC	MC
0	___	___	___	___	
					___
1	___	___	___	___	
					___
2	___	___	___	___	
					___
3	___	___	___	___	
					___
4	___	___	___	___	
					___
5	___	___	___	___	
					___
6	___	___	___	___	
					___
7	___	___	___	___	
					___
8	___	___	___	___	
					___
9	___	___	___	___	
					___
10	___	___	___	___	

(e) What is the capacity of this firm?

(f) What is marginal cost at this capacity output?

(g) The equation for this firm's MC curve is:

$$MC = 3 + 2Q$$

(Those students that are familiar with calculus should note that this is the first derivative of the TC curve). To understand why marginal cost is plotted at the midpoints, use the equation for MC to calculate MC at outputs of 5, 5.5, and 6. Compare these answers with the marginal cost you derived in (d), which was calculated by taking the difference in TC between outputs of 5 and 6.

Appendix Exercises

The following exercises are based upon material in the appendix to this chapter. Complete these only after reading that material.

A-1. This question highlights the different price-quantity implications for a profit maximizer, satisficer and a sales maximizer. The diagram in Figure 7-5 presents the demand and cost conditions faced by a firm.

Figure 7-5

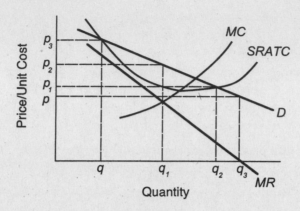

(a) What would be the choice of price and output for a profit maximizer? _____
(b) What would be the range of price and output for a profit satisficer who is content to cover opportunity costs as a minimum? _____
(c) What could be the price and output of a sales maximizer who is willing to accept losses for short periods (assume sufficient economies of scale so that *LRAC* is declining)? _____

A-2. As in the previous question, this exercise emphasizes the different output decisions of firms based upon their goals. In this case you are given the firm's profit function.

Assume that a firm is capable of making a reasonable projection of its profits (π) as it expands output (Q) and that this relationship is given by the following profit function:

$$\pi = 7Q - Q^2 - 6$$

(a) For values of $Q = 1, 2, 3, 3.5, 4, 5,$ and 6, plot the profit function on the grid in Figure 7-6.

Figure 7-6

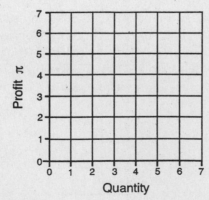

(b) If a satisficing firm has a profit target of 4, what range of output will that firm accept?

(c) What output is consistent with profit maximization?

(d) If the firm were a sales maximizer and constrained to have profits of a least 2, approximately what output would it choose?

A-3. To suggest why economists tend to be dissatisfied with non-maximizing models for price-output decisions, this problem extends the analysis of Exercise 9. In doing that exercise, you should already have noted that the satisficing firm has a rather wide range of outputs to choose from.

Note the following: the profit function is the difference between $TR = 17Q - Q^2$ and $TC = 10Q + 6$; $MR = 17 - 2Q$; and, the demand curve is $P = 17 - Q$.

(a) Confirm that the profit-maximizing output is 3.5, at which the price is 13.5.

(b) Now allow fixed costs to increase by 1 so that $TC = 10Q + 7$. How are the decisions for satisficer, profit maximizer, and sales maximizer altered? You may use the grid in Figure 7-7 to help derive your answers.

(c) Now change the total cost function to $11Q + 6$ to test the effect of a change in marginal costs. You should get straightforward answers for the maximizers, but what about the satisficer?

Figure 7-7

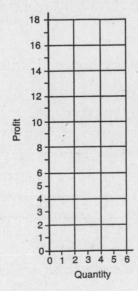

(d) Now assume that the original cost conditions return, but with a favourable demand shift to $P = 17 - 0.5Q$ (which also increases the demand elasticity at every price). Work out the decisions for the maximizers. How might the profit satisficer deal with the wide range of choices that meet the criterion that profits be at least 4?

PRACTICE MULTIPLE CHOICE TEST

1. When a firm uses its own funds to finance a project,
   (a) the cost of these funds is zero because they are fixed costs.
   (b) profits are greater because the firm does not have to borrow.
   (c) the forgone interest that could have been earned by these funds is an imputed cost of the project.
   (d) future profits diminish when revenues are used to replace internal investment funds.
   (e) profits are greater because interest does not have to be paid.

2. Depreciation, defined as the loss of value of an asset from its use in production,
   (a) is clearly a monetary cost.
   (b) is a function *only* of wear and tear in use.
   (c) is not an economic cost if the asset has no market value or alternative use.
   (d) does not apply to used equipment.
   (e) does not affect economic profit so long as the asset has been fully paid for.

3. Suppose that you own a dairy store that makes and sells homemade ice cream, using an ice cream maker that has no alternative use and no resale value. It cost $1,500 when it was purchased 15 years ago. The opportunity cost of its use is
   (a) $100, representing the annual depreciation.
   (b) zero.
   (c) some number greater than zero but under $100, representing the annual depreciation.
   (d) the amount of imputed interest on the cost of a replacement machine.
   (e) its replacement cost.

4. Which of the following is not an imputed cost?
   (a) Use of a firm's own funds.
   (b) Depreciation.
   (c) A return that compensates for risk taking.
   (d) An owner-manger's time.
   (e) The cost of an asset with no resale value.

5. A firm has total revenues of $100,000, total monetary outlays of $75,000, and an opportunity cost of capital of $25,000. It is correct to say that
   (a) economic profits are $25,000.   (b) normal profits are $25,000.
   (c) accounting profits are zero.   (d) accounting profits are negative.
   (e) economic profits are zero.

6. Which of the following is an example of a short run production decision?
   (a) A firm decides to relocate.
   (b) A contractor decides to work its crew overtime to finish a job.
   (c) A railway decides to eliminate all passenger service.
   (d) A paper company installs antipollution equipment.
   (e) An airline expands its fleet of aircraft.

7. If marginal product is falling, marginal product
   (a) is always less than average product.
   (b) is always equal to average product.
   (c) is always greater than average product.
   (d) can be greater than, equal to, or less than average product.
   (e) is negative.

8. A firm's wage bill in the short run equals its
   (a) short run total costs.   (b) total variable costs.
   (c) total fixed costs.   (d) marginal costs.
   (e) average total cost multiplied by output.

Questions 9 to 13 refer to Figure 7-8, which illustrates a firm's average total cost (*ATC*) and average variable cost (*AVC*) curves.

Figure 7-8

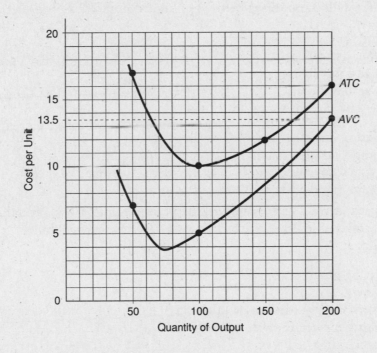

9. When the firm is producing 200 units of output, total costs in the short run are
   (a) $3,200.   (b) $2,700.
   (c) $16.   (d) $13.50.
   (e) Indeterminable with data provided.

10. When output equals 100 units, marginal cost is
    (a) $5.   (b) $15.
    (c) $10.   (d) $500.
    (e) Indeterminable with data provided.

11. At a total product of 200 units, *AFC* is
    (a) $2.50.   (b) $13.50.
    (c) $16.   (d) $2,700.
    (e) Indeterminable with data provided.

12. If the level of production is 50 units, *TFC* is
    (a) $350.   (b) $7.
    (c) $500.   (d) $10.
    (e) Indeterminable with data provided.

13. At an output of 200, *TFC* is
    (a) $500   (b) $3,200
    (c) $2.50   (d) $2,700
    (e) Indeterminable with data provided.

14. This firm's capacity is
    (a) $10.
    (b) $500.
    (c) 200 units of output.
    (d) 100 units of output.
    (e) cannot be determined with information provided.

15. Total cost is $30 at 10 units of output and $32 at 11 units of output. In this range of output, marginal cost is
    (a) equal to average total cost.
    (b) greater than average total cost.
    (c) less than average total cost.
    (d) less than average fixed cost.
    (e) Indeterminable with the information provided.

16. The law of diminishing marginal returns implies
    (a) decreasing average variable costs.   (b) increasing marginal costs.
    (c) decreasing marginal revenue.   (d) increasing average fixed costs.
    (e) decreasing average fixed cost.

SOLUTIONS

Chapter Review

1.(c) 2.(e) 3.(b) 4.(e) 5.(d) 6.(d) 7.(b) 8.(b) 9.(a) 10.(a) 11.(b) 12.(c) 13.(c) 14.(c) 15.(d) 16.(a) 17.(d) 18.(b) 19.(e) 20.(d) 21.(a) 22.(a) 23.(c) 24.(b) 25.(a) 26.(d) 27.(c) 28.(b) 29.(e) 30.(c) 31.(a) 32.(b) 33.(d)

Exercises

1. No, Sally would have been $2,000 better-off by working and investing separately. In deciding whether or not to continue it is current alternatives that count: Can she still get $25,000 in the old job (or another)? Can she sell her business assets for $20,000 and reasonably expect a $2,000 return? What are Sally's expectations regarding sales increases next year?

2. (a) $15,000.
   (b) Harry's imputed costs include forgone annual interest on the $25,000 investment (assuming that he could recover it), and $20,000 opportunity cost for his own salary.

(c) Total costs would be accounting costs of $80,000 plus forgone interest earnings of $2,500 and $20,000 salary.

(d) A *loss* of $7,500 is indicated for the past year.

3. (a) $1,000.

(b) $200, the amount of market value given up by using the machine one more year.

4. (a) Direct costs:

Licence	$ 3,000
Interest payments on loan	600
Bulk purchase	8,000
Promotion, gas, etc.	2,500
Indirect costs:	
Depreciation of van	2,000
Total direct and indirect costs	**$16,100**

(b) Imputed costs:

Interest forgone on savings	$ 450
Risk compensation	1,000
Forgone lifeguard earnings	3,000
Total imputed costs	**$4,450**

(c) Net profit before taxes = revenue − (direct costs + indirect costs) = $24,000 − $16,100 = $7,900.

Net profit after taxes = $7,900 × 0.50 = $3,950.

(d) Economic profit after taxes = net income after taxes − imputed costs = $3,950 − $4,450 = −$500.

(e) Economic profit before taxes = revenue − imputed costs − (direct + indirect costs) = $24,000 − $4,450 − $16,100 = $3,450.

Economic profit after taxes = $3,450 × 0.50 = $1,725.

Monique is more likely to undertake this enterprise if the business tax is applied to economic profits instead of net profit. By taxing net income, Revenue Canada does not allow Monique to deduct real (albeit imputed) costs and thereby converts her economic profit into a loss of $500.

5. (a)

Variable Factor	Total Product	Average Product	Marginal Product
1	10	10	
			150
2	160	80	
			170
3	330	110	
			150
4	480	120	
			120
5	600	120	
			70
6	670	112	
			10
7	680	97	

Figure 7-9

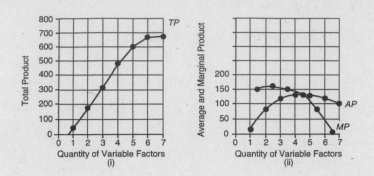

(c) Maximum *MP* is 170, which obtains for the third unit of the variable factor (plotted at 2.5 units). Thus diminishing returns begin after employment of the third variable factor.

6. (a)

Units of Variable Factor	Total Product	Marginal Product	Average Product	Total Cost	Marginal Cost	Total Cost
0	0		0.0	$30		∞
		2			$5.00	
1	2		2.0	40		$20.00
		3			3.33	
2	5		2.5	50		10.00
		2			5.00	
3	7		2.3	60		8.57
		1			10.00	
4	8		2.0	70		8.75
		0			∞	
5	8		1.6	80		10.00

(b) **Figure 7-10**

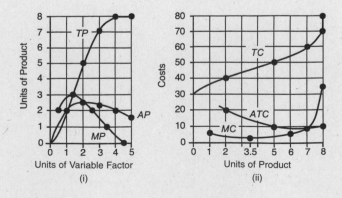

7. (a) 8.   (b) 5.
   (c) 7.

EXTENSION EXERCISES

E-1. (a)

Output	MC	TVC	TC	AVC	ATC
0		$0	$100	—	—
	$50				
1		50	150	$50.00	$150
	40				
2		90	190	45	95
	50				
3		140	240	46.67	80
	100				
4		240	340	60	85
	200				
5		440	540	88	108

(b) **Figure 7-11**

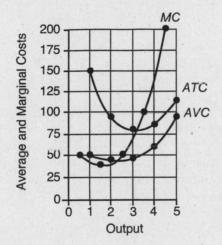

E-2. (a) 30.
       (b) $TVC = 3Q + Q^2$.
       (c) $ATC = TC/Q = (30 + 3Q + Q^2)/Q = 30/Q + 3 + Q$.

(d)

Q	TVC	TFC	TC	ATC	MC
0	$0	$30	$30	—	
					$4
1	4	30	34	34	
					6
2	10	30	40	20	
					8
3	18	30	48	16	
					10
4	28	30	58	14.5	
					12
5	40	30	70	14	
					14
6	54	30	84	14	
					16
7	70	30	100	14.3	
					18
8	88	30	118	14.8	
					20
9	108	30	138	15.3	
					22
10	130	30	160	16	

(e)   Somewhere between output levels 5 and 6.
(f)   14.
(g)   The marginal costs of outputs 5, 5.5, and 6 are 13, 14, and 15, respectively. The difference in *TC* between outputs 5 and 6 is 14, which is precisely the *MC* at the midpoint of 5.5 units of output.

Appendix Exercises

A-1.   (a) P_2 and q_1;
       (b)   from p_3 and q to p_1 and q_2;
       (c) p and q_3.

A-2.   (a)   **Figure 7-12**

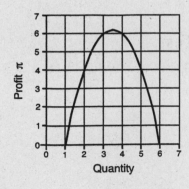

(b) From $Q = 2$ to $Q = 5$.

(c) $Q = 3.5$.

(d) $Q = 5.5$ (approximately).

A-3. (a) In this case, marginal cost is constant at 10. Setting $MC = MR$ yields $10 = 17 - 2Q$, which solves for $Q = 3.5$; $P = 17 - Q$, or 13.5.

(b) This has the effect of shifting the profit curve down a vertical distance of $1 at each level of output. The resulting profit curve is labeled b in the following graph. The output of the profit maximizer is unaffected. The output of the satisficer with a profit target of $4 now ranges from 2.5 to 4.5, approximately. The sales maximizer who has a profit target of $2 reduces output to approximately 5.25.

(c) The resulting profit curve is labeled c in the graph. The profit maximizer produces three units, and the sales maximizer produces four units. The satisficer can no longer attain the minimum profit level of $4. The closest it can come is $3, which is achieved when the profit-maximizing output of three units is produced.

Figure 7-13

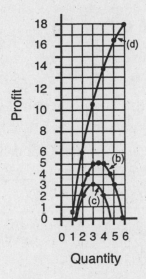

(d) The resulting profit curve is labeled d in the graph. As requested in Exercise 9, the profit curve is plotted only up to an output level of six units, which is the output of both the profit maximizer and the sales maximizer (actually, each would like to increase output beyond six units). The satisficer produces anywhere between (approximately) 1.25 and 6 units, despite the substantial difference in profits over this range.

Practice Multiple Choice Test

1.(c) 2.(c) 3.(b) 4.(e) 5.(e) 6.(b) 7.(d) 8.(b) 9.(a) 10.(c) 11.(a) 12.(c) 13.(a) 14.(d) 15.(c) 16.(b)

CHAPTER 8

PRODUCERS IN THE LONG RUN

(LO) *LEARNING OBJECTIVES*

1 Understand why cost minimization requires firms to equate the marginal product per dollar spent for all factors.

2 Explain the principle of substitution, and why it implies that firms will use more of factors whose prices have fallen (and use less of factors whose prices have increased).

3 Recognize the relationship between short-run and long-run cost curves.

4 Understand that changes in the economic environment often lead firms to innovate to improve their technology.

CHAPTER OVERVIEW

This chapter examines the behaviour of producers in both the long run and the very long run. There are no fixed factors in the long run, so a given output can be produced using different combinations of inputs. Some input combinations are **technically efficient**; some of these are also economically efficient. Profit-maximizing firms will substitute among factors to achieve the combination that provides **cost minimization**. This occurs when inputs are used in quantities such that the marginal product per dollar of expenditure is the same for each.

A **long-run average cost (*LRAC*) curve** represents the boundary between attainable and unattainable levels of cost for a given technology. The shape of the *LRAC* curve depends upon the relationship between inputs and outputs as the scale of a firm's operation changes. **Increasing, constant** and **decreasing returns** lead, respectively, to decreasing, constant and increasing long run average costs. Long and short run cost curves are related. Every point on the *LRAC* curve corresponds to a different combination of factors and, therefore, to a different short run average total cost (*SRATC*) curve. The *LRAC* curve is the **envelope** of the *SRATC* curves.

In the very long run, **technological change** leads to increases in **productivity**. Innovation is the key to productivity growth. New production techniques, improved inputs, and new products are types of innovations that have historically driven productivity growth.

CHAPTER REVIEW

The Long Run: No Fixed Factors

After studying this section, you should be able to: appreciate the relationship between profit maximization and cost minimization; apply the principle of substitution in explaining a firm's input use; explain why increasing returns (economies of scale) occur; discuss the relationship between long run average cost and economies of scale; understand the relationship between the long run and short run average cost curves. The key to understanding the technical material in this section is the relationship between the short and long run cost curves. Remember that a change in labour induces a movement along a *SRATC*, while a change in both labour and capital is generally required to move along the *LRAC* curve. Further, a movement along a *LRAC* curve is equivalent to a shift in the *SRATC* curve.

1. In addition to choosing the level of output, a firm in the long run must also select
   (a) the appropriate technology.
   (b) the amount of overtime for its labour force.
   (c) the cost-minimizing combination of inputs.
   (d) the profit-maximizing quantity of labour to employ with its fixed plant.
   (e) All of the above.

2. The cost-minimizing factor mix is obtained when
   (a) the marginal products of all factors are equalized.
   (b) the marginal product per dollar expended on each factor is equalized.
   (c) the marginal product of each factor divided by total expenditure on that factor is equalized across all factors.
   (d) the cost of employing an additional unit of each factor is equalized across all factors.
   (e) each factor's marginal cost is equalized.

3. A firm's long run average cost curve depicts
   (a) what costs will be attainable with technological improvement.
   (b) the lowest attainable unit costs when all factors are variable.
   (c) a firm's profit-maximizing output choices.
   (d) the lowest attainable average cost when all factor prices vary.
   (e) the lowest attainable average cost when technology is variable.

4. The long run average cost curve is determined by
   (a) technology and tastes.   (b) long run supply.
   (c) population growth.   (d) technology and input prices.
   (e) All of the above.

5. If the long run average cost curve is upward sloping, the firm is experiencing
   (a) long run decreasing returns.   (b) diseconomies of scale.
   (c) increasing costs.   (d) All of the above.
   (e) None of the above.

6. One possible explanation for economies of scale is
   (a) invention and innovation.
   (b) the introduction of new, improved inputs.
   (c) a decrease in a factor price.
   (d) increased specialization of production tasks.
   (e) technological improvement.

The Very Long Run: Changes in Technology

In the very long run, the relationship between inputs and output is itself variable due to technological change. Technological change is measured by productivity growth (e.g., output per unit of labour) and is an important source of rising living standards over time. This is a nontechnical section that identifies three sources of technological change.

7. Which of the following is the best measure of productivity?
   (a) Total output.
   (b) Total output per hour.
   (c) Total output per unit of resource input.
   (d) Total output per dollar of cost.
   (e) Total output per dollar of revenue.

8. Which of the following is *not* a type of technological change?
   (a) Process innovation.   (b) New production techniques.
   (c) Product innovation.   (d) Improved inputs.
   (e) Economies of scale.

9. The very long run
   (a) introduces changes in factor prices.
   (b) always involves a greater range of output than the short run or the long run.
   (c) applies to a period in which new production methods can be introduced.
   (d) extends long run analysis to higher production levels.
   (e) introduces allowance for variable plant size.

10. An *economically efficient* method of production is one that
   (a) uses the smallest number of resource inputs.
   (b) necessarily involves the use of roundabout methods of production.
   (c) produces a given output at minimum cost.
   (d) cannot also be technologically efficient.
   (e) minimizes the use of scarce capital.

Appendix to Chapter 8—Isoquant Analysis

This appendix develops a formal model of cost minimization in the long run. Isoquant analysis is analytically similar to indifference curve analysis which was covered in the appendix to Chapter 6. In reading this appendix, you should first understand the characteristics of isoquant and isocost curves, and then focus on understanding the cost-minimizing input combination. This occurs when a given isoquant is tangent to an isocost curve. The tangency implies that the marginal rate of technical substitution equals relative prices, which is equivalent to the condition in the first section of this chapter that the marginal product per dollar spent on each factor is equal all across factors.

11. If the marginal rate of (technical) substitution is +2 at a point on an isoquant,
   (a) the ratio of factor prices is +1:2.
   (b) the ratio of factor prices is –2:1.
   (c) the ratio of marginal products is 2:1.
   (d) the ratio of factor prices is +2.
   (e) one factor of production has negative marginal product.

12. An isocost line for two factors C and B (their respective prices are P_C and P_B) could have which of the following equations?
    (a) $BC = \$100$.
    (b) $\$100 = P_C + P_B$.
    (c) $\$100 = P_B B + P_C C$.
    (d) $\$100 = P_B P_C$.
    (e) $BC = P_B B + P_C C$.

13. If two factors C and B are graphed in the same unit scale with C on the vertical axis, and an isocost line has a slope $= -2$, then
    (a) $P_B = 2P_C$.
    (b) $P_C/P_B = 2$.
    (c) $C = 2B$.
    (d) $B = 2C$.
    (e) $P_B B = 2P_C C$.

14. At the point of tangency of the isocost line in question 13 with an isoquant,
    (a) the desired factor combination has 2C for each B.
    (b) the marginal product of factor B is twice that of C.
    (c) the desired factor combination has 2B for each C.
    (d) the marginal product of factor C is twice that of B.
    (e) the marginal rate of substitution is -0.5.

EXERCISES

1. **Efficiency**

   The important distinction between technical and economic efficiency is emphasized in the following exercise.

   A firm has four alternative methods of producing 100 gizmos. Each method represents different combinations of three factors: labour, lathe time, and raw materials. The inputs required by each method are given in the following table.

	Production Method			
	A	B	C	D
Labour hours	100	90	60	80
Lathe hours	25	75	80	70
Raw materials (kg)	160	150	120	100

   (a) Assume the price per unit of each factor is \$1. Determine the cost of each production method and indicate which is economically efficient.

   (b) Suppose the price of an hour of lathe time increases to \$2 (other prices remaining constant), what method (s) would a profit-maximizing firm now use?

   (c) Which of these methods is technically inefficient? Explain.

2. Cost Minimization

The focus of this question is the condition for cost minimization given in equations [8-1] and [8-2] of the text. If you are uncertain about it, review the associated discussion in the text.

Three firms are able to combine capital (K) and labour (L) in various ways, resulting in the marginal products as shown in the following table. (Note that higher number combinations substitute more capital for less labour, which decreases MP_K and increases MP_L.) All firms face the same factor prices: the price of a unit of capital is $10, and the price of labour is $5 per unit.

Combination Number	Firm A MP_K	Firm A MP_L	Firm B MP_K	Firm B MP_L	Firm C MP_K	Firm C MP_L
1	10	1	6	3	25	2
2	8	2	5	4	20	4
3	6	3	4	6	14	7
4	4	4	3	8	10	8
5	2	5	2	10	5	10

(a) Firm A is currently using combination 3, Firm B is using combination 2, and Firm C is using combination 4. Which firm is minimizing its costs? Explain.

(b) How would the firms that are not currently minimizing costs have to alter their use of capital and labour to do so?

3. The *LRAC* Curve

This exercise gives you practice in calculating the long run average cost curve. At the beginning of some time period, a firm is producing 1,000 bottles of wine per month by using 5 units of capital (K) and and 100 units of labour (L). The price of capital is $20, and the price of labour is $4 per unit. As the firm increases its output over a period of time, the following changes in the use of capital and labour are observed:

Output per month	K	L
2,000	10	180
4,000	18	300
6,000	25	400
8,000	34	650
10,000	60	1,000

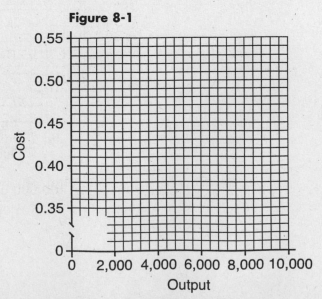

Figure 8-1

(a) Calculate and graph the long run average cost curve.

(b) At what output level do long run increasing returns cease?

4. **The Relationship Between *SRATC* and *LRAC***

The purpose of this exercise is to highlight the relationship between short and long run average cost curves. It does so by making a simplifying assumption that technology only permits two possible short run cost curves.

A firm is operating in an industry in which it is technologically possible to construct only two classes of plant. The first, Class A, is highly automated and requires an initial investment of $1,000,000; production in this plant takes place at a marginal cost of $3 per unit of output. The Class B plant employs a more labour-intensive production process and therefore requires a relatively smaller fixed cost of $500,000. However, this class of plant has a relatively higher marginal cost of $4 a unit. Thus the total cost curve for each class of plant can be represented by the following equations:

$$\text{Class A plant: } TC_A = \$1,000,000 + 3Q$$

$$\text{Class B plant: } TC_B = \$500,000 + 4Q$$

(a) Plot the firm's long run average cost curve (i.e., the lowest attainable average cost for each output with plant size variable).

Figure 8-2

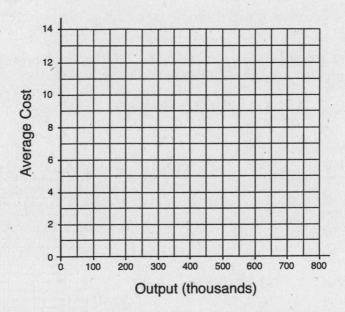

(b) If this firm plans to produce 400,000 units of output, which plant should it employ? Explain.

(c) Over what range of output do economies of scale occur for each class of plant? Why?

5. Well into the post-World War II period, Inco (then International Nickel) possessed monopoly power based on the rich nickel ore body around Sudbury, Ontario. However, discoveries elsewhere gradually eroded its power to control prices. During the metal slump of the early 1980s, Inco posted losses of $1 billion (1981–1984). In 1981, Inco introduced a technique of "bulk mining" columns of ore 300 feet high. Only two tunnel shafts were required. The upper shaft was used for crews to drill the ore column and deposit explosives; the lower shaft, 300 feet below, was used to load the fallen ore. This innovation replaced a technique of drilling 20-foot sections. As a result, Inco made a profit of $45 million in 1985 (even though nickel prices remained depressed and volume static) with 21,000 employees as compared to 35,000 in 1981.

(a) Economists would term this a _____ run development, which is characterized by (upward/downward) shifts of the _____ run and _____ run cost curves.

(b) Assuming the same volume of output, labour productivity increased by roughly _____ percent between 1981 and 1985.

(c) Does this problem lend credence to the adage that "necessity is the mother of invention"? Explain.

Appendix Exercises

The following exercises are based on material in the appendix to this chapter. Read the appendix before attempting them.

A-1. This exercise is designed to derive the cost-minimizing input combination for a given output represented by its isoquant.

The table that follows shows six methods of producing an output of 10 widgets per month by using different combinations of capital and labour.

(a) Complete the last three columns in the table.

Method	Units of Capital	Units of Labour	Δ Capital	Δ Labour	Estimated MRS of Capital for Labour
A	10	80	_____	_____	_____
B	15	58	_____	_____	_____
C	25	40	_____	_____	_____
D	40	24	_____	_____	_____
E	58	15	_____	_____	_____
F	80	9	_____	_____	_____

(b) On the graph in Figure 8-3, plot the isoquant indicated by the data in the table. (Assume these are the only feasible methods, and connect the points by straight line segments.)

Figure 8-3

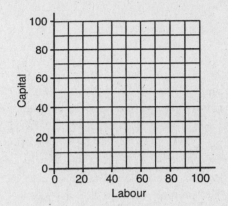

(c) For each of the following price combinations, calculate the slope of the isocost line P_L/P_K, and determine the economically efficient method of production by drawing in the minimum isocost line.

	Price of Labour	Price of Capital	P_L/P_K	Method
(1)	$1,000	$ 500	_____	_____
(2)	1,000	1,000	_____	_____
(3)	1,000	2,000	_____	_____

A-2. The following exercise gives you practice using isoquant analysis.

The graph in Figure 8-4 depicts isoquants for several levels of output that could be produced with different combinations of capital and labour.

Figure 8-4

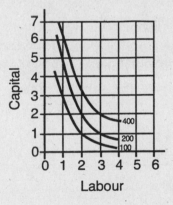

(a) If the relative price of labour to capital were 1, how many units of capital and labour would this firm employ to produce 100 units of output (at minimum cost)?

(b) If the price of capital were to change to one-half its original level, and the firm wanted to produce 200 units of output at minimum cost, how much capital and labour would it now employ? Explain.

(c) By examination of these three isoquants, what (if anything) can be said about returns to scale?

PRACTICE MULTIPLE CHOICE TEST

1. The profit-maximizing combination of capital (K) and labour (L) occurs when these factors are employed such that
   (a) $MP_K/P_K = MP_L/P_L$.   (b) $MP_K/K = MP_L/L$.
   (c) $MP_K/P_L = MP_L/P_K$.   (d) $P_K K = P_L L$.
   (e) $MP_K/P_K K = MP_L/P_L L$.

2. Suppose that the marginal product of capital in a particular firm is 5 and that of labour is 10, and the price of capital is $2 and that of labour is $1. To minimize costs, this firm will
   (a) substitute more capital for less labour.
   (b) substitute more labour for less capital.
   (c) not alter its factor mix.
   (d) hire more capital and keep labour constant.
   (e) reduce labour employment.

Questions 3 and 4 refer to the following table, which presents four possible combinations of capital (K) and labour (L) and their associated marginal products. Each combination produces exactly 100 units of output. Assume that the firm wishes to minimize production costs.

Combination	K	MP_K	L	MP_L
A	14	12	1	10
B	12	14	3	7
C	8	16	4	4
D	6	20	7	2

3. If the ratio of the price of capital to the price of labour is 2, this firm will employ combination
   (a) A.   (b) B.
   (c) C.   (d) D.
   (e) Either C or D.

4. If the relative price of capital to labour falls, the firm may (depending on the magnitude of the fall) wish to use combination
   (a) A.   (b) B.
   (c) C.   (d) D.
   (e) Indeterminable with data provided.

5. Constant long run average costs for a firm means that
   (a) there are greater advantages to small than to large plants.
   (b) an unlimited amount of output will be produced.
   (c) any scale of production costs the same per unit as any other.
   (d) total cost is independent of the level of output.
   (e) marginal cost equals zero.

6. Suppose a firm doubles employment of all of its factors and, as a result, output increases from 100 units to 300 units. This firm is operating under
   (a) diseconomies of scale.   (b) long run decreasing returns.
   (c) decreasing costs.   (d) decreasing total cost.
   (e) increasing costs.

7. A firm experiencing long run increasing returns that decides to increase output should do so by
   (a) substituting more labour and less capital.
   (b) employing a new technology.
   (c) employing less of each factor.
   (d) building smaller plants.
   (e) building larger plants.

8. An upward shift in the family of short run cost curves as well as the long run average cost curve could be explained by
   (a) economies of scale.
   (b) an increase in the fixed factor such as plant size.
   (c) an increase in a factor price.
   (d) a larger capital-labour ratio.
   (e) technological improvement.

9. When a firm seeks to minimize the cost of producing a given output, it does not need to know
   (a) the technically efficient input combinations.
   (b) the economically efficient input combinations.
   (c) its production function.
   (d) the prices of inputs.
   (e) the maximum level of profits.

10. In a country where labour is relatively abundant and capital is scarce, it is likely that
    (a) firms will use capital intensive production methods, *ceteris paribus*.
    (b) virtually any combination of inputs would be economically efficient.
    (c) firms will employ labour intensive production techniques.
    (d) there is a strong incentive to introduce labour-saving innovations.
    (e) Both (c) and (d) are correct.

11. Assume a local garage employs 10 units of labour and 50 units of capital to produce 400 oil changes. Currently, the price of labour is $10 per unit and the price of capital is $5 per unit, and the MP_L equals 2 and the MP_K equals 6. Given these circumstances, the firm
    (a) is both profit-maximizing and cost-minimizing.
    (b) should increase the use of both inputs.
    (c) could lower its production costs by decreasing labour input and increasing capital input.
    (d) could lower its production costs by increasing labour input and decreasing capital input.
    (e) should decrease the use of both inputs.

12. If capital costs $8 per unit and labour costs $4 per unit, and a firm's marginal product of capital is 4 and the marginal product of labour is 8, this firm should
    (a) employ more capital and labour.
    (b) employ less capital and labour.
    (c) employ more capital and less labour.
    (d) employ less capital and more labour.
    (e) not change its current factor use.

13. Due to China's higher population density, the price of land (relative to the price of labour) is higher in China than in Canada. Consider Canadian and Chinese rice producers who have access to the same technologies. The Canadian firm will use the two inputs, land and labour, in such a way that its land/labour ratio is
    (a) equal to that of the Chinese firm.
    (b) lower than that of the Chinese firm.
    (c) higher than that of the Chinese firm.
    (d) equal to the relative prices of land and labour.
    (e) indeterminable with information provided.

14. Increasing returns to scale
    (a) means that output rises proportionately less than inputs, increasing per unit cost of production in the short run.
    (b) means that output rises proportionately more than inputs resulting in increasing per unit costs.
    (c) means that output rises proportionately more than inputs, resulting in lower per unit costs in the long run.
    (d) has the same meaning as increasing costs of production.
    (e) none of these.

15. In the long-run a firm's production will take place
    (a) at the minimum point of the *LRAC*.
    (b) at the tangency of the relevant *SRATC* and the *LRAC*.
    (c) anywhere along the *LRAC*.
    (d) between the highest and lowest points of the *LRAC*.
    (e) none of the above.

16. Points below the long-run average cost curve
    (a) may represent actual cost and production levels in the short run.
    (b) represent less efficient cost levels than points on the long-run average cost curve.
    (c) are attainable only when all factors are variable.
    (d) represent unattainable cost levels.
    (e) are attainable if the firm minimizes its costs according to the "principle of substitution."

Questions 17 to 21 refer to the following diagram which depicts a firm's *LRAC* and selected *SRATC* curves.

Figure 8-5

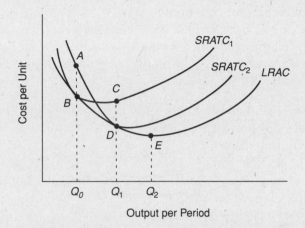

17. If this firm is producing at point *B*, we could say that it
    (a) is maximizing its profits.
    (b) minimizing the cost of producing Q_O.
    (c) can increase profits by moving to point *A*.
    (d) can lower its costs by moving to point *A*.
    (e) minimizes costs at point *E*.

18. The firm is currently producing at point *A*. If it increases its employment of labour, it will move toward
    (a) any point on $SRATC_2$.
    (b) *B*.
    (c) *C*.
    (d) *D*.
    (e) none of the above.

19. The firm is currently producing at point *B*. An increase in its capital may be represented by
    (a) a movement to *A*.
    (b) staying at point *B*.
    (c) a movement to *C*.
    (d) an upward shift in the *LRAC* curve.
    (e) none of the above.

20. A technological improvement can be characterized by
    (a) a movement from either *A* to *B* or *C* to *D*.
    (b) a movement from either *B* to *A* or from *D* to *C*.
    (c) a shift from $SRATC_1$ to $SRATC_2$.
    (d) an upward shift in the *LRAC* curve.
    (e) a downward shift in the *LRAC* curve.

21. Output beyond Q_2 is experiencing
    (a) diseconomies of scale.
    (b) decreasing returns.
    (c) increasing costs.
    (d) all of the above.
    (e) none of the above.

Appendix

Questions 22 to 24 refer to Figure 8-6 which depicts several of a firm's isocost and isoquant curves.

Figure 8-6

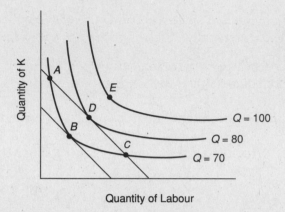

22. A firm will minimize the costs of producing 80 units of output at point
    (a) A
    (b) B
    (c) C
    (d) D
    (e) E

23. Suppose the firm is currently producing at point B and the price of labour increases. If the firm wants to minimize the cost of producing the same level of output, a possible input combination is at point
    (a) A
    (b) B
    (c) C
    (d) D
    (e) E

24. Suppose the firm is currently producing at point B and the prices of both labour and capital increase by 25%. If the firm wants to minimize the cost of producing the same level of output, the firm's chosen input combination would be at point
    (a) A
    (b) B
    (c) C
    (d) D
    (e) E

SOLUTIONS

Chapter Review

1.(c) 2.(b) 3.(b) 4.(d) 5.(d) 6.(d) 7.(c) 8.(e) 9.(c) 10.(c) 11.(c) 12.(c) 13.(a) 14.(b)

Exercises

1. (a) Method D is economically efficient. Method A costs $285, B costs $315, C costs $260, and D costs $250.

   (b) Method A, which costs $310. (Method B now costs $390, C costs $340, and D costs $320.)

   (c) Method B is technically inefficient since method D uses fewer units of each factor. Thus method B would not be economically efficient under any set of factor prices.

2. (a) Firm A is minimizing costs since, with combination 3, the ratio of the marginal products of capital and labour are equal to the ratio of their cost per unit of the factor employed (6/3 = 10/5).

   (b) Firm B would have to move to combination 1 by using less capital, and thereby raise the MP_K, and more labour, thereby reducing the MP_L. Firm C would have to move to combination 3, increasing MP_K (reducing capital use) and decreasing MPL (increasing labour use).

3. (a) **Figure 8-7**

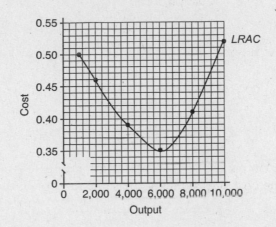

   (b) 6,000.

4. (a) **Figure 8-8**

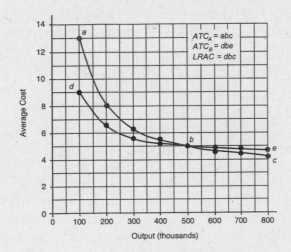

   (b) Class B. With a Class A plant, it would cost $2.2 million to produce 400,000 units but only $2.1 million with a Class B plant.

   (c) Economies of scale occur over the entire range of output from 1 to infinity. Each total cost curve is characterized by a fixed cost and constant marginal cost. It is easy to determine that average variable cost is also constant (and equal to marginal cost). Under these conditions, average total cost will continuously decrease as output increases because average variable cost is not rising to offset the impact of a declining average fixed cost.

5. (a) Very long; downward; short; long.
   (b) 67%. Since 3/5 of the number of workers are producing the same output, productivity increased to 5/3 its original level or, equivalently, by 2/3.
   (c) The losses with the erosion of monopoly power and the slump in the metal market created the necessity.

6. (a)

Method	Δ Capital	Δ Labour	Estimated MRS of Capital for Labour
A	—	—	—
B	+5	−22	−0.23
C	+10	−18	−0.56
D	+15	−16	−0.94
E	+18	−9	−2.00
F	+22	−6	−3.67

(b) **Figure 8-9**

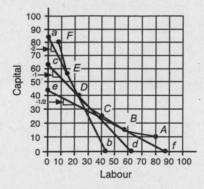

(c) For price combination 1, the relative price of labour to capital is 2, and the minimum isocost line for producing 100 widgets is *ab* in the graph. The tangency of the isocost line and the straight line segment joining E and D implies that either method E or D could be employed. Combination 2 has a price ratio of 1, and a minimum isocost line *cd*, which implies method D. Combination 3 has a price ratio of 0.5, a minimum isocost line *ef*, which implies that method B should be employed.

7. (a) One unit of capital and two units of labour.
   (b) The slope of an isocost line is now −2, which yields a tangency with the isoquant representing 200 units of output at approximately two units of capital and two units of labour.
   (c) These isoquants indicate economies of scale. Take any factor mix such as two units each of capital and labour and double each to four units. Since factor prices are constant, doubling all factors serves to double total cost exactly. However, the combination of four units of each factor lies above the isoquant representing 400 units of output. Therefore, doubling all factors results in more than double the output. A doubling of costs and a more than doubling of output implies that long run average cost is decreasing.

Practice Multiple Choice Test

1.(a) 2.(b) 3.(b) 4.(a) 5.(c) 6.(c) 7.(e) 8.(c) 9.(e) 10.(c) 11.(c) 12.(d) 13.(c) 14.(c) 15.(b) 16.(d) 17.(b) 18.(d) 19.(a) 20.(e) 21.(d) Appendix 22.(d) 23.(a) 24.(b)

PART FOUR

MARKETS, PRICING, AND EFFICIENCY

CHAPTER 9

COMPETITIVE MARKETS

LEARNING OBJECTIVES

1 Distinguish between competitive markets and competitive firm behaviour.

2 Know the key assumptions of the theory of perfect competition.

3 Explain the difference between an individual firm's demand curve and the industry demand curve for a perfectly competitive market.

4 Understand the rules for profit-maximizing behaviour.

5 Identify whether firms are making losses or profits in the short run.

6 Explain the role that entry and exit play in a competitive industry's long run equilibrium.

7 Understand how competitive industries respond to long run changes in demand.

CHAPTER OVERVIEW

Market structure affects the degree to which individual firms can influence their product's price. In **perfectly competitive markets**, firms produce a **homogeneous product** and are **price-takers**. There is no need for firms in a perfectly competitive market structure to actively engage in competitive behaviour.

All profit-maximizing firms produce that level of output where (a) price is at least as great as average variable cost, and (b) marginal cost equals marginal revenue. Since firms are price-takers in perfectly competitive markets, their marginal revenue equals price. Thus, profit-maximizing firms in these markets equate marginal cost to price.

In the short run, firms will cease production entirely if revenues from the sale of output do not cover the variable costs of production but will continue to operate if revenue is above variable costs. This insight explains why some firms continue to employ less efficient, vintage technologies, and why some firms may continue to operate in declining industries even though they may be experiencing losses.

Perfect competition is also characterized by *freedom of entry and exit*. In the long run, profits or losses will lead to the entry or exit, respectively, of capital into or out of the industry. Freedom of entry and exit drives the competitive industry to a long run equilibrium of zero profits, and results in the firm's production level corresponding to minimum average cost. We will see in later chapters that these are important properties that help explain the widespread appeal of perfect competition as a market structure.

CHAPTER REVIEW

Market Structure and Firm Behaviour

Many students are surprised to hear that perfectly competitive firms do not actively engage in competitive behaviour. This is due to a confusion between competitive market structure and competitive behaviour. When reading this section, focus on the reason why perfectly competitive firms are price-takers and do not therefore engage in competitive behaviour.

1. A perfectly competitive market structure is best described by firms that
   (a) allocate a substantial share of their budget to advertising.
   (b) engage in cutthroat competition by denigrating each others' products.
   (c) are subjected to government controls ensuring fair competition.
   (d) do not actively advertise or undercut their competitors' prices.
   (e) actively undercut their competitors' prices.

2. Which of the following characteristics is not an important determinant of the type of market structure?
   (a) The number of sellers and the number of buyers.
   (b) Whether the firms are foreign-owned transnational corporations.
   (c) The firm's ability to influence demand by advertising.
   (d) The ease of entry and exit in the industry.
   (e) The similarity of competitors' products.

The Theory of Perfect Competition

After reading this section, you should be able to explain why it is reasonable for each firm in a perfectly competitive market to behave as though it faces a perfectly elastic demand curve, even though the market demand curve is downward sloping. The explanation is that these firms are price-takers which is implied by the first three assumptions of perfect competition. Note also that average revenue, marginal revenue and price are all equal for firms in these markets.

3. The assumption that each firm in a perfectly competitive market is a price-taker basically means that
   (a) market price is independent of the level of industry output.
   (b) each firm's supply curve is perfectly elastic.
   (c) the industry supply curve is perfectly elastic.
   (d) regardless of how much an individual firm produces, it will never have any impact on market price.
   (e) for reasonable variations in a single firm's output, the impact on market price is negligible.

4. Which one of the following characteristics of a market would you expect to be *inconsistent* with price-taking behaviour?
   (a) There are a large number of firms in the industry.
   (b) Each firm produces a product that is somehow distinguishable from that of its competitors (e.g., in terms of quality or brand name).
   (c) Each firm's share of total industry output is insignificant.
   (d) Each firm behaves as though it faces a perfectly elastic demand curve.
   (e) Firms do not actively engage in competitive behaviour.

5. A firm that faces a perfectly elastic demand curve has a
   (a) linear total revenue curve with a slope equal to the market price.
   (b) horizontal total revenue curve.
   (c) constant total revenue regardless of the level of output.
   (d) total revenue curve shaped like an inverted U.
   (e) negatively sloped total revenue curve.

6. In a perfectly competitive market, each firm's demand curve is coincident with the
   (a) average revenue curve.
   (b) marginal revenue curve.
   (c) horizontal line drawn at the market price.
   (d) All of the above.
   (e) None of the above.

Short Run Decisions

Make sure you fully understand the conditions under which a profit-maximizing firm will produce a positive level of output and when it will shutdown production; it is worthwhile rereading the two rules for profit maximization presented in the text. (*TIP*: A firm's decision to shut down does not mean that it goes out of business, but rather that it reduces output to zero—going out of business is a long run decision). The firm's short run equilibrium obtains when it produces the output which maximizes its profit at a given price. The set of such short run equilibria generated by different prices traces out the firm's short run supply curve. Review Figure 9-7 in the text to understand how a firm may be making positive, zero or negative profits in the short run even though it is maximizing profits.

7. If output occurs where marginal cost equals marginal revenue, then
   (a) the last unit produced adds the same amount to costs as it does to revenue.
   (b) the firm is maximizing profits.
   (c) there is no reason to reduce or expand output, as long as TR is greater than or equal to TVC.
   (d) the difference between TR and TC is maximized.
   (e) All of the above.

8. A profit-maximizing firm, regardless of market structure, should shut down production and suffer a short run loss equal to its fixed cost if
   (a) average revenue is less than average variable cost.
   (b) average revenue is less than average total cost but greater than average variable cost.
   (c) total revenue is less than total cost but greater than total variable cost.
   (d) its economic profits are negative and smaller in absolute value than total fixed cost.
   (e) profits are negative.

9. Should it decide to produce a positive output, any profit-maximizing firm should produce the output level for which
    (a) the incremental change in revenue equals the incremental change in costs.
    (b) total revenue exceeds total costs.
    (c) average revenue equals average total costs.
    (d) average costs are minimized.
    (e) total revenue equals total costs.

10. A perfectly competitive firm does not try to sell more of its product by lowering its price below the market price because
    (a) this would be considered unethical price chiseling.
    (b) its competitors would not permit it.
    (c) its demand is inelastic, so total revenue would decline.
    (d) it can sell whatever it produces at the market price.
    (e) consumers might believe this firm's product to be inferior, and therefore cease buying it.

11. Assuming that Rule 1 for profit maximization is satisfied, a perfectly competitive firm is maximizing short run profits when it produces that output where
    (a) price equals average total cost.
    (b) price equals short run marginal cost.
    (c) short run marginal cost equals average total cost.
    (d) marginal revenue equals average variable cost.
    (e) All of the above.

12. A firm producing a positive output level, covering variable costs but making a loss in the short run,
    (a) is not maximizing profits.
    (b) should definitely shut down.
    (c) should exit the industry.
    (d) should either expand or contract its plant size.
    (e) may nonetheless be doing the best that it can with respect to profits.

Long Run Decisions

Profits are a signal for resource allocation. If profits are positive (negative) firms will enter (exit) a perfectly competitive market. If profits are zero, resources are just covering their opportunity cost, and there is no incentive for entry or exit. Bear in mind that we are referring to economic profit. Review the conditions for long run equilibrium in perfect competition. It is useful to compare them to the conditions for short run equilibrium. After reading this section you should be able to explain its central lesson: how the pursuit of profits eliminates profits. The long run supply curve for a perfectly competitive industry may slope upwards, downwards or be horizontal. Make sure that you understand all three cases.

13. The existence of positive profits in a perfectly competitive industry
    (a) is a signal for existing firms to lower their price.
    (b) is a signal for existing firms to maintain their plant size.
    (c) provides an incentive for new firms to enter the industry.
    (d) encourages all firms to expand their production levels.
    (e) signals firms to increase price.

14. Long run equilibrium in a perfectly competitive industry is characterized by
    (a) each firm in the industry earning maximum attainable profits.
    (b) each firm in the industry making zero economic profits.
    (c) no firm desiring to enter or exit this industry.
    (d) no firm desiring to alter its plant size.
    (e) All of the above.

15. The conditions for long run competitive equilibrium include all but which of the following?
    (a) $P = AVC$.   (b) $P = MC$.
    (c) $P = SRATC$.   (d) $P = LRAC$.
    (e) $MR = MC$.

16. Long run economic profits will not exist in a perfectly competitive industry because
    (a) new firms will enter the industry and eliminate them.
    (b) corporate income taxes eliminate profits.
    (c) competitive firms are too small to be profitable.
    (d) increasing costs will eliminate profits in the long run.
    (e) firms in this industry engage in cutthroat price cutting.

17. A competitive industry's long run supply curve is
    (a) the sum of each firm's short run supply curve.
    (b) the sum of each firm's $LRAC$ curve.
    (c) the set of long run market equilibria induced by changes in demand.
    (d) upward sloping so long as factor prices are constant.
    (e) perfectly elastic in a declining cost industry.

EXERCISES

1. This exercise gives you practice in reading profit information from a firm's cost curves. Figure 9-1 depicts the short run cost structure of a hypothetical, profit-maximizing firm that operates in a perfectly competitive industry.

   Figure 9-1

   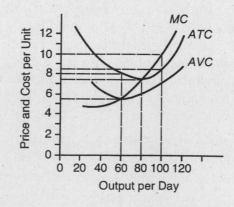

(a) Use the firm's cost structure to complete the following table.

If Market Price is	$10.00	$7.50	$5.50
(i) profit-maximizing output is	_____	_____	_____
At this output,			
(ii) total revenue is	_____	_____	_____
(iii) total costs is	_____	_____	_____
(iv) profit is (+ or -)	_____	_____	_____
(v) marginal revenue is	_____	_____	_____
(vi) marginal cost is	_____	_____	_____
(vii) average total cost is	_____	_____	_____
(viii) profit per unit is	_____	_____	_____

(b) Why is neither $10.00 nor $5.50 the long run market price?

2. The purpose of the following question is to determine if a firm is maximizing short run profits and, if not, what adjustments it should make. You are provided with raw data that is numerical as opposed to diagrammatic (as was the case in Exercise 1 above).

Consider the following information regarding output levels, costs, and market price for two perfectly competitive firms operating in different industries. Each firm has an upward-sloping marginal cost curve.

Firm A: output = 5,000   total variable cost = $2,500
              price = $1.00   total fixed cost = $2,000
                                marginal cost = $1.20

Firm B: output = 5,000   average total costs = $1.00
              price = $1.20   (and, at the minimum level)

	Firm A	Firm B
(a) Are these firms making profits?	_____	_____
(b) If so, how much?	_____	_____
(c) Are these firms making maximum profits?	_____	_____
(d) Should these firms produce more, less, or the same output? Explain.	_____	_____

3. *This Is Nuts!*

Some students may feel that it is unreasonable for a competitive firm to behave as though it faces a horizontal demand curve when it knows the market demand curve is downward sloping. This exercise is designed to demonstrate the reasonableness of this assumption.

Suppose the output of peanuts in the United States is 2 million tons in a given year. One of the many producers, Mr. Shell, has experienced a doubling of his output over his previous year's output of 40 tons. All other producers report no change in their output. The market elasticity of demand is estimated to be 0.20.

(a) Calculate the effect on the world price of peanuts from Mr. Shell's increase in output (in percentage terms).

(b) Calculate the elasticity of demand Mr. Shell's firm faces.

(c) Does your answer for (b) indicate that the firm is likely to act as a price taker? Explain.

4. The Industry's Short Run Supply Curve

This is a quick exercise that derives the industry's short run supply curve from its firms' cost curves.

The graphs in Figure 9-2 present the marginal cost curves of three firms which, for simplicity, are assumed to be the only firms in a perfectly competitive industry. Minimum average variable costs for the three firms are as follows: Firm A, $3; Firm B, $5; Firm C, $7. Further, minimum average total costs are as follows: Firm A, $5; Firm B, $7; Firm C, $8.

Figure 9-2

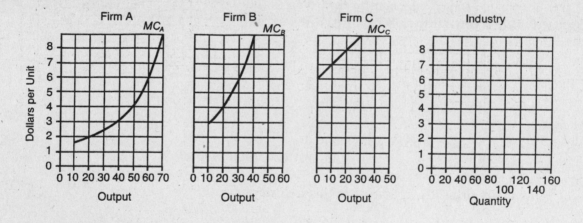

(a) Derive the industry short run supply curve, and plot it in the industry grid.

(b) If market price were $6.50, what quantity would be supplied by this industry, and what would be the output of each of the three firms? (approximate answers)

(c) For each of the three firms, indicate if it would be making a profit or a loss.

5. The Long Run Equilibrium

This exercise walks you through some of the long run adjustments that take place in a perfectly competitive market in response to a change in demand (we ignore adjustments that current firms may make to plant size). This is an important exercise! Successful completion of it reflects a good understanding of much of the analytical material in this chapter.

All firms in the gadget industry, as well as potential entrants, have the cost structure depicted in panel (i) of Figure 9-3 (the notation is identical to that in the text). Panel (ii) shows the industry's short run supply curve S and the current market demand curve D.

(a) What are equilibrium price and quantity in the gadget market?

(b) What is the output of each firm in this industry, and what is the resulting level of profit?

Figure 9-3

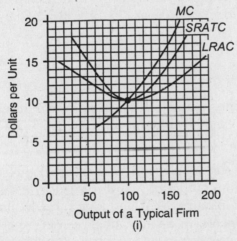
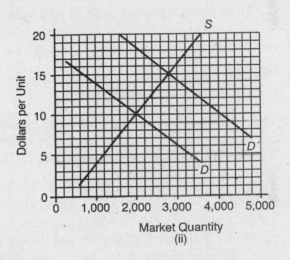

(c) How many firms are operating in this industry?

(d) Is the industry in long run equilibrium? Explain.

(e) Now suppose that the demand for gadgets shifts to D'. What are the new equilibrium market price and quantity in the short run?

(f) What is the short run quantity response of each firm in the industry?

(g) What is each firm's short run profit?

(h) Explain what will happen to the industry short run supply curve once sufficient time has elapsed for entry and exit to occur.

(i) Once the new long run equilibrium is established, what are the market price and quantity?

(j) What are the levels of output and associated profit of each firm in the new long run equilibrium?

(k) How many firms are now in this gadget industry?

6. **Long Run Equilibrium, Again!**

This exercise also examines long run adjustments in a perfectly competitive industry. This time you are given adjustments in the industry and are asked to depict the firm's adjustments—the opposite of the previous exercise.

An industry's short run supply (SRS) and long run supply (LRS) curves are depicted in panel A of Figure 9-4. The industry's initial equilibrium output of X is disturbed by a shift in demand to D'D'. The new short run equilibrium output is Y, and long run equilibrium output is Z. Show these equilibria and the adjustments for an individual firm in panel B. Use the firm's demand, short run marginal and average total cost, and long run average cost curves. Denote the firm's corresponding outputs as x, y and z.

Figure 9-4

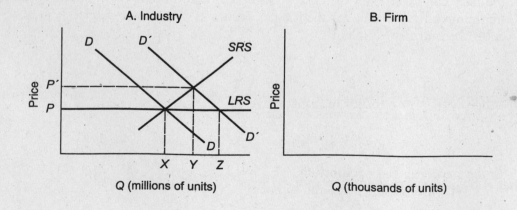

EXTENSION EXERCISE

E-1.   **The Impact of a Technological Improvement**

This exercise addresses the impact of a change in technology in a perfectly competitive market. For simplicity we shall consider only two vintages of technology, the old and the new. For the moment, assume that the new technology has not yet been invented, so that all firms employ the current (soon to be old) production technology that results in the cost structure depicted in panel (i) of Figure 9-5. To keep the graph tidy, the *LRAC* curve has not been drawn; however, you should assume that minimum efficient scale for these firms occurs at 10 units of output. Panel (ii) provides the market demand curve (*D*) and the industry short run supply curve (*S*).

Figure 9-5

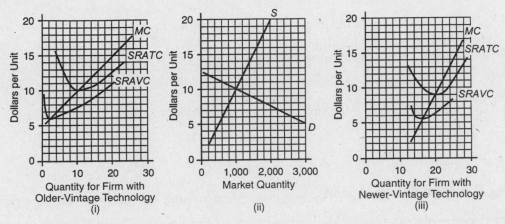

(a)   What are the industry's long run equilibrium price and quantity?

(b)   What is each firm's output and profit level in the long run equilibrium? How many firms are in the industry?

(c)   Now suppose that a new technology is invented so that any firm now entering this industry can do so with the cost structure depicted in panel (iii). Assume that the minimum efficient scale for these firms occurs at 20 units of output. Will new firms enter the industry? Explain.

(d)   When will entry into this industry cease?

(e)   In the new long run equilibrium,
(i)   what are market price and quantity?

(ii) what are the output level and profit of firms using the newer-vintage technology?

(iii) what are the output level and profit of firms employing the older-vintage technology?

(iv) how many firms in the industry use the newer technology and how many use the older, less efficient technology?

(f) Should all of the plants using the less efficient technology be replaced by those with the newer production technology?

PRACTICE MULTIPLE CHOICE TEST

Questions 1 to 8 refer to Figure 9-6, which depicts the short run cost curves of a perfectly competitive firm.

Figure 9-6

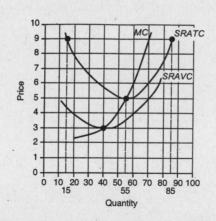

1. If the current market price is $9, the profit-maximizing output of this firm is
   (a) 15.   (b) 70.
   (c) 55.   (d) 85.
   (e) 40.

2. At this output, total costs are equal to
   (a) $135.   (b) $765.
   (c) $630.   (d) $420.
   (e) $350.

3. The firm's total profit is equal to
   (a) $210.   (b) $220.
   (c) $280.   (d) $70.
   (e) Indeterminable with data provided.

4. Should the market price fall to $4, this firm will
   (a) shut down and make zero profit.
   (b) shut down and suffer a loss equal to total fixed cost.
   (c) continue operating in the short run and suffer a loss that is less than its total fixed cost.
   (d) produce 55 units and make a loss equal to total variable cost.
   (e) produce 40 units and suffer a loss equal to its total fixed cost.

5. This firm's maximum attainable profit level would equal zero if
   (a) the industry were in short run equilibrium.
   (b) it produces any output where marginal cost equals marginal revenue.
   (c) the market price were $5.
   (d) the market price were $3.
   (e) it were to shut down.

6. This firm would shut down production if the market price were below
   (a) $5.   (b) $3.
   (c) marginal cost.   (d) average total cost.
   (e) Indeterminable with data provided.

7. The short run supply curve for this firm is its
   (a) marginal cost curve.
   (b) marginal cost curve at or above $3.
   (c) marginal cost curve at or above $5.
   (d) SRATC curve at or above $5.
   (e) SRAVC curve at or above $3.

8. With a market price of $5, an output of 55 units would be the firm's long run profit-maximizing output if
   (a) the firm expected price to rise in the future.
   (b) its long run average cost curve is minimized at 55 units of output.
   (c) other firms were barred from entering this industry.
   (d) this firm could not exit the industry.
   (e) the firm was experiencing decreasing returns to scale.

9. When all firms in a perfectly competitive industry are producing at minimum efficient scale and just covering costs,
   (a) it is physically impossible for existing firms to increase output.
   (b) new firms could enter, produce at minimum efficient scale, and also cover their costs.
   (c) profits could be made only with larger plants.
   (d) the industry is in long run equilibrium.
   (e) some firms will exit the industry.

10. Which of the following characteristics is true of a perfectly competitive industry that is subject to continuous technological change?
(a) Only plants of recent vintage and thus greater efficiency will operate.
(b) The market price equals the minimum average total cost of the most efficient plants.
(c) The market price equals the minimum average total cost of the least efficient plant still in use.
(d) Plants with a greater than average level of efficiency will make positive profits.
(e) Any plant without the most recent and efficient technology will be closed immediately.

11. In which of the following situations should a profit-maximizing firm leave its output unaltered?
(a) $MR > MC$ and $TR > TC$.   (b) $MR = MC$ and $TR > TVC$.
(c) $MR > MC$ and $TR = TC$.   (d) $MR < MC$ and $TR < TC$.
(e) $MR = MC$ and $TR < TVC$.

12. If a competitive industry faced a steady decrease in demand, economic theory predicts that in the long run
(a) firms will gradually leave the industry, thereby shrinking its productive capacity.
(b) firms will modernize plant and equipment in order to increase efficiency.
(c) existing firms will expand output levels as a means of recovering losses.
(d) the industry will expand with newer, more efficient firms entering.
(e) Both (b) and (d) are correct.

13. Suppose the following data are observed for a perfectly competitive firm: output = 5,000 units, market price = $1, fixed costs = $2,000, total variable costs = $1,000, and marginal cost = $1.25. To maximize profits the firm should
(a) reduce output.
(b) expand output.
(c) shut down.
(d) increase the market price.
(e) not change output.

14. At its current level of output, a perfectly competitive firm's average variable cost is $8.00, average total cost is $10.00, and marginal cost is $9.00. If the market price is $10.00, this firm can increase profits by
(a) shutting down production.
(b) decreasing output.
(c) increasing output.
(d) increasing the market price.
(e) not changing output. This firm is at its profit-maximizing position.

15. If a perfectly competitive firm is producing where price equals average total cost and average total cost is greater than marginal cost, the firm should
(a) reduce output.
(b) expand output.
(c) shut down.
(d) increase the market price.
(e) not change output.

16. If a perfectly competitive market is in short-run equilibrium and each firm has $P > SRATC$, then in the long-run
    (a) individual firms will increase their output.
    (b) new firms will enter the market.
    (c) the market supply curve will become less elastic.
    (d) existing firms will continue to earn economic profits.
    (e) all of the above.

17. A long-run competitive equilibrium is impossible if
    (a) the industry supply curve slopes upward.
    (b) all firms are producing where $P = ATC$.
    (c) the industry's long-run supply curve slopes downward continuously.
    (d) all firms have downward-sloping $LRAC$ curves at all levels of output.
    (e) all firms have U-shaped $LRAC$ curves.

Questions 18 to 23 refer to the following diagram which depicts cost curves for a firm in a perfectly competitive market

Figure 9-7

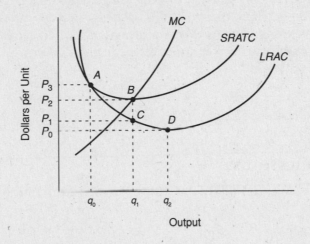

18. If this firm were producing at point A, it is
    (a) maximizing profits.
    (b) minimizing the cost of producing Q_0.
    (c) in a short run equilibrium.
    (d) in a long run equilibrium.
    (e) not employing an efficient combination of capital and labour to produce q_0.

19. If market price were P_2 and this firm were at point B, it
    (a) should move to point A to maximize short run profit.
    (b) should move to point A to maximize long run profit.
    (c) is maximizing short run profit.
    (d) will not want to change its capital in the long run.
    (e) is minimizing the long run cost of producing Q_1.

20. If market price were initially P_2, this firm would eventually be in a long run equilibrium at point
    (a) A.
    (b) B.
    (c) C.
    (d) D.
    (e) none of the above.

21. If market price were P_2,
   (a) short run profits would be maximized at B.
   (b) short run profits would be zero.
   (c) this firm will expand its capital.
   (d) other firms will enter the industry.
   (e) all of the above.

22. If factor prices in this industry were constant and market price is initially P_2, the long run equilibrium will obtain at
   (a) P_3 and Q_0.
   (b) P_2 and Q_1.
   (c) P_1 and Q_1.
   (d) P_0 and Q_2.
   (e) indeterminate with information provided.

23. If factor prices decreased as industry output increased and market price were initially P_2, the long run equilibrium will obtain at
   (a) P_2 and Q_1.
   (b) P_1 and Q_1.
   (c) P_0 and Q_0.
   (d) some price greater than P_0.
   (e) some price less than P_0.

SOLUTIONS

Multiple Choice Questions

1.(d) 2.(b) 3.(e) 4.(b) 5.(a) 6.(d) 7.(e) 8.(a) 9.(a) 10.(d) 11.(b) 12.(e) 13.(c) 14.(e) 15.(a) 16.(a) 17.(c)

Exercises

1. (a) (i)   100; 80; 60.   (ii) $1,000; $600; $330.
       (iii) $850; $600; $480.   (iv) $150; 0; –$150.
       (v) $10.00; $7.50; $5.50.   (vi) $10.00; $7.50; $5.50.
       (vii) $8.50; $7.50; $8.00.   (viii) $1.50; 0; –$2.50.
    (b) At $10.00, profits will induce entry; at $5.50, losses will induce exit of firms, so the industry supply curve would shift.

2. (a) Yes, for both firms
    (b) Firm A: $500; Firm B: $1,000
    (c) No, for both firms. Neither firm is producing where $P = MC$ (note that for Firm B, $MC = \$1$ because at minimum ATC, $ATC = MC$).
    (d) Firm A should produce less output. At current output $P < MC$; since P is constant for a perfectly competitive firm and MC is positively sloped, a decrease in output changes MC toward P. For Firm B, $P > MC$; this firm will therefore maximize profits by producing more output.

3. (a) The market elasticity of demand (η) is given by the formula

$$\eta = \frac{\text{percentage change in output}}{\text{percentage change in price}}$$

Here,

$$0.20 = \frac{40/2,000,000}{\text{percentage change in price}}$$

Thus, the percentage change in price = 0.0001.

(b) The firm's elasticity of demand is the percentage change in the output of the firm divided by the percentage change in the price [calculated in (a)]. This is equal to

$$\frac{40/60}{.0001} = 6,667$$

(c) Yes. For practical purposes the elasticity is infinity (perfectly elastic), and reasonable changes in the firm's output have no effect on price.

4. (a) **Figure 9-8**

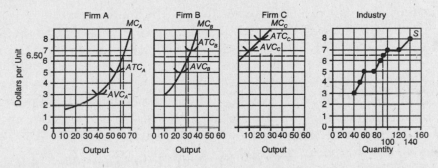

Each firm's short run supply curve corresponds to the portion of its MC curve that is greater than or equal to AVC. Thus no firm produces at a price less than $3. Between $3 and just slightly below $5, only Firm A produces output. When the price hits $5, Firm B abruptly raises output from zero to approximately 25 units—this explains the horizontal segment of the industry supply curve at $5. Similarly, the discrete jump in output by Firm C when price reaches $7 explains the other horizontal segment of the industry supply curve. As the number of firms in the industry increases, these discrete jumps in output by additional firms coming on line would become small relative to total industry output, so the industry supply curve would be much smoother.

(b) At a market price of $6.50, Firm A would produce approximately 62.5 units and Firm B, approximately 32.5 units. Since the market price would be less than Firm C's AVC (at every level of output), it would shut down and produce no output in the short run. Thus the quantity supplied by the industry at this price would be approximately 95 units.

(c) Firm C would make a loss equal to its fixed cost. Firm A would make a profit, but we do not have enough information to determine how much. At 62.5 units of output, we do not know the level of Firm A's ATC. However, we do know that the ATC curve is rising at this output because it is to the right of minimum ATC. Since ATC is rising, MC(=P) is greater than ATC, and profit is therefore positive. For Firm B, price is greater than AVC (same reason as before) but less than ATC. Firm B is therefore making a loss that is less than its fixed cost. Again, we cannot determine the magnitude of the loss because the information provided does not indicate the level of AVC at 32.5 units of output.

5. Figure 9-9

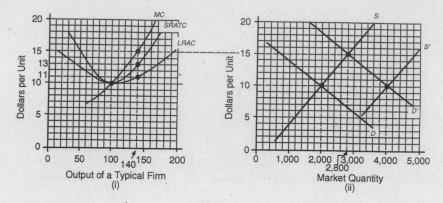

(i) Output of a Typical Firm

(ii) Market Quantity

(a) $10 and 2,000 units, respectively.

(b) Each firm produces 100 units of output (i.e., where $MC = MR = P = \$10$). Since at an output of 100 units average revenue (P) equals $SRATC$, profits are therefore equal to zero.

(c) 20 (= 2,000/100).

(d) Yes. The typical firm is producing where $MC = MR$ and is on its $LRAC$ curve; thus it is producing the profit-maximizing output at the lowest attainable cost. Further, since the level of economic profit is zero, there is no incentive for new firms to enter or old firms to exit.

(e) $15 and 2,800 units, respectively.

(f) At a market price of $15, each existing firm increases output to 140 units where $P = MC$.

(g) Each firm's total revenue is $2,100 (i.e., $15 × 140). The average total cost of producing 140 units (given that the firm cannot adjust plant size) is $13. Thus total cost is $1,820 (i.e., $13 × 140). Therefore, short run profit for each firm is $2,100 − $1,820 = $280.

(h) Since industry profits are positive, new firms will enter. This entry is captured in the graph by the industry short run supply curve shifting to the right and thereby lowering price.

(i) Long run equilibrium obtains when each firm is doing the best that it can and there is no incentive for further entry. Both conditions are satisfied when price is again equal to $10 at the intersection of the new demand curve D' and a new industry short run supply curve (e.g., S' in the graph). The associated equilibrium market quantity is 4,000 units.

(j) Each firm produces 100 units and earns an economic profit equal to zero, which is the same as the initial long run equilibrium position of each firm in (b).

(k) The difference with the initial long run equilibrium is that there will be more firms in the industry; specifically, there will be 40 firms (4,000/100).

6. Figure 9-10

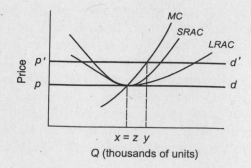

Q (thousands of units)

Extension Exercise

E-1. **Figure 9-11**

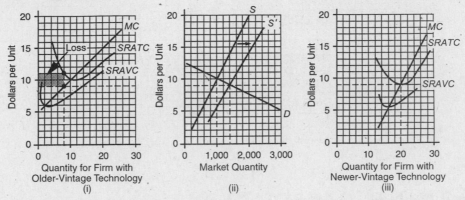

(a) $10 and 1,000 units, respectively.

(b) Each firm produces 10 units of output and makes zero profits. There are 100 firms in the industry (i.e., 1,000/10).

(c) Yes. A firm entering with the new technology faces the same price as the existing firms, and by producing 21 units (where $MR = MC$ for the newer plants), it can make a positive profit; at this output, average revenue is greater than average total cost.

(d) Entry will cease when profits of a potential entrant are driven to zero. This occurs when the market price is $9, implying that plants of recent vintage would operate at minimum efficient scale.

(e) (i) $9 and 1,400 units, respectively.

(ii) 20 units of output and zero profit.

(iii) 8 units of output and a loss of $16.

(iv) Since total revenue exceeds total variable cost for plants employing the older technology, all 100 of these firms remain in the industry. Total output by these firms is therefore 800 units (100 × 8), which leaves 600 units that are produced by the newer vintage plants (1,400 – 800). Each of these produces 20 units, so there are 30 plants with the new technology.

(f) No. The market value of the output of each of these firms is $72 (i.e., $9 × 8), greater than the value of resources that are currently used to produce this output (i.e., total variable cost), which is $63.

Practice Multiple Choice Test

1.(b) 2.(d) 3.(a) 4.(c) 5.(c) 6.(b) 7.(b) 8.(b) 9.(d) 10.(b) 11.(b) 12.(a) 13.(a) 14.(c) 15.(b) 16.(b) 17.(d) 18.(b) 19.(c) 20.(d) 21.(e) 22.(d) 23.(e)

CHAPTER 10

MONOPOLY

LEARNING OBJECTIVES

1 Explain why marginal revenue is less than price for a profit-maximizing monopolist.

2 Recognize the importance of entry barriers in allowing monopolists to maintain positive profits in the long run.

3 Understand how firms can form a cartel in which they restrict industry output and increase price and profits.

4 Explain the different forms and consequences of price discrimination.

CHAPTER OVERVIEW

In a **monopoly** market structure, a single firm faces the entire market demand curve. The monopoly maximizes profits by producing the output where *marginal revenue* equals *marginal cost*, just as competitive firms would do. However, a downward-sloping market demand curve means that, in the case of monopoly, marginal revenue is less than price. Therefore, the most profitable output for a monopolist results in a price that exceeds marginal cost.

A monopoly does not necessarily earn positive profits. In the short run, profits depend on the relative magnitudes of price and average cost at the profit-maximizing output. In the long run, monopoly power is limited by the possible entry of other firms. A monopolist will attempt to protect its monopoly position with **barriers to entry**. In the very long run, monopoly power is limited by the development of substitute products, a process known as **creative destruction**.

The potential for profit provides an inducement for otherwise competitive firms to agree to jointly behave as a monopoly. Firms that form such agreements are called **cartels**. Cartels are, however, unstable as there is an incentive for individual members to cheat on the agreement.

A monopolist may increase profits if it is able to practice **price discrimination** across buyers, markets, or even units of output. Price discrimination enables the firm to capture some (or in the extreme case, all) of the consumer surplus.

CHAPTER REVIEW

A Single-Price Monopolist

After studying this section you should be able to: explain the relationship between price and marginal revenue for a monopolist; solve for the monopolist's profit-maximizing output and associated profit level; explain how in the long run the monopoly can only be sustained by barriers to entry which may be natural or created; and, appreciate how the very long run process of creative destruction can erode monopoly power. When reading this section, contrast the monopoly equilibrium with that of perfect competition.

1. A fundamental feature of a monopolistic market is that the firm
   (a) can sell any quantity it desires at current market price.
   (b) can obtain any price for any quantity of output.
   (c) faces a perfectly inelastic demand curve.
   (d) faces the price and quantity trade-off depicted by market demand.
   (e) Both (a) and (b) are correct.

2. For the single-price monopolist, the average revenue curve
   (a) is a horizontal line drawn at the market price.
   (b) is the same as the market demand curve.
   (c) is the same as the marginal revenue curve.
   (d) has the same price intercept as the demand curve, but is twice as steep.
   (e) does not exist.

3. If average revenue declines as output increases, marginal revenue must
   (a) increase.
   (b) also decline and be less than average revenue.
   (c) also decline because it is equal to average revenue.
   (d) also decline and be greater than average revenue.
   (e) decline, but may be less than, equal to or greater than average revenue.

4. Since the profit-maximizing monopolist produces that output where marginal cost equals marginal revenue, we can conclude that
   (a) $P = MC$.   (b) $P = MR$.
   (c) $P > MC$.   (d) $P < MR$.
   (e) $P > ATC$.

5. A single-price monopoly is able to make positive profits only if the average total cost curve
   (a) intersects the demand curve.
   (b) is tangent to the demand curve.
   (c) declines over a substantial portion of market demand.
   (d) lies above the marginal revenue curve.
   (e) lies above the demand curve.

6. Barriers to entry, which sustain a monopoly, may be due to *all but which* of the following?
   (a) Economies of scale.   (b) Patent laws.
   (c) Long-run increasing average costs.   (d) Large set-up costs.
   (e) Licensing.

7. Natural barriers to entry
   (a) include patent laws and exclusive franchises.
   (b) most commonly arise through economies of scale.
   (c) result from an increasing long run average cost curve.
   (d) imply that small firms have lower ATC curves than larger firms.
   (e) must be sustained by government regulation.

8. The process of "creative destruction" refers to
   (a) the threat of price-cutting behaviour.
   (b) the inherent instability of cartels.
   (c) an early declaration of bankruptcy as a means of avoiding debts.
   (d) the takeover of a competitive industry by a monopoly.
   (e) the replacement of one monopoly by another through invention and innovation.

Cartels as Monopolies

This section discusses the cartelization of a competitive industry. It establishes that although cartels can maximize joint profits for a group of firms, there is an individual incentive for member firms to cheat on the cartel. The key to this section is an understanding of the difference between the interests of cartel member firms as a group, and the interests of an individual firm in the cartel (i.e., maximization of joint profits versus individual profits).

9. A cartel increases the industry's profits by
   (a) fully capturing all economies of scale.
   (b) ceasing all active competitive behaviour with respect to price.
   (c) agreeing to sell all current output at an agreed-upon fixed price.
   (d) decreasing industry output and thereby increasing market price.
   (e) agreeing to produce more, but sell at a higher price.

10. Which of the following is *not* a problem associated with enforcement of a successful cartel?
    (a) Entry of new firms.
    (b) Government restrictions on output.
    (c) Preventing cartel members from violating the agreed-upon production level.
    (d) Convincing other firms to join the cartel.
    (e) Monitoring the output of cartel members.

11. Economic theory predicts cartels to be unstable because
    (a) there is an incentive for individual firms to produce beyond their quota.
    (b) governments will invariably dismantle them.
    (c) although industry profits increase, the profits of individual firms decrease.
    (d) individual firms have an incentive to produce less than the restrictions imposed on them by the cartel.
    (e) the industry output that maximizes joint profits for the cartel tends to exceed that of a competitive market.

A Multiprice Monopolist: Price Discrimination

When studying price discrimination, focus on developing an understanding of when price discrimination is possible, how the firm practices it, and the implications for profits and efficiency.

12. Which of the following is the *best* example of price discrimination?
    (a) Some air travellers pay lower air fares as standby passengers.
    (b) A telephone company charges lower rates for long-distance calls after midnight than during the day.
    (c) A local transit company allows senior citizens, the unemployed, and children to ride at reduced fares.
    (d) The London underground charges each individual according to the distance travelled.
    (e) A cinema charges lower prices on Tuesdays than on Fridays or Saturdays.

13. Price discrimination is possible because
    (a) different individuals are willing to pay different amounts for the same commodity.
    (b) each individual is willing to pay a different amount for each successive unit of the same commodity.
    (c) different individuals have different incomes.
    (d) demand curves slope downwards.
    (e) Both (a) and (b) are correct.

14. Price discrimination increases a monopoly's profits because it
    (a) increases the willingness of households to pay for a good.
    (b) allows the firm to capture some consumer surplus.
    (c) allows the firm to exploit economies of scale more fully.
    (d) shifts the demand curve the firm faces.
    (e) restricts output.

15. Perfect price discrimination implies that
    (a) demand is perfectly elastic.
    (b) demand is perfectly inelastic.
    (c) supply is perfectly elastic.
    (d) the firm produces a lower output than it would as a single price monopolist.
    (e) the firm sells each unit at a different price and captures all consumer surplus.

EXERCISES

1. The equilibrium for a single price monopolist is quickly reviewed in this exercise.

   The demand curve and selected cost curves of a single price monopolist are depicted in the following graph.

   Figure 10-1

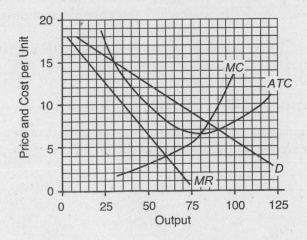

(a) At what output are the firm's profits at a maximum? _____
(b) What is the price at this output? _____
(c) What is total revenue at this output? _____
(d) What are the corresponding total costs? _____
(e) What is the level of profits? _____
(f) What range of output would yield some positive profit? _____

2. The objective of the following exercise is to demonstrate that the output at which a monopolist's marginal revenue equals marginal cost is the output that maximizes the difference between its total revenue and total costs (i.e., profit). This exercise involves numerical calculations—some students may wish to use a spreadsheet to expedite calculations.

The following data are taken from *Solitary Inc.*, a fictitious monopolistic firm.

(a) Calculate *Solitary Inc.*'s marginal cost (MC), marginal revenue (MR), total revenue (TR), and profit to complete the table.

Output	Total Cost	Price	Quantity Demanded	TR	MR	MC	Profit
0	$20	$20	0	___			___
					___	___	
1	24	18	1	___			___
					___	___	
2	27	16	2	___			___
					___	___	
3	33	14	3	___			___
					___	___	
4	43	12	4	___			___
					___	___	
5	57	10	5	___			___
					___	___	
6	75	8	6	___			___

(b) Plot Solitary Inc.'s average revenue (AR), MR, and MC in panel (i), TC and TR in panel (ii).

Figure 10-2

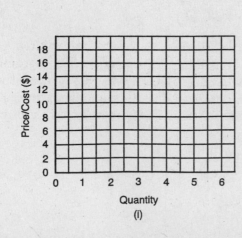

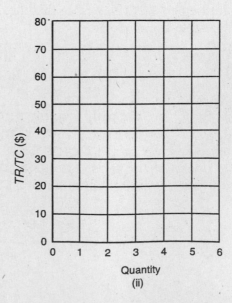

(c) What is the profit-maximizing output (whole units)? _____
(d) At what price will the monopolist sell the product (whole units)? _____
(e) What are the monopolist's economic profits? _____
(f) Are any of these answers different across the two diagrams? _____

3. The following graph shows the cost and revenue curves for a monopolist.

Figure 10-3

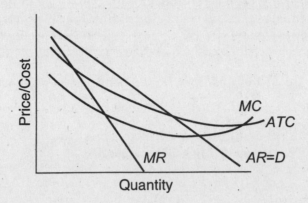

(a) Illustrate on the graph the price the profit-maximizing monopolist will set and the quantity that will be sold. (Label the P_M and Q_M.)
(b) Indicate monopoly profits by shading-in the appropriate area.
(c) Suppose that the monopolist, to be allocatively efficient, sets price equal to marginal cost. Label the price P_E and the output Q_E. Would this output be sustainable in the long run? Explain.

4. **Price Discrimination on the *Double-Loop Monster!***

This exercise provides an example of price discrimination between two groups of consumers who have different demands for the same commodity.

A local amusement park has estimated the following demand curves for its new roller coaster ride, the Double-Loop Monster:

$$Q_a = 1,000 - 125P_a$$

$$Q_c = 8,000 - 2,000P_c$$

where Q_a and Q_c are the daily quantity demanded of rides by adults and children, respectively, and P_a and P_c are the price per ride charged to each of these groups. The marginal cost of every additional rider on the *Double-Loop Monster* is calculated to be $1, regardless of the age of the rider. Use the grids that follow to determine the profit-maximizing prices for the amusement park. Indicate (approximately) the number of rides taken by each group.

Figure 10-4

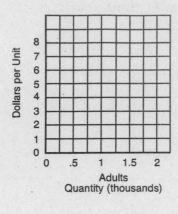
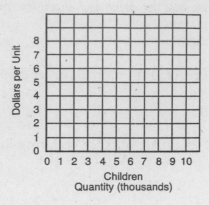

Adults
Quantity (thousands)

Children
Quantity (thousands)

5. Cartels

The implications of collusion by (otherwise perfectly competitive) firms that form a cartel to maximize joint profits are investigated in this exercise.

The graph on the left of Figure 10-5 presents the cost structure for one of many identical firms in a perfectly competitive industry. On the right you are given the market demand curve and the industry supply curve, which (you should recall) is the horizontal summation of the marginal cost curves of all firms in the industry.

Figure 10-5

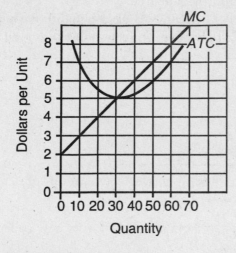
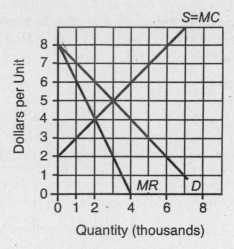

(a) Suppose that the industry is in long-run competitive equilibrium.

   (i)   What are market price and quantity?

   (ii) What is the output of each firm?

   (iii) What is the profit of each firm?

(b) Now suppose that all firms in the industry collude by forming a cartel to maximize joint profits. What market price and quantity maximize profits for the cartel?

(c) What output would the cartel instruct each firm to produce?

(d) What is the level of profits for each firm in the cartel?

(e) Given the market price established by the cartel, what output would an individual firm like to produce? What are the associated profits? Explain.

6. **The Single Price Monopoly Versus the Perfect Price Discriminator**

This exercise compares the equilibrium of the single price monopolist to that of the perfect price discriminator.

The diagram in Figure 10-6 applies to a monopoly. AL is the market demand curve and AK the marginal revenue curve. EH is the long-run supply curve for the industry as well as the $LRAC$ curve for the monopolist. (There are no economies of scale so that $LRAC = LRMC$).

Figure 10-6

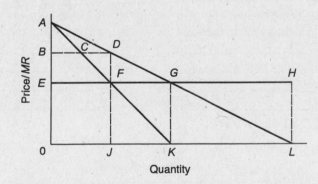

(a) Assume that the monopolist sets a single price and maximizes profits. Determine the following:
   (i) the monopoly price _____ and output _____.
   (ii) consumer surplus at that price _____.
   (iii) economic profits at that price _____.
(b) Assume that a discriminating monopolist is able to obtain the maximum price for each unit. Determine the following:
   (i) the price range, from _____ to _____.
   (ii) output _____.
   (iii) consumer surplus _____.
   (iv) economic profits _____.

PRACTICE MULTIPLE CHOICE TEST

1. As long as marginal cost is positive, a monopolist will be operating
   (a) on the elastic portion of the demand curve.
   (b) where demand is unit-elastic and total revenue is therefore at a maximum.
   (c) on the inelastic portion of the demand curve.
   (d) on any portion of the demand curve, depending on the supply curve.
   (e) where demand is perfectly inelastic.

2. A linear downward-sloping demand curve has a marginal revenue curve that is
   (a) also linear, with the same price intercept as the demand curve and half the quantity intercept.
   (b) coincident with the average revenue curve.
   (c) horizontal at market price.
   (d) also linear, with half the slope of the demand curve.
   (e) (a) and (d) are both correct.

3. In perfect competition, the industry short-run supply curve is the horizontal summation of the marginal cost curves (above AVC) of all of the firms in the industry. In monopoly, the short-run supply curve
   (a) is the single firm's marginal cost curve.
   (b) is the portion of the single firm's marginal cost curve that lies above average variable cost.
   (c) is the downward-sloping segment of the average total cost curve.
   (d) is the upward-sloping segment of the MC curve.
   (e) does not exist.

Questions 4 to 7 refer to the following graph, which depicts the marginal cost curve of a monopoly and the market demand it faces.

Figure 10-7

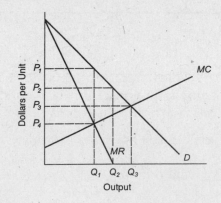

4. The monopolist's profit-maximizing output is
   (a) Q_1.   (b) Q_2.
   (c) Q_3.   (d) greater than Q_1 but less than Q_3.
   (e) Indeterminable with data provided.

5. The price set by the monopolist for the profit-maximizing output is
   (a) P_1.   (b) P_2.
   (c) P_3.   (d) P_4.
   (e) Indeterminable with data provided.

6. The level of output that corresponds to maximum revenue is
   (a) Q_1.   (b) Q_2.
   (c) Q_3.   (d) greater than Q_3.
   (e) Indeterminable with data provided.

7. A monopolist that is able to practise perfect price discrimination will produce output
   (a) Q_1.   (b) Q_2.
   (c) Q_3.   (d) greater than Q_3.
   (e) Indeterminable with data provided.

8. Suppose a firm's minimum efficient scale (MES) occurs at an average total cost of $4 and an output of 4 million units, while quantity demanded at a price of $4 is 3 million units. Given that the demand curve is downward-sloping, one can conclude that
   (a) the firm is a natural monopoly.
   (b) the firm's profits can be sustained only if it creates barriers to entry.
   (c) it is always impossible to make positive profits regardless of the output level.
   (d) the firm always breaks even.
   (e) the firm will exit the industry.

9. Which of the following is *not* true of price discrimination?
   (a) Output is generally larger than under a single-price monopoly.
   (b) Any given level of output yields a larger revenue.
   (c) To be successful, resale must be impossible or prevented.
   (d) Lower-income individuals must be charged lower prices.
   (e) Consumer surplus decreases.

10. If a firm can sell 10 units of output for $15 each or eleven units at $14 each, the additional revenue from selling the eleventh unit is
    (a) $14.   (b) $4.
    (c) $15.   (d) $154.
    (e) $1.

Questions 11 to 15 refer to Figure 10-8 which depicts the demand and supply facing an entire industry in Panel (i) and the cost structure for a typical firm in the industry in Panel (ii). Assume that each firm is identical and small relative to the entire market.

Figure 10-8

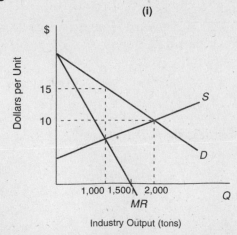

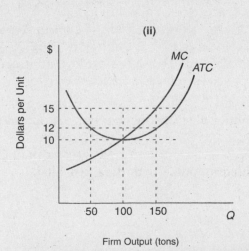

11. If firms do not cooperate but behave as price-takers, the market equilibrium price and quantity would be _____ and each firm's output and profit would be _____.
    (a) $15 and 1,000 tons; 150 tons and $450.
    (b) $15 and 1,000 tons; 100 tons and $300.
    (c) $10 and 2,000 tons; 100 tons and $1,000.
    (d) $10 and 2,000 tons; 150 tons and $450.
    (e) $10 and 2,000 tons; 100 tons and zero.

12. Now suppose these firms cooperate with each other so as to maximize joint profits by forming a cartel. The market price and quantity are now
    (a) $15 and 1,000 tons.
    (b) $15 and 1,500 tons.
    (c) $15 and 2,000 tons.
    (d) $10 and 2,000 tons.
    (e) Indeterminable with data provided.

13. Suppose the cartel agreement reduces each firm's output by the same proportion as the reduction in industry output. An individual firm's output and profit under such an agreement would be
    (a) 50 tons and $250.
    (b) 50 tons and $150.
    (c) 50 tons and $zero.
    (d) 100 tons and $500.
    (e) 100 tons and $300.

14. If an individual firm cheats on the cartel, it would produce _____ of output and make _____ profit.
    (a) 100 tons; $500.
    (b) 50 tons; $750.
    (c) 150 tons; $450.
    (d) 150 tons; $750.
    (e) 100 tons; $300.

15. The number of firms in this industry is
    (a) 10.
    (b) 20.
    (c) 50.
    (d) 1.
    (e) Indeterminable with the data provided.

16. Under perfect price discrimination
    (a) the firm captures all of the consumer surplus.
    (b) each unit is sold at a different price (assuming a downward-sloping demand curve).
    (c) the firm achieves more profit than it could with a single price.
    (d) the firm produces an allocatively efficient output.
    (e) all of the above.

17. Suppose the elasticity of demand for electricity by residential customers of B.C. Hydro is 0.8 while that of industrial customers is 1.2. B.C. Hydro could practice price discrimination by charging
    (a) residential customers a higher price per kWh.
    (b) industrial customers a higher price per kWh.
    (c) the group with the larger quantity demanded a higher price per kWh.
    (d) the group with the smaller quantity demanded a higher price per kWh.
    (e) Insufficient data to determine.

18. Price discrimination between two markets will result in
    (a) equal marginal revenues across markets.
    (b) equal marginal cost across markets.
    (c) marginal revenue equal marginal cost in each market.
    (d) a lower price in the market with the relatively more elastic demand.
    (e) all of the above.

SOLUTIONS

Multiple Choice Questions

1.(d) 2.(b) 3.(b) 4.(c) 5.(a) 6.(c) 7.(b) 8.(e) 9.(d) 10.(b) 11.(a) 12.(c) 13.(e) 14.(b) 15.(e)

Exercises

1. (a) 60.
    (b) $11.
    (c) $660.
    (d) $480.
    (e) $180.
    (f) output: 30 to 90 units; price ranges from $15 to $7.

2. (a)

Output	TR	MR	MC	Profit
$0	$0			$–20
		$18	$4	
1	18			–6
		14	3	
2	32			5
		10	6	
3	42			9
		6	10	
4	48			5
		2	14	
5	50			–7
		–2	18	
6	48			–27

(b) **Figure 10-9**

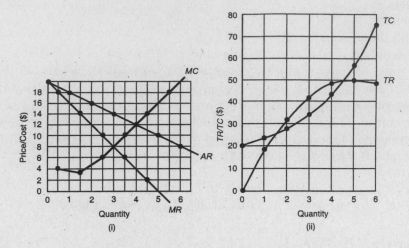

(c) 3 units.

(d) $14 (price to sell output where $MR = MC$).

(e) At 3 units of output, TR is $42, TC is $33, and profits are $9.

(f) No, they are identical.

3. (a) and (b) **Figure 10-10**

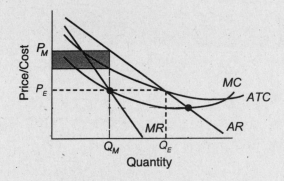

(c) No, it would not, because the ATC exceeds the price, so business could not be sustained for long.

4. **Figure 10-11**

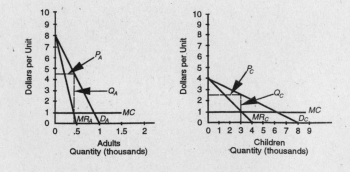

5. (a) (i) $5 and 3,000 units, respectively.
   (ii) 30 units.
   (iii) zero profits.
   (b) $6 and 2,000 units, respectively.
   (c) 20 units; where *MC* of each firm equals market *MR* of $4.
   (d) $10. At 20 units of output, average revenue is $6 and average total cost is $5.50.
   (e) The output of any individual firm constitutes an insignificant share of total output (in this example, one-hundredth), so market price is negligibly affected by changes in any single firm's output. Therefore, each firm behaves as a price taker and would like to produce 40 units where marginal cost is equal to marginal revenue for the firm. The resulting profit level would be $20 = ($6 − $5.50) × 40.

6. (a) (i) *OB*, *OJ*   (ii) *ABD*   (iii) *BDFE*
   (b) (i) *OA* to *OE*   (ii) *OK*   (iii) zero   (iv) *AEG*

Practice Multiple Choice Test

1.(a) 2.(a) 3.(e) 4.(a) 5.(a) 6.(b) 7.(c) 8.(a) 9.(d) 10.(b) 11.(e) 12.(a) 13.(b) 14.(c) 15.(b) 16.(e) 17.(a) 18.(e)

CHAPTER 11

IMPERFECT COMPETITION

LEARNING OBJECTIVES

1   Recognize that most industries in Canada have either a large number of small firms or a small number of large firms.

2   Understand that imperfectly competitive firms distinguish their product from those of their competitors and often engage in non-price competition.

3   Explain the key elements of the theory of monopolistic competition.

4   Recognize how free entry drives profits to zero in the long run.

5   Understand why strategic behaviour is a key feature of oligopoly.

6   Use the basic tools of game theory to explain the difference between cooperative and noncooperative oligopoly outcomes.

CHAPTER OVERVIEW

Much of the production in the Canadian economy takes place in industries where firms cannot be considered as either price-takers or monopolists. These firms operate in an imperfectly competitive market framework which can be classified into two broad groups—those markets with a large number of relatively small firms, and those with a small number of relatively large firms. **Concentration ratios**, which measure the fraction of total market sales controlled by the few largest sellers in a market, are used to classify markets into these groups.

Monopolistic competition is characterized by many relatively small firms actively competing with each other by **differentiating their products** in some way. For example, there are many different brands of products such as soap and cereal, and many different characteristics to services such as convenience stores and restaurants. Monopolistic competition produces a wider range of products but at a higher cost per unit than perfect competition.

Oligopolistic industries are characterized by a small number of firms, each of which accounts for a significant fraction of their industry's production. There can be vigorous interfirm competition in oligopoly which results in a **noncooperative outcome** as firms adopt strategic behaviour in an effort to increase their individual profits. The **cooperative outcome** results when firms maximize joint profits which is achieved through **collusion**. Oligopolistic firms may erect entry barriers into the industry. Just as actual entry may reduce profits in an oligopoly, the theory of **contestable markets** suggests that potential entry can also serve to reduce profits.

CHAPTER REVIEW

The Structure of the Canadian Economy

After reading this section, you should be able to explain how imperfectly competitive market structures differ from the perfectly competitive and monopoly models. You will also understand that market definition poses a basic weakness in the use of concentration ratios.

1. A concentration ratio is intended to measure
   (a) how much of an industry is concentrated in central Canada.
   (b) the number of firms in an industry.
   (c) how much production in a given market is controlled by a few firms.
   (d) how much of a given industry is concentrated in the hands of foreign-owned trans-national corporations.
   (e) the proportion of an industry that concentrates on export markets.

2. Neither the model of perfect competition nor that of monopoly provides a completely satis-factory description of the Canadian economy because there are significant sectors of the economy with
   (a) many small firms that still have some price-setting ability.
   (b) only a few large firms.
   (c) many firms, but with a disproportionate amount of production concentrated in the hands of a few.
   (d) many small firms each selling a differentiated product.
   (e) All of the above.

3. A concentration ratio that measures the proportion of Canadian production accounted for by the largest four firms in Canada, may provide a misleading indicator of market power because
   (a) the relevant market may be local instead of national.
   (b) the relevant market may be global instead of national.
   (c) the number four is arbitrarily chosen.
   (d) there may be a duopoly in the industry.
   (e) Both (a) and (b) are correct.

Imperfectly Competitive Market Structures

After reading this section you should understand why firms that produce differentiated products face downward sloping demand curves that allow them to administer price. These firms may also engage in several forms of non-price competition.

4. Firms that sell a differentiated product (such as Burger King and Harvey's Hamburgers) each
   (a) face a downward-sloping demand curve.
   (b) have some ability to administer price.
   (c) receive information on market conditions through changes in quantity sold at the set price.
   (d) tend to absorb transitory fluctuations in demand by changing output and holding prices constant.
   (e) All of the above.

5. In the sense used in this chapter, administered prices are
   (a) prices determined by international forces.
   (b) prices controlled by the government.
   (c) prices determined by market forces.
   (d) set by individual firms.
   (e) set by regulatory agencies such as marketing boards.

6. Which of the following forms of *competitive behaviour* is observed in imperfectly competitive markets?
   (a) Offering of product guarantees.
   (b) Advertising.
   (c) Offering competing product standards.
   (d) Creating barriers to entry.
   (e) All of the above.

Monopolistic Competition

When reading this section note that the monopolistically competitive firm's short run equilibrium is similar to that of a monopoly, but that its long run equilibrium differs from both monopoly and perfect competition. Reread the caption to Figure 11-2 of the text if you are uncertain about long run equilibrium in monopolistic competition. You should also understand what gives rise to the excess capacity theorem and the debate concerning its relevance.

7. Which of the following is *not* a characteristic of a market that features monopolistic competition?
   (a) There is a large number of firms.
   (b) Each firm faces a downward-sloping demand curve.
   (c) All firms sell an identical product.
   (d) There is freedom of entry and exit.
   (e) Each firm's marginal revenue curve lies below its demand curve.

8. The excess capacity theorem in monopolistic competition
   (a) means that these firms will not be producing at minimum average total cost in the long run equilibrium.
   (b) implies that the trade-off for product variety is a higher unit production cost.
   (c) arises because of the assumptions of freedom of entry and downward-sloping demand curves.
   (d) is a characteristic of long run equilibrium in this market structure.
   (e) All of the above.

9. An important feature that distinguishes monopolistic competition from perfect competition is that
   (a) monopolistic competitors sell a differentiated product rather than a homogeneous one.
   (b) the monopolistic competitor's demand curve is the same as the market demand curve.
   (c) in long-run equilibrium, monopolistic competitors earn economic profits, whereas perfectly competitive firms do not.
   (d) there are important barriers to entry in monopolistic competition.
   (e) there is only one firm in a monopolistically competitive market structure.

10. Some economists have argued that monopolistic competition is inefficient because
    (a) the long run equilibrium of these firms is characterized by positive profits.
    (b) these firms over-invest in barriers to entry.
    (c) these firms produce an output less than that corresponding to the minimum point on the *LRAC* curve.
    (d) it produces a limited range of product variety.
    (e) All of the above are correct.

Oligopoly

After studying this section, you should: understand that each firm may have an incentive to depart from the cooperative outcome; distinguish among the different types of collusion and their behavioural implications; recognize that in a Nash equilibrium each firm has chosen its best strategy even though there exist other cooperative outcomes all firms would have preferred; appreciate the struggle for market share, types of non-price competition and the competitive advantages of new technology; appreciate that profits in oligopolistic industries can persist in the long run only if there are significant barriers to entry; appreciate the theory of contestable markets; and, be able to discuss the role and importance of oligopolies in the economy.

11. In some markets, there may be room for only a few firms because
    (a) of economies of scale.
    (b) the industry produces a homogeneous good.
    (c) individual firms face perfectly elastic demand curves.
    (d) a rising *LRAC* curve
    (e) All of the above.

12. A noncooperative (Nash) equilibrium among oligopolistic firms
    (a) tends to be unstable because each firm has an incentive to cut price and increase output.
    (b) is the same outcome that a single monopoly firm would reach if it owned all the firms in the industry.
    (c) results in each firm producing more, but earning less than it would in a cooperative equilibrium.
    (d) maximizes joint profits for the firms in the industry.
    (e) is characterized by each firm having an incentive to change its output.

13. Which of the following contributed to OPEC's collapse as an output-restricting cartel in the late 1980s?
    (a) New productive capacity by non-OPEC countries.
    (b) Individual OPEC members producing in excess of their quotas.
    (c) Development of substitute products and new technologies that were more efficient in their use of oil.
    (d) All of the above.
    (e) Both (b) and (c) are correct.

14. Which of the following is a cause of "bigness" of firms?
    (a) Mergers.   (b) Takeovers.
    (c) Firm-created entry barriers.   (d) Economies of scale.
    (e) All of the above.

15. Brand proliferation creates a barrier to entry by
    (a) reducing production costs for existing firms.
    (b) increasing the minimum efficient scale of a potential entrant.
    (c) allowing existing firms to fully exploit economies of scale.
    (d) enabling existing firms to operate at minimum efficient scale.
    (e) All of the above.

16. Which of the following qualify as possible barriers to entry that oligopolistic firms may erect?
    (a) Production of many competing brands of a good by a single firm.
    (b) Large advertising budgets.
    (c) A credible threat to engage in tacit collusion.
    (d) Contestable markets.
    (e) Both (a) and (b) are correct.

17. Economic profits can exist in an oligopolistic industry in the long run because of
    (a) natural barriers to entry.
    (b) barriers created by existing firms.
    (c) barriers created by government policy.
    (d) economies of scale.
    (e) All of the above.

18. According to the theory of contestable markets,
    (a) the mere threat of potential entry encourages oligopolists to hold profits near the competitive level.
    (b) firms must actually enter an industry if prices and outputs are to be held near the competitive level.
    (c) many firms in an industry make it contestable.
    (d) high costs of entry make markets more contestable.
    (e) Both (a) and (d) are correct.

EXERCISES

1. **Monopolistic Competition**

   The following diagram shows selected cost and revenue curves facing a firm that is operating in a monopolistically competitive industry characterized by ease of entry, product differentiation, and a large number of firms.

   Figure 11-1

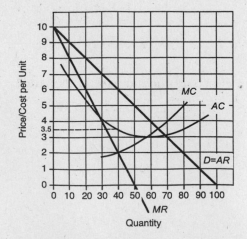

(a) What price will a profit-maximizing firm set? _____

(b) What are the associated profits? _____

(c) Given that entry is relatively easy, is this a long-run equilibrium situation? Explain.

(d) Which curves will be affected and in which direction if this firm increases its advertising expenditures by a fixed amount, thereby causing sales to increase?

(e) If new firms enter this industry, what curves in the graph would be affected the most? Why? What is the *main* implication for this firm?

(f) Explain how the result in (e) illustrates the excess capacity theorem.

2. **Long Run Equilibrium in Monopolistic Competition**

Draw a diagram in Figure 11-2 that illustrates the long run equilibrium of a firm in a monopolistically competitive industry.

Figure 11-2

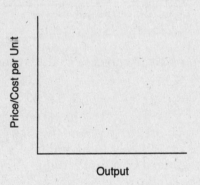

(a) Suppose that demand for the product increases. Show the short run effects on price, output, and profit for the firm. Explain.

(b) What will be the long run effects of the increase in demand?

3. Game Theory and the Nash Equilibrium

This exercise applies game theory to a firm's choice of an advertising budget. Suppose two competitors, Pepsi and Coke, must each select their advertising expenditures. For simplicity, assume there are only two sizes of advertising budgets: moderate and large. The relationship between advertising and profits for each firm is presented in the following payoff matrix which gives each firm's profits for each of its own possible budgets as well as that of the competitors. Note that there are four possible combinations of budgets in the market—these are represented by the four cells in the diagram. Coke's profits are presented in the left circle of each cell, while Pepsi's are in the right circle. [*Note:* Some students may wish to reread the caption to Figure 11-3 in the text to better understand the payoff matrix.]

Figure 11-3

Payoff matrix (profit in millions of dollars)*

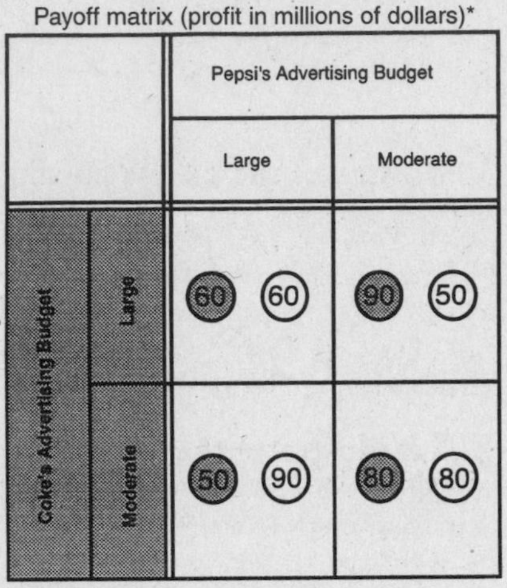

*Coke's profit is in the left shaded circle of each cell, Pepsi's is in the right circle.

(a) If Pepsi and Coke colluded on their choices of advertising budgets, which would they select? Explain.

(b) Is the cooperative outcome in (a) likely to be stable? Explain.

(c) What is the noncooperative (i.e., Nash) equilibrium in this game? Explain.

4. Strategic Behaviour, or *Stabbed in the Back!*

This question also uses game theory to examine cooperative and noncooperative outcomes. In this case you are asked to construct the payoff matrix.

Two firms, EverSharp and TripleEdge, are the only producers of bayonets. They have each been invited to submit a sealed bid on a large contract to supply bayonets to the military. They can bid only one of two prices: a high price or a low price. The high price is expected to yield a profit of $10 million, while the low price will yield a profit of $7 million. If they both submit the same price, they share the contract and the profits equally. If they bid different prices, the firm with the lower bid gets the entire contract.

(a) Construct the payoff matrix.

(b) What would the outcome be under cooperative behaviour? Explain.

(c) What would the outcome be under strategic behaviour? Explain.

5. *Read All About It!*

Use the economic analysis developed in this and the previous chapters to discuss each of the following events described in newspaper headlines.
(a) "Prices of Petroleum Products Rise as OPEC Restricts Oil Supplies" (1974)
   "Oil Prices Plummet with OPEC Price War" (1985)
   "OPEC Ministers Unable to Agree on New Production Quotas" (1993)
   "OPEC Maintains Discipline Over Production Levels" (1999)

(b) "GM Announces Price Hikes for 1992 Models; Ford and Chrysler Expected to Follow" (1991)

(c) "Personal Computer Price War Spurs Buying Spree" (1992)

(d) "Independent Gas Retailers Spur Price Wars in Southwestern Ontario" (1998)

(e) "Local Retailers Compete with Large Chains by Personalizing Service" (1999)

PRACTICE MULTIPLE CHOICE TEST

1. An important prediction of monopolistic competition is that the long-run profit- maximizing output of the firm is
   (a) where price exceeds average total cost. .
   (b) less than the point at which average total cost is at a minimum.
   (c) less than the point at which average total cost equals average revenue.
   (d) less than the point at which marginal cost equals marginal revenue.
   (e) where price equals marginal revenue.

Questions 2 and 3 refer to Figure 11-4.

Figure 11-4

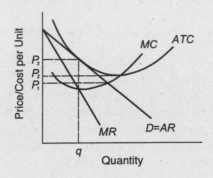

2. The profit-maximizing firm in monopolistic competition will set its price equal to
   (a) P_1.   (b) P_2.
   (c) P_3.   (d) minimum MC.
   (e) marginal cost.

3. The situation described by price P_3 and output q is
   (a) a long-run equilibrium in perfect competition since there are no economic profits.
   (b) a long-run equilibrium in monopolistic competition.
   (c) unstable; new firms will enter the industry to eliminate economic profits.
   (d) unstable; firms will exit because profits are zero.
   (e) not the profit-maximizing equilibrium for a monopolistic competitor.

4. The feature that distinguishes perfect competition from all other market structures is that competitive firms
   (a) face negatively sloped demand curves.
   (b) sell an identical product and are price takers.
   (c) actively compete through various forms of nonprice competition such as advertising.
   (d) administer their prices.
   (e) make zero profits in long run equilibrium.

5. Tacit cooperation among firms refers to
   (a) a legally binding contract to collude.
   (b) explicit collusion agreement.
   (c) an implicit understanding to cooperate in their joint interests
   (d) is a stable agreement because no single firm can do better by violating the agreement.
   (e) isn't worth the paper it's printed on.

6. The key difference between oligopolists and firms that operate in all other market structures is that oligopolists
   (a) are guaranteed long run profits.
   (b) produce an identical product but administer prices.
   (c) take explicit account of the impact of their decisions on competing firms.
   (d) do not engage in strategic behaviour.
   (e) do not engage in tacit collusion.

7. The cooperative, joint profit-maximizing outcome in oligopoly
   (a) is a long run equilibrium so long as there are barriers to entry.
   (b) will be unstable because each firm has an incentive to produce more output to increase profits.
   (c) results in allocative efficiency.
   (d) maximizes the output of each firm.
   (e) is an equilibrium so long as collusion is explicit as opposed to tacit.

8. Cooperation among oligopolistic firms that affects prices
   (a) is an effective agreement because it is a legal contract.
   (b) results in long run joint profit-maximizing equilibrium and stability in the industry.
   (c) tends to break down through strategic behaviour and technological innovation.
   (d) is more likely the greater the number of firms in the industry.
   (e) is more likely the weaker are the industry's barriers to entry.

9. Advertising expenditures can create a barrier to entry by
   (a) increasing costs for new entrants.
   (b) raising the minimum efficient scale of production.
   (c) allowing existing firms to announce to potential entrants the intention to engage in predatory pricing.
   (d) making a market contestable.
   (e) Both (a) and (b).

10. The equilibrium payoffs in the Prisoner's Dilemma
    (a) are a Nash equilibrium.
    (b) result from noncooperative behaviour.
    (c) are such that no individual prisoner can do better by changing its plea.
    (d) All of the above.
    (e) None of the above.

11. The observation that some oligopolistic firms sometimes sell at below cost is explained as
    (a) non-maximizing behaviour.
    (b) predatory pricing.
    (c) administered pricing.
    (d) non-price competition.
    (e) tacit cooperation.

12. The lower the _____, the greater the _____ an oligopolistic market.
    (a) price; profit in.
    (b) price; cooperation among firms in.
    (c) sunk cost of entry; contestability of.
    (d) degree of cooperation among firms; level of joint profit in.
    (e) advertising expenditure; minimum efficient scale of firms in.

13. According to the theory of monopolistic competition, a firm that lowers its price will
    (a) gain some but not all buyers in the market due to product differentiation.
    (b) increase its profits.
    (c) gain all of the market due to the nature of the demand curve facing the firm.
    (d) not affect its profits.
    (e) induce other firms to raise their prices.

14. The notion that monopolistic competition is systematically inefficient is *invalid* because consumers benefit
    (a) from lower prices.
    (b) from an increased variety of products.
    (c) because of an increase in quantity available.
    (d) from products becoming more homogeneous.
    (e) from lower production costs.

15. The long run equilibrium of a monopolistically competitive firm has all of the following characteristics except
    (a) $P = ATC$.
    (b) $MR = MC$.
    (c) ATC is increasing.
    (d) $ATC >$ minimum average cost.
    (e) ATC curve is tangent to the demand curve.

16. Which of the following applies to *both* monopolistic competition and perfect competition?
    (a) Firms produce a standardized product.
    (b) Non-price competition is common.
    (c) Absence of significant barriers to entry.
    (d) Each firm is a price-taker.
    (e) Short run equilibrium characterized by zero profits.

17. By taking into account the expected reaction of their competitors, oligopolists are exhibiting
    (a) tacit behaviour.
    (b) collusive behaviour.
    (c) cooperative behaviour.
    (d) noncooperative behaviour.
    (e) strategic behaviour.

18. Which of the following statements about Nash equilibrium is *false*?
    (a) A Nash equilibrium is an example of a non-cooperative equilibrium.
    (b) In a Nash equilibrium, all players are maximizing their payoffs given the current behaviour of the other players.
    (c) In a Nash equilibrium, all players are better off than they would be with any other combination of strategies.
    (d) A Nash equilibrium is self-enforcing.
    (e) Both (c) and (d) are false.

19. Which of the following is *not* a characteristic of an oligopolistic market structure?
    (a) Products of different firms may or may not be differentiated.
    (b) The price policies of the largest firm will impact on price policies of other firms in the industry.
    (c) There are relatively large numbers of sellers.
    (d) The concentration ratio is high.
    (e) Prices are typically administered.

20. Which of the following statements about oligopolistic behaviour is *false*?
    (a) There is a wide range of oligopolistic behaviour.
    (b) Oligopoly prices will generally exceed marginal cost.
    (c) Oligopoly may be the best available market structure when MES is large.
    (d) Oligopoly profits are unlikely to persist in the long run.
    (e) Oligopolists engage in strategic behaviour.

21. The firms in a highly "contestable" market set price _____ the perfectly competitive level in order to _____.
    (a) near; deter potential entry
    (b) near; keep sunk costs of entry high
    (c) well above; deter potential entry
    (d) well above; maximize their profit
    (e) below; force losses on competitors

22. Consider an example of the prisoner's dilemma where 2 firms are making sealed bids on a contract and each firm is allowed to bid either $150 or $350. If both firms bid the same price, the job is shared equally and each firm earns half the value of its bid. Otherwise the lowest bidder wins the contract and receives the full value of its bid. The cooperative outcome in this situation is
    (a) both firms bid $150.
    (b) both firms bid $350.
    (c) one firm bids $150, the other bids $350.
    (d) there is no cooperative equilibrium in this situation.
    (e) either (a) or (b).

23. Given the information in question 22, the Nash equilibrium is
    (a) both firms bid $150.
    (b) both firms bid $350.
    (c) one firm bids $150, the other bids $350.
    (d) there is no cooperative equilibrium in this situation.
    (e) either (a) or (b).

SOLUTIONS

Multiple Choice Questions

1.(c) 2.(e) 3.(e) 4.(e) 5.(d) 6.(e) 7.(c) 8.(e) 9.(a) 10.(c) 11.(a) 12.(c) 13.(d) 14.(e) 15.(b) 16.(e) 17.(e) 18.(a)

Exercises

1. (a) $6.00.
    (b) ($6.00 – $3.50) × 40 = $100.00.
    (c) No. The entry of new firms will reduce economic profits.
    (d) The *ATC* curve rises. To the extent that advertising is effective, the *D* curve will shift rightward, with the *MR* curve shifting accordingly. The *MC* curve will be unchanged since, in this case, advertising is a fixed amount.
    (e) The average revenue (demand) and marginal revenue curves for this firm would shift leftward, and economic profits would be reduced.

(f) Leftward shifts of the downward-sloping demand curve would eventually result in a tangency with the declining part of *ATC*. This tangency must occur at an output that is less than capacity (defined as output at which *ATC* is minimized).

2. Long run equilibrium is illustrated at price P_o and output q_o in Figure 11-5.

Figure 11-5

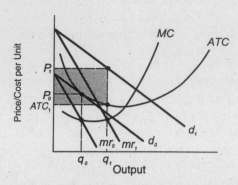

(a) This firm will get a share of the increased demand for the industry's product, so its demand curve shifts to the right (d_1 in Figure 11-5). Because the associated *mr* curve also shifts to the right, the profit-maximizing output increases (to q_1), as do its price (P_1) and profits (the shaded area).

(b) The positive profits induce other firms to enter, thereby reducing the firm's market share. This is represented by a leftward shift in the firm's individual demand curve until it is again tangent to its average total cost curve. Thus, output and price will decrease, and profit will again be zero.

3. (a) Joint profits are maximized if both firms adopt moderate advertising budgets. In this case profits for each firm are $80 million, so that joint profits are $160 million.

(b) No, the cooperative outcome of both firms adopting moderate budgets is unstable. Each firm can do better if it switches to a large budget while its competitor retains moderate expenditures. In the payoff matrix, a firm adopting a large budget would obtain profits of $90 million, while the competitor which remains with the moderate budget receives $50 million.

(c) The noncooperative equilibrium obtains when each firm selects the large advertising budget. Note that this outcome results in the lowest possible joint profits. However, it is a Nash equilibrium because no firm can do better given the choice of its competitor.

4. (a) Here are the payoffs: if both firms bid high prices, they each get $5 million; if they both bid low, they each get $3.5 million; and , if one firm bids high and the other low, the low bidder gets $7 million and the high bidder gets $0 million. See Figure 11-6 for the matrix.

Figure 11-6

Payoff Matrix (Profit in Millions of Dollars)

		Ever Sharp's Bid	
		Low	High
Triple Edge's Bid — High		0 7	5 5
Triple Edge's Bid — Low		3.5 3.5	7 0

(b) Combined profits are greatest if they both submit a high price. Thus, collusion would yield each firm a profit of $5 million.

(c) If the firms do not collude, they each will submit a low bid, thereby sharing the contract and receiving profits of $3.5 million each. This is the Nash equilibrium. Consider TripleEdge's (TS) logic. If EverSharp (ES) bids low and TS bids high, TS gets nothing, whereas if TS also bids low , it receives $3.5 million. If ES were to bid high and TS also bids high, TS would receive $5 million, whereas if TS bids low, it would get the entire contract for $7 million profit. Thus, it is always in TS's strategic interests to bid low. A symmetric logic applies to ES's strategy.

5. (a) OPEC drastically restricted supply in 1974, eventually raising the price above U.S. $35 per barrel. A combination of factors including new entrants, innovative substitutes and cheating by cartel members caused the price to drop in the 1980s to a low of $10 per barrel. In the early 1990s OPEC members were still unable to agree on enforceable output quotas, and the price of a barrel remained low. At the time of writing (July 1999), OPEC has been able to increase the price per barrel of crude by 75% since the beginning of the year to U.S. $21. How long OPEC can maintain discipline among its members is anyone's guess.

(b) This is a classic example of strategic pricing behaviour by the "Big Three" U.S. automakers. It appears that Ford and Chrysler chose to follow the leader in setting their prices: a form of tacit collusion. However, increased competition from transnational producers has limited the ability of the Big Three to administer prices.

(c) This particular price war was triggered by the develpment of a 386 microprocessor by American Micro Devices that was compatible with Intel's which, until then, had a virtual monopoly on the production of 386 chips. Intel responded by slashing prices. This is a good example of innovative pressures in oligopoly.

(d) The independent retailers have been attempting to increase their market share by offering lower prices. This is sometimes precipitated by entry or surplus production at the refinery. Brand name retailers respond by matching or even undercutting prices—a series of price decreases ensues, often resulting in temporary losses, until prices return to their normal levels.

(e) This is an excellent example of nonprice competition. Local retailers often cannot offer a good at the same price as large chains which receive volume discounts on their purchases (e.g., Wal-Mart). Thus, the local retailers are attempting to differentiate their product from that of the chains by offering more personal service.

Practice Multiple Choice Test

1.(b) 2.(c) 3.(b) 4.(b) 5.(c) 6.(c) 7.(b) 8.(c) 9.(e) 10.(b) 11.(b) 12.(c) 13.(a) 14.(b) 15.(c) 16.(c) 17.(e) 18.(c) 19.(c) 20.(d) 21.(a) 22.(b) 23.(a)

CHAPTER 12

ECONOMIC EFFICIENCY
AND PUBLIC POLICY

LO *LEARNING OBJECTIVES*

1 Explain the difference between productive and allocative efficiency.

2 Understand why perfect competition is allocatively efficient, whereas monopoly is allocatively inefficiency.

3 Understand the alternative methods of regulating a natural monopoly.

4 Gain a basic knowledge of Canadian competition policy.

CHAPTER OVERVIEW

Economists distinguish between two kinds of **efficiency: productive** and **allocative**. Productive efficiency occurs when output is being produced at the lowest attainable per unit cost. This requires, first, that firms be on (rather than above) their relevant cost curves and second, that all firms in the industry have the same marginal cost. Allocative efficiency involves producing the right mix of products. This occurs when price equals marginal cost for every product. When an economy's resources have been efficiently allocated, it is impossible to find an alternative allocation that can make at least one person better off without making someone else worse off. Such an allocation is called *Pareto efficient*.

We have studied several alternative market structures in the last three chapters; this chapter compares their relative efficiencies. While productive efficiency holds in all of the market structures we have studied, allocative efficiency obtains only in perfect competition. This is established by examination of the conditions for efficiency as well as the sum of consumer and **producer surplus.**

The goal of economic efficiency provides the rationale for promotion of competitive markets by government. There are two broad types of policies designed to promote allocative efficiency in monopolistic and imperfectly competitive markets: *economic regulation* and *competition policy*. Regulation of price and entry conditions are used in both monopolistic and oligopolistic market structures. Competition policy applies more to the latter.

Canadian competition policy seeks to prevent the unwarranted exploitation of market power. Although it has been subjected to several major reforms over the last century, it has always recognized the need for firms to be large in relation to the domestic market if economies of scale are to be exploited.

CHAPTER REVIEW

Economic Efficiency

When reading this section note that productive efficiency refers first to an individual firm and then to the industry, whereas allocative efficiency refers to the entire economy. After completing this section you should have a good understanding of the conditions required for an economy to be on its production possibility curve, as well as the conditions for being at the Pareto efficient point on that curve. Note that allocative efficiency maximizes the sum of consumer and producer surplus.

1. Resources are allocated efficiently when
   (a) there are no unemployed resources.
   (b) all firms are producing at the lowest attainable cost.
   (c) prices are as low as possible.
   (d) no alternative allocation of resources makes at least one household better off without making another household worse off.
   (e) profits are maximized.

2. If two firms are producing the same product with different marginal costs, then
   (a) a reallocation of output between the firms can lower the industry's total cost.
   (b) neither firm is producing its output at the lowest attainable cost.
   (c) some resources must be unemployed.
   (d) each firm is being wasteful.
   (e) one firm is not maximizing profits.

3. Allocative efficiency holds when
   (a) price equals marginal cost.
   (b) the consumer valuation of the last unit produced equals the value of resources used to produce this unit.
   (c) the sum of consumers' and producers' surplus is maximized.
   (d) it is impossible to reallocate resources in such a way as to make one individual better off, without making someone else worse off.
   (e) All of the above.

4. Productive efficiency holds
   (a) when $P = MC$ for perfect competition.
   (b) only for perfect competition and monopolistic competition where long run profits are zero.
   (c) for natural monopolies where economies of scale are fully exploited.
   (d) throughout the market economy where the objective of firms is to maximize profits.
   (e) when firms produce that output where the ATC curve is at a minimum.

5. Producers' surplus is defined as
   (a) profits.
   (b) retained earnings.
   (c) total revenue less total costs.
   (d) total revenue less total variable costs.
   (e) total revenue less total fixed costs.

6. The deadweight loss of monopoly is
    (a) its fixed cost.
    (b) any negative profit due to cyclical decreases in demand.
    (c) the forgone total surplus due to the allocatively inefficient monopoly output level.
    (d) the cost of maintaining effective barriers to entry.
    (e) the extra administrative costs of operating a large firm.

Economic Regulation to Promote Efficiency

The implications of marginal and average cost price regulations for a natural monopoly depend upon whether the firm is operating on the downward or upward sloping portion of its *ATC* curve. (You might want to return to Figure 12-6 of the text for a quick review.) This section develops an appreciation of several key issues in the debate concerning regulation of oligopolies.

7. Average cost pricing for a falling-cost natural monopoly results in
    (a) zero profits.
    (b) allocative efficiency.
    (c) production at the optimal output.
    (d) $P = MC$.
    (e) All of the above.

8. The larger the minimum efficient scale of firms, *ceteris paribus*,
    (a) the more likely a concentrated market will improve productive efficiency.
    (b) the greater the tendency toward natural monopoly.
    (c) the greater the advantages of large-scale production.
    (d) the fewer the number of firms comprising an industry.
    (e) All of the above.

9. Cross-subsidization refers to
    (a) the taxation of growing industries to subsidize declining ones.
    (b) the use of profits from one of a firm's products to subsidize another of its products at a price below cost.
    (c) transfers of profits between crown corporations and private firms in the same industry.
    (d) transfers from rising-cost natural monopolies to falling-cost natural monopolies.
    (e) taxation of private sector firms to subsidize public sector enterprises.

10. If a natural monopoly is regulated to charge a price that is set equal to marginal cost where the marginal cost curve intersects the demand curve and is less than average cost, the resulting level of output is
    (a) allocatively efficient, and a positive profit is earned.
    (b) allocatively efficient, but the firm must be paid a subsidy or it will go out of business.
    (c) less than the allocatively efficient level, and profits are zero.
    (d) less than the allocatively efficient level, but negative profits are earned.
    (e) greater than the allocatively efficient level, but negative profits are earned.

11. The original philosophy behind the regulation of natural monopolies such as public utilities
    (a) was to guarantee consumers a low price.
    (b) involved government ownership in key economic sectors.
    (c) was to achieve the advantages of large-scale production but prevent the monopoly from restricting output and raising price.
    (d) was to erect dependable and effective barriers to entry.
    (e) to protect domestic industries from foreign competition.

12. A two-part tariff is one means of allowing a _____ cost natural monopoly to cover the _____ resulting from _____-cost pricing.
    (a) declining; loss; average.
    (b) increasing; loss; average.
    (c) increasing; efficiency cost; marginal.
    (d) declining; loss; marginal.
    (e) declining; efficiency cost; marginal.

13. Which of the following is *not* one of the forces encouraging deregulation and privatization in advanced industrial nations?
    (a) The experience that many regulatory bodies serve to reduce competition rather than increase it.
    (b) The growing evidence that nationalized industries do not enhance productivity growth or allocative efficiency.
    (c) Increased pressures from world competition.
    (d) The conclusion that industrial performance improves when an oligopoly is replaced by a nationalized monopoly.
    (e) Concern over cross subsidization that is often required by regulatory agencies.

14. In practice, many regulatory agencies have pursued policies that
    (a) are aimed at protecting the consumer.
    (b) reflect a concern for existing firms and limiting the entry of potential competitors.
    (c) concern the trade-offs between domestic and foreign trade policy.
    (d) deal with work safety and environmental issues.
    (e) defend the market mechanism against monopoly control.

Canadian Competition Policy

After reading this section you will have a better appreciation of the historical development of competition policy in Canada, as well as an understanding of its current structure and objectives.

15. The lack of effective combines enforcement in Canada prior to 1986 was partly due to
    (a) the inability of civil actions to cope with complex economic issues.
    (b) the passage of the Combines Investigation Act as criminal rather than civil legislation.
    (c) the fact that the fines were rather small.
    (d) the reluctance of Canadian courts to assess economic evidence.
    (e) Both (b) and (d) are correct.

16. The 1976 amendments to the Combines Investigation Act included *all but which* of the following?
    (a) Claims of product quality must be based upon adequate tests.
    (b) Prohibiting producers from advertising a bargain price without reasonable quantities.
    (c) Prohibition of mergers.
    (d) Extension of the act to include service industries.
    (e) Allowance for civil as opposed to criminal actions.

17. The trend in the 1980s towards deregulation and privatization was based on all of the following realizations *except*:
    (a) increased global competition.
    (b) regulatory agencies often reduced competition.
    (c) replacement of a private monopoly with a crown corporation improves the industry's performance.
    (d) publically owned industries achieve less economic efficiency than privately owned ones.
    (e) replacement of privately owned oligopolies with a publicly owned monopoly worsens the industry's performance.

18. The Minister of Finance disallowed the proposed banking mergers in 1999 on the grounds that
    (a) there were no additional economies of scale to be gained.
    (b) Canadian banks already compete effectively in world financial markets.
    (c) the established network of branch banks is a massive entry barrier.
    (d) Canadian banks have been making excess profits.
    (e) Canadian banks can compete with foreign banks through the internet.

EXERCISES

1. **Allocative Efficiency and the Sum of Consumer and Producer Surplus**

   In Figure 12-1, *DD* is the market demand curve, and *DM* is the associated marginal revenue curve. *AN* is the supply curve for a competitive industry but also the marginal cost curve for a monopolist.

   Figure 12-1

   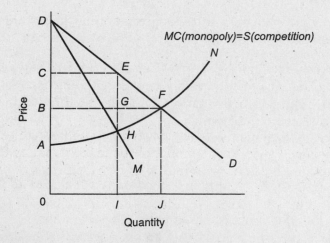

   (a) For perfect competition, predict the following:
       (i) equilibrium price _____ and quantity _____.
       (ii) consumer surplus _____.
       (iii) producer surplus _____.
       (iv) the sum of producer and consumer surplus _____.
   (b) For monopoly, predict the following:
       (i) equilibrium price _____ and quantity _____.
       (ii) consumer surplus _____.
       (iii) producer surplus _____.
       (iv) the sum of producer and consumer surplus _____.

(c) The surplus transferred from consumers to producers with monopolization of a competitive industry is _____.

(d) The deadweight loss from monopoly is _____.

2. The following exercise compares the impact of an increase in cost on a perfectly competitive market with a monopolized market.

A perfectly competitive market is illustrated in the first panel of Figure 12-2, while a monopolistic market is presented in the second. Note that each market faces an identical demand curve.

Figure 12-2

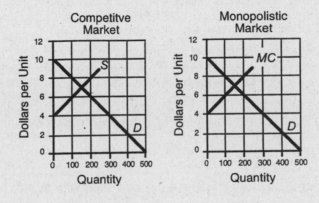

(a) What are the equilibrium levels of price and output in the perfectly competitive market? In the monopoly market?

(b) What shift in the monopolist's MC curve (relative to perfect competition) is required to have the levels of price and output the same in both market structures?

(c) Starting from the equilibrium situations depicted in (a), illustrate that both price and quantity would change by less in the monopolistic market than in the perfectly competitive in response to an increase in marginal costs by $2 per unit of output.

3. **Regulatory Pricing**

This exercise reviews the implications of regulatory pricing. The following graph depicts a market demand curve and a firm's cost structure. The latter is characterized by constant marginal cost (MC) and a large set-up cost so that average total cost (ATC) is continuously declining over market demand. The firm is therefore a natural monopoly.

Figure 12-3

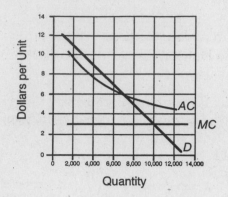

(a) What is the allocatively efficient level of output? Why?

(b) What are the unregulated monopolist's profit-maximizing price and quantity in this market and the associated profit level?

(c) What is the resulting deadweight loss?

(d) Suppose that a regulatory agency attempted to induce this monopolist to produce the allocatively efficient output by restricting price to equal marginal cost. Would the agency be successful? Why or why not?

(e) As an alternative, suppose that the agency imposes "average cost pricing" on the monopolist. What is the regulated price and the resulting quantity?

(f) Compare the level of profits and deadweight loss under "average cost pricing" with that under "marginal cost pricing" from (d).

4. **The Monopolization of a Competitive Industry**

This exercise investigates the impact on consumer and producer surplus from the monopolization of an otherwise perfectly competitive market.

The demand curve for a product is $Q^d = 90,000 - 1,000P$, where P (price) is expressed in dollars. In a competitive market, the supply curve is given by $Q^s = 2,000P - 45,000$ (with supply being zero at $P \leq \$22.50$). Remember, the competitive supply curve is the horizontal summation of the firm's marginal cost curves above the minimum average variable cost (here, $22.50).

(a) Determine the equilibrium price and quantity of the product necessary for allocative efficiency. (Use the grid in Figure 12-4 or solve algebraically.)

(b) Indicate consumer and producer surpluses (total net benefits, in dollars) under allocative efficiency.

Figure 12-4

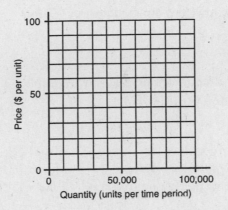

(c) Suppose that the market for this product were monopolized. The monopolist's counterpart to the competitive supply curve is $MC = 22.5 + 0.0005Q$. [Note the graphic identity of MC in this graph to S in part (a)]. Determine the quantity that would be supplied by the monopolist and the market price. Indicate the associated consumer and producer surpluses on the grid in Figure 12-5.

Figure 12-5

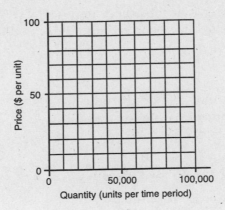

(d) Compare producer surplus, consumer surplus, and total net benefits in (c) with those obtained in (b).

5. **The Market for Taxicab Medallions in NYC**

An interesting example of how government policies serve to promote monopoly power is provided by laws requiring licensing of taxicabs. New York City passed such a law in 1937, freezing the number of taxicab licences (medallions) at 11,797—taxicabs without medallions are not supposed to pick up people who hail cabs from the street. Prior to the law, free entry had been allowed. In 1937 the price of taxicab medallions was near zero, since existing cabs were "grandfathered": existing operators were granted a medallion by virtue of already being in the industry. New entrants had to purchase a medallion from an existing owner at whatever price the market determined. As demand for taxi services rose, the market value of a medallion rose, reaching $100,000 in December 1985. About 1,600 medallions are traded each year, with banks often giving mortgages for their purchase.

(a) Use a graph to illustrate why the price of medallions has increased over time. Why is the increase in market price likely to continue?

(b) What does the market value of a medallion represent?

(c) What effect has the emergence of "gypsy" cabs (illegal cabs without medallions) in the city had on the taxicab market and the market value of a medallion? How would unrestricted entry affect the market value of a medallion?

(d) In April 1985, New York's Mayor Koch proposed increasing the number of medallions by 10 percent of the existing number. The new medallions were to be made available by auction. Earlier Koch had proposed giving each medallion owner a second medallion which the owner could either use or sell. Contrast these two plans.

PRACTICE MULTIPLE CHOICE TEST

1. A major difference between equilibrium in a competitive industry and a monopoly is that
   (a) the monopoly produces where $MR = MC$, but the perfect competitor does not.
   (b) perfect competitors achieve productive efficiency, but monopolies do not.
   (c) the perfect competitor produces where $P = MC$, but the monopoly does not.
   (d) the monopoly achieves allocative efficiency but perfect competition does not.
   (e) All of the above.

Questions 2 to 5 refer to Figure 12-6 in which the supply curve refers to a perfectly competitive industry and the marginal cost curve refers to a monopoly.

Figure 12-6

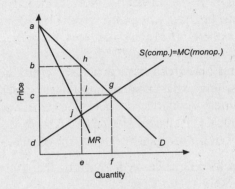

2. The allocatively efficient levels of output and price are
   (a) *e* and *b*, respectively.   (b) *e* and *c*, respectively.
   (c) f and *c*, respectively.   (d) f and *a*, respectively.
   (e) *e* and *d*, respectively.

3. If this industry were to switch from perfect competiton to a monopoly, the changes in price and quantity would be
   (a) +*cb* and –*fe*, respectively.   (b) –*bc* and –*fe*, respectively.
   (c) +*db* and +*ef*, respectively.   (d) +*dc* and +*ef*, respectively.
   (e) +*ca* and –*fe*, respectively.

4. Under monopoly, producer surplus is area
   (a) *bdjh*.   (b) *bdgh*.
   (c) *cdg*.   (d) *adj*.
   (e) *adg*.

5. If price increases from *c* to *b*, and therefore quantity demanded is reduced from f to *e*, consumer surplus is reduced by area
   (a) *hig*.   (b) *bcih*.
   (c) *hjg*.   (d) *bcgh*.
   (e) *efgh*.

6. The condition of allocative efficiency is satisfied only under perfect competition because only this market structure results in
   (a) long run profits equal to zero.
   (b) *P = MC*.
   (c) complete freedom of entry and exit.
   (d) maximization of profits through cutthroat competition.
   (e) productive efficiency.

7. Productive efficiency requires that
   (a) each firm produces its output at the lowest possible cost.
   (b) each firm employ factors such that the ratio of their marginal products is equal to the ratio of their prices.
   (c) the total cost of producing the industry's output is minimized.
   (d) marginal cost of production be equalized across all firms in the industry.
   (e) All of the above.

8. In reviewing a proposed merger, the Competition Bureau is obliged to consider
   (a) potential efficiency gains.
   (b) degree of foreign competition.
   (c) barriers to entry.
   (d) degree of competition after the merger.
   (e) All of the above.

Questions 9 to 15 refer to Figure 12-7 which depicts a firm with a constant marginal cost curve and a declining average total cost (e.g., due to some large entry cost).

Figure 12-7

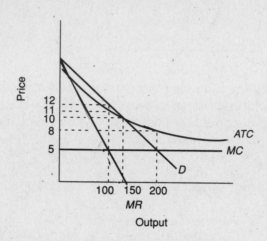

9. The firm depicted above can be classified as
   (a) a constant cost natural monopoly.
   (b) a declining cost natural monopoly.
   (c) an oligopoly.
   (d) monopolistically competitive.
   (e) perfectly competitive.

10. If this firm were *not* subject to regulation, its output and profit would be
    (a) 100 units; $100.
    (b) 150 units; $750.
    (c) 100 units; $700.
    (d) 100 units; $12.
    (e) 200 units; $600.

11. If this firm were *not* subject to regulation, the resulting deadweight loss would be
    (a) zero.
    (b) $100.
    (c) $350.
    (d) $700.
    (e) $1,000.

12. If this firm were subject to marginal cost price regulation, its output and profit would be
    (a) 100 units; $100.
    (b) 100 units; $0.
    (c) 100 units; $700.
    (d) 200 units; $0.
    (e) 200 units; –$600.

13. If this firm were subject to average cost price regulation, its output and profit would be
    (a) 100 units; $100.
    (b) 150 units; $0.
    (c) 150 units; $750.
    (d) 150 units; -$750.
    (e) 200 units; $0.

14. The deadweight loss resulting from marginal cost pricing and average cost pricing are
    (a) $150 and $150, respectively.
    (b) $100 and $150, respectively.
    (c) $0 and $125, respectively.
    (d) $125 and $150, respectively.
    (e) $0 and $100, respectively.

15. Suppose the firm is regulated by the following two-part tariff. If it produces 200 units, it is permitted to sell the first 100 units of output at whatever price it wishes, but any output after that is subject to marginal cost pricing. The profit of this firm would be
    (a) $0.
    (b) $200.
    (c) $150.
    (d) -$150.
    (e) -$600.

SOLUTIONS

Chapter Review

1.(d) 2.(a) 3.(e) 4.(d) 5.(d) 6.(c) 7.(a) 8.(e) 9.(b) 10.(b) 11.(c) 12.(d) 13.(d) 14.(b) 15.(e) 16.(c) 17.(c) 18.(c)

Exercises

1. (a) (i) B,J; (ii) area BDF; (iii) area ABF; (iv) area ADF.
   (b) (i) C,I; (ii) area CDE; (iii) area ACEH; (iv) area ADEH.
   (c) area CBGE.
   (d) area HEF.

2. (a) **Figure 12-8**

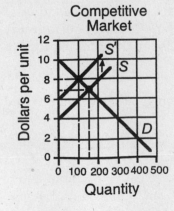

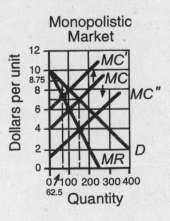

The initial equilibrium in perfect competition obtains at a price of $7 and a quantity of 150 units. The monopoly equilibrium is derived by first drawing the monopolist's marginal revenue curve (same price intercept and half the quantity intercept as the demand curve), which equals MC at an output of 100 units, implying a price of $8.

(b) The equilibrium in perfect competition obtains at a price of $7 and a quantity of 150 units. For these to be the profit-maximizing price and quantity of the monopolist, the market MR curve and the monopolist's MC curve must intersect at a quantity of 150. This requires (for a uniform shift) that MC be $3 lower per unit of output—for illustration, MC''.

(c) In panel (i), shift the supply curve a vertical distance of $2 to S'; the new equilibrium price is $8 and quantity is 100. In panel (ii), shift the MC curve a vertical distance of $2 to MC'; equate MR and MC' to obtain the new profit-maximizing price of $8.75 and quantity of 62.5 (approximately). Thus both price and quantity change less in the monopoly situation.

3. **Figure 12-9**

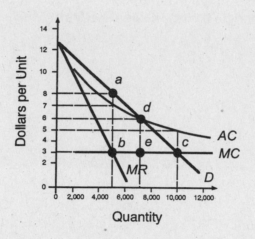

(a) 10,000. Because the value of the resources used to produce the 10,000th unit (i.e., MC) equals the value that households place on the consumption of this unit.

(b) $8; 5,000 units; and, $5,000.

(c) area abc = ($8 − $3) (10,000 − 5,000)/2 = $12,500.

(d) If the market price were $3 and the firm produced 10,000 units, TR would be $30,000. But AC would be $5, which implies a TC of $50,000. Therefore, the firm would be making a loss of $20,000; it would eventually go out of business unless the loss was offset by a subsidy from the government.

(e) Price could be regulated at $6, which would yield a market quantity of 7,000 units.

(f) Under average cost pricing in (e), profits are zero but the deadweight loss is area dec = ($6 − $3) (10,000 − 7,000)/2 = $4,500. Marginal cost pricing in (d) does not yield any deadweight loss, but the firm is forced to incur an operating loss.

4. (a) Set demand equal to supply and solve for price (45) and output (45,000). (See panel (i) of Figure 12-10 below.)

(b) Consumer surplus is area (a) and producer surplus is area (b) in panel (i); $1,012,000 and $506,250, respectively.

(c) Price is h and quantity is 27,000. In panel (ii), consumer surplus is shown by the triangle ehg; producer surplus is the quadrangle khgf.

(d) Under competitive conditions, consumer surplus (CS) is more and producer surplus (PS) is less than under monopoly. For example, CS in (c) is the area ehg in panel (ii), which is less than triangle (a) in panel (i). Net benefits (consumer plus producer surplus) are less under monopoly. The amount of the reduction (the so-called deadweight loss) is shown by the triangle *ifg* in panel (ii).

Figure 12-10

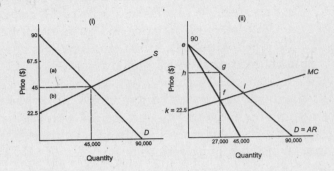

5. (a) Supply is fixed, or perfectly inelastic. As demand increases over time, the price will be driven up.

Figure 12-11

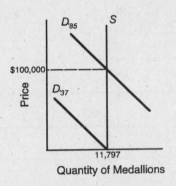

(b) It represents the present value of the stream of future profits obtainable from owning and operating a cab in New York City.

(c) Entry is characterized by a rightward shift in the supply curve, thereby eroding the price of a medallion. While gypsy cabs operate illegally, authorities in New York have for the most part ignored them in recent years: they have therefore reduced the market value of a medallion. With free entry, the supply curve will shift to the right until it intersects current demand at a medallion price of zero.

(d) A 10 percent increase in the quantity of medallions would lower their price, but not by as much as a doubling of their number. Thus, current owners would suffer less of a capital loss with the first plan. On the other hand, current owners gain nothing with the first plan since the medallions are auctioned off, while under the second plan they would receive a second medallion free. The relative magnitudes of these offsetting effects would determine their preferred plan.

Practice Multiple Choice Test

1.(c) 2.(c) 3.(a) 4.(a) 5.(d) 6.(b) 7.(e) 8.(e) 9.(b) 10.(a) 11.(c) 12.(e) 13.(b) 14.(c) 15.(b)

PART FIVE

FACTOR MARKETS

CHAPTER 13

FACTOR PRICING AND FACTOR MOBILITY

LEARNING OBJECTIVES

1 Understand the size and functional distributions of income.

2 Explain a profit-maximizing firm's demand for a factor.

3 Understand the determinants of the elasticity of factor demand.

4 Explain the role of factor mobility in determining factor supply.

5 Distinguish between temporary and equilibrium factor-price differentials.

6 Explain the concept of economic rent, and how it is related to factor mobility.

CHAPTER OVERVIEW

This chapter discusses the theory of how factor prices are determined. As you might expect, equilibrium factor prices are determined by the forces of demand and supply in markets for factors of production.

The demand for a factor is a **derived demand**. The decisions by firms on how much to produce and how to produce it imply specific demand for the various factors of production. This "derived demand" provides the link between goods markets and factor markets. The product of **marginal physical productivity** and marginal revenue is called **marginal revenue product**. The *MRP* curve is the demand curve for a variable factor. The degree of responsiveness of the quantity of factor demanded to a change in factor price is called the **elasticity of factor demand**. The elasticity of factor demand is the percentage change in factor use associated with a percentage change in the factor's price. Factor demand will be more elastic the greater the elasticity of demand for the product, the more slowly marginal productivity declines as output expands, the easier it is to substitute among factors, and the greater the factor's share of total costs.

The supply of a factor to a particular industry or occupation is more elastic than its supply to the whole economy because one industry can bid units away from other industries. The elasticity of supply to a particular use depends on **factor mobility**, which tends to be greater the longer the time allowed for a reaction to take place.

With factor mobility, factor returns will tend to be equalized among uses. A difference in returns for different units of any one factor may reflect a temporary situation. Factors may earn an economic rent until that gap is eliminated. Conversely, the differences in factor prices may reflect an equilibrium situation that will persist due to qualitative differences in the factors or nonmonetary advantages of jobs to workers.

CHAPTER REVIEW

Income Distribution

Classical economists focused on the **functional distribution of income,** defined as the distribution of national income among the major factors of production (land, labour, capital). Modern economists, who are interested in income inequality between individuals, have concentrated on the **size distribution of income.** A Lorenz curve shows how much of total income is accounted for by given proportions of the nation's families—that is, in fairly simple terms, the Lorenz curve illustrates the inequality of income in a particular country. What would the Lorenz curve look like if there were complete equality of income in a nation?

1. The functional distribution of income
   - (a) emphasizes the function of income in attracting workers.
   - (b) is concerned with income distribution by socioeconomic class.
   - (c) can be graphically shown by a Lorenz curve.
   - (d) shows income shares of factors of production.
   - (e) deals with the transfer earnings portion of total factor incomes.

2. Complete equality of income distribution would appear on a Lorenz curve as a
   - (a) diagonal line.
   - (b) convex line.
   - (c) concave curve.
   - (d) single point.
   - (e) series of points below the diagonal.

The Demand for Factors

What condition determines whether a firm will hire one extra unit or use one less unit of any factor of production? The profit-maximizing marginal decision rule boils down to the condition that a firm will hire a factor up to the point where the marginal cost of the factor is equal to the marginal revenue product of the factor. In the special case of competitive goods and factor markets, the equation can be written as $w = MPP \times p$, where the symbol p represents the good's price per unit and w is the unit price of the factor.

The *MRP* curve of a variable factor is the firm's derived demand curve of that variable factor. As the factor price changes, the quantity of factor demand will change (a movement along a given *MRP* curve). If either *MPP* or p change, the *MRP* curve will shift.

Make sure you can identify each of the **four economic conditions that determine factor demand elasticity,** and that you understand how it affects the elasticity of factor demand.

3. The marginal revenue product of a factor is
   (a) the change in revenue from selling the extra output produced by an additional unit of a factor.
   (b) average physical productivity of the factor multiplied by product price.
   (c) the change in revenue from selling one more unit of output.
   (d) equal to the market price of the product that is produced by the factor.
   (e) its marginal physical product times the factor's price.

4. The marginal physical product of labour is
   (a) total output divided by total labour in use.
   (b) the change in output divided by the change in labour use.
   (c) total labour in use divided by total output.
   (d) the change in labour use divided by the change in output.
   (e) None of the above.

5. A perfectly competitive, profit-maximizing firm hires a factor up to the point at which
   (a) the factor's price equals its marginal revenue product.
   (b) the marginal cost of hiring the factor equals the additional revenue obtained from that factor's marginal contribution to output.
   (c) the factor's price equals its marginal physical product times the product's price.
   (d) All of the above.
   (e) None of the above.

6. Perfectly competitive, profit-maximizing firms that employ any factor until marginal revenue product equals its price will hire
   (a) additional units of the factor if its price falls, other things equal.
   (b) more of the factor if the price of the product it produces falls, other things equal.
   (c) less of the factor if technology changes such that factor productivity rises, other things equal.
   (d) additional units of the factor if the factor's price exceeds its marginal revenue product.
   (e) the same quantities of all factors.

7. Which of the following explains why a profit-maximizing, competitive firm's demand curve for labour slopes downward? As the quantity of labour employed rises,
   (a) the marginal physical product of labour eventually falls.
   (b) the firm's marginal revenue declines as output increases.
   (c) the marginal cost of hiring another unit of labour increases.
   (d) All of the above.
   (e) None of the above.

8. If the quantity demanded for a factor of production decreases by 10 percent when its price increases by 8 percent, the elasticity of demand for the factor is
   (a) –18.0.   (b) 1.25 percent.
   (c) –0.80.   (d) –2.00.
   (e) –1.25.

9. Which of the following is *not* true about the demand for a factor of production?
   (a) It is more elastic the greater the elasticity of demand for the final product.
   (b) It is more elastic in cases where technology dictates its use in fixed proportions with other factors.
   (c) It is less elastic the less its importance in producing a good.
   (d) It is more elastic the greater its substitutability with alternative inputs.
   (e) None of the above are correct.

10. Which of the following is likely to shift the demand curve for carpenters to the right?
    (a) A decrease in carpenters' wages.
    (b) An increase in carpenters' wages.
    (c) An increase in the demand for residential construction.
    (d) A decrease in carpenters' marginal physical productivity at all levels of employment.
    (e) None of the above.

The Supply of Factors

The supply of factors and the elasticity of the factor supply can be determined at three different levels of aggregation; for the economy as a whole, for a particular industry or occupation, and for one firm. The key determinant of supply elasticity is factor mobility within and among the three levels of aggregation. The section *Applying Economic Concepts 13-1* provides an interesting discussion of the "brain drain" of Canadian workers to the United States.

11. A highly mobile factor of production
    (a) is one that shifts easily between uses in response to small changes in incentives.
    (b) displays supply inelasticity in most uses.
    (c) is one that possesses skills that are used by only one firm.
    (d) will tend to have a large proportion of its earnings made up of economic rents.
    (e) Both (a) and (d).

12. The elasticity of the supply of a factor will be lowest when
    (a) a factor moves from Ford of Canada to Chrysler Canada.
    (b) a factor moves from the steel industry to the automobile parts manufacturing industry.
    (c) a doctor moves from one country to another.
    (d) a carpenter moves from Brandon to Winnipeg.
    (e) the factor is perfectly mobile between all uses.

13. As a factor of production, agricultural land
    (a) is considered to be highly immobile in both a physical and an economic sense.
    (b) is the only factor that is paid economic rents.
    (c) is mobile in an economic sense because it has many alternative uses as a factor of production.
    (d) is completely immobile because it cannot be moved.
    (e) ceases to be considered a factor of production if it is used for purposes other than farming.

14. The discussion of the increased "brain drain" of skilled workers from Canada to the United States in *Applying Economic Concepts 13-1* suggests that
    (a) Canada receives no inflows of skilled workers from the United States.
    (b) some observers argue that the brain drain generates short-term and long-term costs for Canada.
    (c) better job prospects are unimportant determinants of the migration to the United States.
    (d) government budget cuts have led to higher wages for Canadian public-sector workers.
    (e) None of the above are correct.

The Operation of Factor Markets

In a competitive factor market, equilibrium levels of employment of the factor and its unit price are determined by the intersection of the demand and supply curves. The product of factor price times quantity is the factor's total income. Variations in factor prices can occur temporarily or they can persist for long periods of time (equilibrium differentials).

Equal net advantage is a theory of the allocation of the total supply of factors to particular uses. Owners of factors will choose the use that produces the greatest net advantage, allowing for both the monetary and nonmonetary advantages of a particular employment.

Any excess that a factor earns over the minimum needed to keep it at its present use (its **transfer price**) is called its **economic rent**. When the supply curve for a factor is perfectly inelastic, all earnings are economic rents since a perfectly inelastic supply curve implies that there are no alternative uses for this factor. When the supply curve for a factor is perfectly elastic, all earnings are transfer income (there are no economic rents). When the supply curve for a factor is upward sloping, the difference between the equilibrium factor price and the transfer price for a particular level of factor use is economic rent. As the mobility of a factor decreases, the share of the factor payment that is economic rent increases.

15. Which of the following will unambiguously increase the equilibrium wage rate of economists?
(a) The demand curve for economists shifts to the left.
(b) Both the demand and supply curves for economists shift to the right.
(c) Both the demand and supply curves for economists shift to the left.
(d) The supply curve for economists shifts to the right.
(e) The demand curve for economists shifts to the right and the supply curve shifts to the left.

16. Assume that a temporary differential exists such that wages in occupation A are higher than those in occupation B. According to the hypothesis of equal net advantage, we would expect
(a) all nonmonetary advantages to be equalized between the two occupations.
(b) workers to move from occupation A to occupation B.
(c) the differential wage to be eliminated eventually as movers move from B to A.
(d) the wage differential to be long-lasting particularly if workers are highly mobile.
(e) None of the above are correct.

17. Equilibrium differentials in factor prices may reflect
(a) intrinsic differences in factor characteristics.
(b) acquired differences in factor characteristics.
(c) nonmonetary advantages in uses of the factor.
(d) All of the above.
(e) None of the above.

18. Which of the following is not an example of an equilibrium differential in a factor price?
(a) Land in downtown Toronto is more expensive than land in the suburbs.
(b) Wages in the Alberta construction trades are higher than elsewhere in the country because of a booming Albertan economy.
(c) Individuals working in isolated communities tend to be paid more than their counterparts in the more accessible cities.
(d) A dentist is paid more than a dental hygienist.
(e) Certain workers receive higher wages because of greater working hazards.

19. Economic rent
(a) refers exclusively to the income of landowners.
(b) is taxable under the income tax law, whereas transfer earnings are not.
(c) is earned only by completely immobile factors.
(d) is the excess of income over transfer earnings.
(e) refers exclusively to the income of capital.

20. All payments to certain workers would be economic rents if
    (a) their supply curve were perfectly elastic.
    (b) they were perfectly mobile between alternative uses.
    (c) their supply curve were upward sloping.
    (d) the demand by firm for their services were elastic.
    (e) None of the above are correct.

21. A politician who earns $100,000 and who estimates she might earn $70,000 in her occupation before she was elected, is currently receiving
    (a) economic rents of $100,000.
    (b) transfer payments of $100,000.
    (c) economic rents of $70,000.
    (d) transfer payments of $30,000.
    (e) economic rents of $30,000.

22. One would expect which of the following parties to view most of the payment to Carlos Delgado of the Toronto Blue Jays as transfer earnings?
    (a) The Toronto Blue Jays.
    (b) The professional baseball industry.
    (c) University professors.
    (d) National transfer payment recipients.
    (e) None of the above.

EXERCISES

1. This exercise demonstrates that the "law" of diminishing returns yields a downward-sloping factor demand curve for a profit-maximizing firm that sells its product in a perfectly competitive market. It also shows the conditions that cause shifts in the demand curve for the factor. The following table is partly completed to assist you. Three cases are illustrated: Case B reflects a lower product price than for case A. Case C assumes that labour productivity is different from that in cases A and B. The marginal physical productivity of labour is denoted as MPP, and the product price per unit is p.

Units of Labour	Output	MPP	p	Case A MRP	p	Case B MRP	MPP	p	Case C MRP
1	50	50	$30	$1,500	$27	$1,350	60	$30	$1,800
2	63	13	30	390	27	351	15	30	450
3	75	12	30	360	27	324	14	30	420
4	85	10	30	300	27	270	12	30	360
5	94	___	30	___	27	___	11	30	___
6	99	___	30	___	27	___	7	30	___

(a) Complete the table and plot all three MRP curves in Figure 13-1.

(b) Explain why the MRP curve slopes downward in all three cases.

(c) For case A, what is the firm's quantity demanded for workers if the wage is $360? Explain your answer.

(d) For case A, explain why the firm's hiring would increase if the wage fell from $360 to $270. What is the new profit-maximizing amount of labour?

(e) For case B, what is the firm's quantity demanded for workers if the weekly wage is $270? How does this value compare with that for case A in part (d)?

(f) For every wage rate, explain why the firm's demand for labour is less in case B than in case A.

(g) What effect did the lower product price in case B have on the position and the slope of the demand curve for labour?

(h) For case C, what is the firm's demand for labour when the weekly wage is $360? How does this value compare with that of case A, in part (c)?

(i) Explain why the firm's demand for labour at every wage is greater for case C than for case A.

Figure 13-1

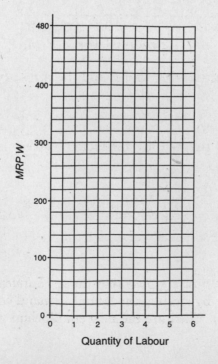

2. Given that *DD* is the demand curve for commercial airplane pilots and *W* is equilibrium monthly salary, draw the supply curves in Figure 13-2 that are consistent with
   (a) none of earnings being economic rent.
   (b) all earnings being economic rent.
   (c) half of earnings being economic rent.

Figure 13-2

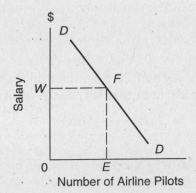

3. Consider Figure 13-3 which represents a labour market for a specific type of worker. The initial demand curve is L^D, but there are two possible supply curves: L^s_A and L^s_B.

Figure 13-3

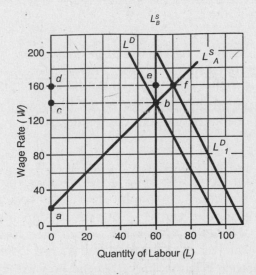

(a) What are the equilibrium values of *W* and *L* and the total payment to this factor in each case?

(b) What is the division of total payment to this factor between economic rent and transfer earnings in each case?

(c) For case A, what is the division between transfer earnings and economic rent for the sixtieth unit of labour? The fortieth?

(d) Assuming that case A holds, now suppose that the government attempts to increase employment in this industry by shifting the labour demand curve to the right (the new labour demand curve is L^D_1). What are the new equilibrium wage and quantity of labour demanded?

(e) By how much does the government policy increase economic rents in this market?

(f) How much of the increase in economic rents goes to labour that was employed before the policy was introduced?

4. (a) A firm's demand for a factor of production is given by its marginal revenue product, and if the price of the factor is given, the quantity demanded can be determined as in Exercise 1. Using the MRP schedules for Firms A and B given here, determine the quantity of machines they will each rent if the rental price is $8.

Quantity of Machines	MRP_A	MRP_B
10	10	8
20	9	6
30	8	4
40	7	2
50	6	0
60	5	0

Quantity of machines rented: Firm A ____; Firm B ____

(b) A single firm may be able to take the rental price as given, but if A and B represent the MRP in two different industries and if the total number of machines available to these two industries is fixed, industry A can acquire more machines only by bidding them away from industry B. Assuming that the stock of machines available is 70, how should they be most efficiently allocated between the two industries?

Quantity of machines rented: Industry A ____; Industry B ____.

(c) You can show the result from (b) graphically by plotting the two MRP curves in the machine market represented by the graph below. The horizontal axis represents the total number of machines available. The MRP of machines in A is measured from the left-hand origin, and the MRP of machines in B is measured from the right-hand origin. The MRP for B is plotted for you. Plot the MRP for A, and determine the rental price where these two curves intersect. What is this price, and how are the machines allocated between the two industries?

Figure 13-4

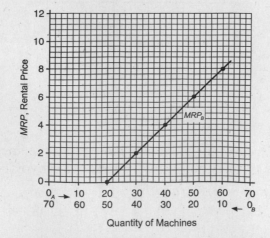

(d) Suppose that the productivity of machines in industry B rises because of technological improvements, and the new MRP schedule in B is as shown below. Plot this curve, and determine the new equilibrium rental price and allocation of machines between the two industries.

Quantity	MRP'_B
10	11
20	9
30	7
40	5
50	3

(e) By how many machines did the MRP curve shift horizontally to the left, and how many additional machines did industry B end up renting? Explain why the number of machines B rents does not rise by as much as the MRP curve shifts to the left.

5. The demand and supply conditions in a competitive factor market are portrayed in Figure 13-5. Two possible demand scenarios are labelled D_1 and D_2. With an initial supply curve of S_0, the current equilibrium values of price and employment are 8 and 40, respectively.

Figure 13-5

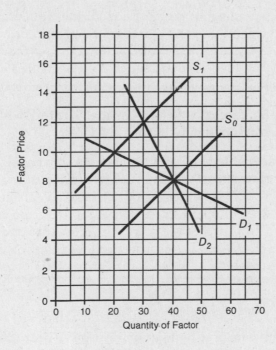

(a) If S_0 holds, what are current total factor earnings? What is the value of economic rents for the thirtieth unit?

(b) Suppose that the supply curve for the factor shifts up to the line labelled S_1. What are the new equilibrium values of price and employment for the two demand scenarios?

(c) Using midpoints between the new and old equilibrium values, calculate the elasticity of demand for both demand curves. Which demand curve has the higher elasticity?

(d) In terms of the elasticity values you have calculated, which demand curve implies, (all else equal),

    (i)   a lower elasticity of demand for the product that this factor produces?

    (ii)   a higher degree of substitutability of other factors for this factor when its price increases?

    (iii) larger increases in the factor's marginal productivity as less of the factor is used?

    (iv) lower total factor earnings at the new equilibrium situation compared with those at the initial equilibrium?

6. This exercise focuses on the Lorenz curve for Canada. The following table provides data on the size distribution of before-tax family income for 1993.

Family Income Rank	Percentage Share of Aggregate Income	Cumulative Percentage of Aggregate
Lowest fifth	6.4	_____
Second fifth	12.0	_____
Middle fifth	17.6	_____
Fourth fifth	24.1	_____
Highest fifth	39.9	_____

Source: *Statistics Canada*, 13-207

(a) Calculate the cumulative income-population distribution for Canada in 1993.

(b) Plot the 1993 Lorenz curve for Canada in Figure 13-6.

Figure 13-6

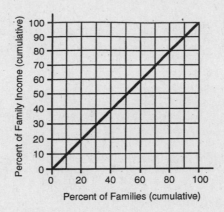

(c) By visual inspection of your Lorenz curve, can you conclude that income in Canada was equally distributed?

EXTENSION EXERCISE

E1.   There are two regional labour markets within a country, X and Y. Workers are equally qualified to perform the same type of job in either region, and they have no nonmonetary preferences with respect to the region in which they work and live. The initial situation in each labour market is portrayed in Figure 13-7, point a for market X and point h for market Y.

Figure 13-7

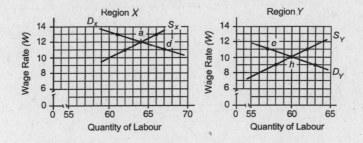

(a)   In terms of the information provided, what type of differential exists between the two markets?

(b)   In terms of the principle of net advantage, explain why labour flows will cause shifts in the labour supply curves such that new equilibria might occur at points d and e.

PRACTICE MULTIPLE CHOICE TEST

Use Figure 13-8 to answer questions 1 and 2:

Figure 13-8

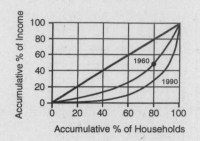

1. The Lorenz curve for a hypothetical economy is given for two different years. Between 1960 and 1990,
   (a) the income distribution became less equal.
   (b) the income distribution became more equal.
   (c) the poverty rate rose.
   (d) the poverty rate fell.
   (e) the employment-income share of total income increased.

2. In 1960, the richest 20 percent of households received
   (a) twice as much income as the poorest 20 percent of households.
   (b) as much income as the other 80 percent of households.
   (c) twice as much income as the other 80 percent of households.
   (d) half as much income as the other 80 percent of households.
   (e) None of the above.

Questions 3 to 6 refer to Figure 13-9. The demand and supply curves apply to a competitive market for a factor of production. Point *A* is the initial market equilibrium situation; other points represent alternative equilibria caused by parallel shifts in either the demand curve or the supply curve, but not both.

Figure 13-9

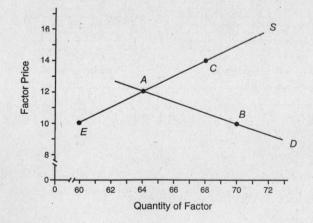

3. At the initial equilibrium situation at point *A*,
   (a) total income paid to the factor is $12.
   (b) total factor earnings are $768.
   (c) the economic rent of the sixty-fourth unit is zero.
   (d) Both (b) and (c).
   (e) None of the above.

4. If the equilibrium in this factor market changed from point A to point B, then
   (a) the supply curve for the factor has shifted to the right.
   (b) total factor earnings are $700.
   (c) the economic rent of the sixty-fourth unit is now positive.
   (d) All of the above.
   (e) None of the above.

5. If the equilibrium in this factor market changed from point A to point C, then
   (a) the new equilibrium unit price of the factor is $14.
   (b) total factor earnings are lower at C than those associated with point A.
   (c) the total demand for the factor decreased.
   (d) Both (a) and (b).
   (e) All of the above.

6. Assuming an equilibrium factor price of $12,
   (a) the sixtieth unit of the factor makes no economic rents.
   (b) the economic rent to the sixtieth unit of the factor is $2.
   (c) the transfer earning to the sixtieth unit of the factor is $10.
   (d) the economic rent to the sixtieth unit of the factor is $10.
   (e) Both (b) and (c) are correct.

Answer questions 7 through 13 by referring to the schedule below which indicates output at various levels of labour use as well as the firm's product price per unit.

Labour	Output	Marginal Physical Product	Price/Unit
0	0	0	2
1	16	16	2
2	36	20	2
3	54	18	2
4	68	14	2
5	80	—	2
6	90	10	2
7	98	8	2
8	104	6	2

7. What is the magnitude of the marginal physical product of the fifth worker?
   (a) 80.   (b) 16.
   (c) 12.   (d) 2.
   (e) 40.

8. The marginal revenue product of the fourth worker is
   (a) $108.   (b) $2.
   (c) $14.   (d) $68.
   (e) $28.

9. The marginal revenue product of the seventh worker is
    (a) greater than the *MRP* of the fourth worker.
    (b) equal to the *MRP* of the second worker.
    (c) less than the *MRP* of the eighth worker.
    (d) equal to $16.
    (e) None of the above.

10. Over the range of the second to the eighth worker, the value of the *MRP*
    (a) decreases due to diminishing marginal physical productivity.
    (b) remains constant at $2.
    (c) decreases because marginal revenue declines as more output is sold.
    (d) Both (a) and (c) are correct.
    (e) increases because total revenue product increases as more output is sold.

11. If the current wage rate per worker were $16, what is the profit-maximizing level of labour use?
    (a) Five workers.
    (b) Eight workers.
    (c) Seven workers.
    (d) Six workers.
    (e) None of the above.

12. If the firm's product price increased from $2 to $3, then
    (a) the *MRP* curve would shift to the right.
    (b) at every level of employment, the value of *MRP* would decrease.
    (c) the firm would hire more workers, assuming the wage paid to workers did not change.
    (d) the wage rate must also increase by 50 percent.
    (e) Both (a) and (c).

13. An increase in the wage rate would
    (a) shift the *MRP* curve to the right.
    (b) trigger the firm to hire more workers.
    (c) shift the *MRP* curve to the left.
    (d) necessarily lead to a decrease in the firm's product price.
    (e) None of the above.

SOLUTIONS

Chapter Review

1.(d) 2.(a) 3.(a) 4.(b) 5.(d) 6.(a) 7.(a) 8.(e) 9.(b) 10.(c) 11.(a) 12.(c) 13.(c) 14. (b) 15.(e) 16.(c) 17.(d) 18.(b) 19.(d) 20.(e) 21.(e) 22.(a)

Exercises

1. (a) Marginal physical product: 9, 5; case A, *MRP* = $270, $150; case B, *MRP* = $243, $135; case C, *MRP* = $330, $210

Figure 13-10

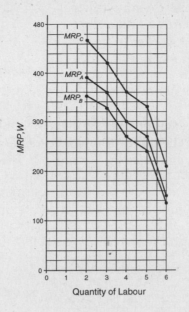

(b) As more labour is employed, marginal physical productivity falls; this is the "law" of diminishing returns.

(c) The firm demands three units of labour. The firm will maximize profits if it equates the marginal cost of obtaining labour ($360) to the marginal revenue product.

(d) Three units of labour no longer represents a profit-maximizing situation since the *MRP* of the third unit of labour is $360 while the wage rate is $270. The firm will hire two more units of labour (a total of five), at which point *MRP* = $270.

(e) For case B, the firm will hire four units of labour, at which point *MRP* = $270. This is one less unit of labour than in case A.

(f) The price (marginal revenue) per unit is less; compare $27 with $30.

(g) The demand curve for labour in case B lies to the left of the demand curve in case A. The shift is not parallel.

(h) For case C, the firm will hire four units of labour, which is one more than in case A, part (c).

(k) The demand for labour in case C will be greater than for case A since the marginal productivity of each unit of labour has increased.

2. (a) Horizontal supply curve at *W*.
   (b) Vertical supply curve at *E*.
   (c) Any of a number of supply curves dividing rectangle *OWFE* into two equal areas; a diagonal straight line from *O* to *F* would be one example.

3. (a) In each case, *W* = $140 and *L* = 60, so total factor payment is $8,400.
   (b) In case A, economic rent is the area below the wage line and above the supply curve (area *abc* in the graph), which equals $3,600 (=(120 × 60) divided by 2). Transfer earnings equal total factor payments minus economic rent or, in this case, $4,800. In case B, there is a perfectly inelastic supply curve, so all $8,400 of factor payments are economic rent.
   (c) For the sixtieth unit of labour, transfer earnings equal the wage rate of $140. The fortieth unit is willing to work for $100 but is paid $140. Therefore, for this unit transfer earnings equal $100 and economic rent is $40.
   (d) The new equilibrium wage and quantity are $160 and 70 units, respectively.
   (e) Economic rents now equal area *adf* in the graph. Thus the increase in economic rent is area *bcdf*, which equals $1,300.

(f) The 60 units of labour employed prior to the policy change receive area *bcde* in additional rents; this equals $1,200.

4. (a) Firm *A*, 30; Firm *B*, 10
   (b) The 70 machines must have the same *MRP* regardless of the industry where they are used. Hence if 50 machines are allocated to industry *A* and 20 to industry *B*, *MRP* will be equalized at 6.
   (c) The two curves intersect at a rental price of $6, where industry *A* rents 50 machines and industry *B* rents 20. See Figure 13-11 for the plotted relationships.
   (d) Industry *A* rents 40 machines, and industry *B* rents 30. The equilibrium rental price increases from $6 to about $7.

Figure 13-11

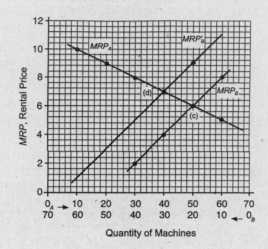

(e) The *MRP* curve shifts to the left by about 15 machines, and industry *B* rents 10 more machines than initially. *B* does not rent 15 more machines because *A* is willing to pay a higher rental price to avoid losing that many machines (rather than $6). If *B* is to match that higher rental price, it would rent only 10 more machines.

5. (a) Total factor earnings are $320. The thirtieth unit is prepared to supply services for $6 but receives $8. Hence, economic rent is $2 for the thirtieth unit.
   (b) For D_1, quantity is 20 and price per unit is $10. For D_2, quantity is 30 and price per unit is $12.
   (c) Elasticity for D_1 = 20/30 × 9/2 = 3.00; elasticity for D_2 = 10/35 × 10/4 = 0.71. Clearly, D_1 has the higher elasticity.
   (d) (i) D_2 (ii) D_1 (iii) D_2 (iv) D_1

6. (a)

Cumulative Population (families)	Cumulative Percentage of Income
Lowest 20 percent	6.4
Lowest 40 percent	18.4
Lowest 60 percent	36.0
Lowest 80 percent	60.1
Lowest 100 percent	100.0

(b) **Figure pj13-12**

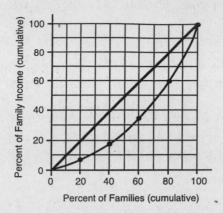

Percent of Families (cumulative)

(c) No; the Lorenz curve for 1993 lies below the diagonal line.

Extension Exercise

E1. (a) There is a temporary differential of $2 per unit of labour since there are no non-monetary considerations, no differences in labour productivity, and no difference in the types of jobs.

(b) There are net advantages between the two regions; workers by moving from Y to X will increase their wage rate. As this flow occurs, the supply curve for labour in region Y will shift to the left and the supply curve in region X will shift to the right. Wages will rise in Y and fall in X. Migration from Y to X will continue until the wage differential is eliminated (wage = $11 in both regions).

Practice Multiple Choice Test

1. (a) 2. (b) 3. (d) 4. (d) 5. (a) 6. (e) 7. (c) 8. (e) 9. (d) 10. (a) 11. (c) 12. (e) 13. (e)

CHAPTER 14

LABOUR MARKETS

LEARNING OBJECTIVES

1 Explain wage differentials in competitive labour markets.

2 Explain the wage differentials that arise in imperfectly competitive labour markets.

3 Understand the effects of legislated minimum wages.

4 Recognize the tradeoff that unions face between employment and wages.

5 Explain why the trend away from manufacturing jobs and toward service jobs is not necessarily a problem for the economy as a whole.

CHAPTER OVERVIEW

In a competitive labour market, wages are set by the forces of supply and demand. Differences in wages in competitive labour markets will arise because some skills are more valued than others, because some jobs are more onerous and risky than others, because of varying amounts of human capital, and because of discrimination based on such factors as gender and race.

Two important noncompetitive labour market situations are presented: (1) a single employer with monopoly power in hiring labour (a **monopsonist**), and (2) a union acting as a monopolist in supplying labour. Compared to a competitive situation, union actions tend to drive up wage rates but only at the cost of reducing employment, while a monopsonist tends to drive down wages and reduce employment. Union entry into a monopsonistic market, however, may result in higher wages and higher employment. A legislated **minimum wage** in a competitive labour market has labour market effects similar to union action.

This chapter also considers how discrimination affects wages and employment opportunities. Direct discrimination affects wages and employment opportunities in part by limiting labour supply in the best-paying occupations and by increasing it in less attractive occupations.

Union membership in Canada as a share of the labour force is about 30%. The **union** goal of increasing wages relative to those for nonunion workers (the union wage premium) can conflict with the goal of increasing employment of union members. The process by which unions and employers reach an agreement is known as **collective bargaining**. The potential effects of unions on productivity and featherbedding are also discussed.

CHAPTER REVIEW

Wage Differentials

There can be temporary and equilibrium differential wages in competitive markets. Variations in working conditions, differences in the amount of investment in human capital, differences in inherited skills, and discrimination by characteristics (like gender or race) will produce wage and income differentials.

Wage differentials also occur in imperfect markets. The textbook discusses two types of imperfectly competitive labour market situations. On the demand side of the labour market, one firm may be a monopsonist. On the supply side, labour supply may be regulated by a single seller (a union). Learn the effects of unions and minimum wages using four basic taxonomies for different market structures for labour supply and labour demand as are shown in the matrix below. Element 3 depicts a situation where a union bargains with a competitive firm or industry. The textbook describes element 4 as the *bilateral monopoly* case. Some of the multiple choice questions that follow refer to this table.

	Competitive Labour Demand	Monopsony Buyer
competitive labour supply	*element 1* competitive, competitive	*element 2* competitive, monopsonist
union labour supply	*element 3* union, competitive	*element 4* union, monopsonist

1. Which of the following, by itself, would tend to generate a higher wage for worker *A* compared to worker *B*?
   (a) Worker *A* has a job that is safer in terms of the chances of injury.
   (b) Worker *A*, of a particular ethnic heritage, has encountered more labour market discrimination.
   (c) Worker *B* has more years of formal education.
   (d) Worker *A* has obtained more on-the-job education than has *B*.
   (e) Both workers are accountants, but worker *B* has more knowledge of computer software than *A*.

2. All workers would receive the same wage if
   (a) All workers were identical in terms of inherited skills, human capital, and on-the-job education.
   (b) the non-monetary advantages and conditions of all jobs were identical.
   (c) All firms operated in competitive labour markets.
   (d) Labour was supplied in perfectly competitive markets.
   (e) All of the above are correct.

3. Which of the following are likely to influence the willingness of individuals to stay in school beyond the years of compulsory eduction?
   (a) The earnings they could have made in the labour market if they had not stayed in school.
   (b) The expectation of higher incomes.
   (c) Tuition fees and costs of attendance such as books and additional living costs.
   (d) The opportunity to have a greater spectrum of jobs that match their career preferences.
   (e) All of the above are correct.

4. If discrimination prevented a certain group of people from entering labour market E but not labour market O,
   (a) the wage rate would be lower than the competitive level in both markets.
   (b) the labour supply curve is farther to the left than it would otherwise be in both markets.
   (c) wage rates will tend to be higher in market E and lower in market O than they would be with no discrimination.
   (d) individuals in labour market E would benefit only if the demand curve for labour is elastic.
   (e) None of the above.

5. Where the supply curve of labour is upward-sloping, the marginal cost curve of labour to the monopsonist
   (a) is the same as the supply curve of labour.
   (b) is the same as the average cost curve of labour.
   (c) lies above the supply curve of labour.
   (d) lies below and parallel to the supply curve.
   (e) intersects the supply curve at the equilibrium wage.

6. A firm that currently pays $8 per hour to each of its ten workers discovers that it must pay $9 to get an eleventh worker. What are the marginal costs to the firm of obtaining the eleventh worker?
   (a) $1.   (b) $9.
   (c) $17.   (d) $19.
   (e) $10.

Questions 7 to 10 refer to the above table.

7. Referring to the situation depicted by *element 1*, a minimum wage that is set above the competitive level will cause which of the following?
   (a) Employment will increase.
   (b) An excess demand for labour will be created.
   (c) Some workers will lose their jobs in this industry.
   (d) Fewer individuals will wish to offer their labour services to this industry.
   (e) None of the above are correct.

8. Referring to the situation depicted by *element 2*, a monopsonist firm
   (a) lowers both the wage rate and employment below their competitive levels.
   (b) lowers the wage rate but not employment below their competitive levels.
   (c) has the same employment level and the same wage as a competitive firm.
   (d) raises the wage rate but decreases employment with respect to their competitive levels.
   (e) raises both the wage rate and employment above their competitive levels.

9. Referring to the situation depicted by *element 3*, which of the following will *not* occur if a union negotiates a wage above the competitive level?
   (a) Employment in the industry will normally fall.
   (b) Those employed will earn a higher wage rate than before.
   (c) A pool of unemployed workers will be created.
   (d) The supply curve of labour will shift to the right.
   (e) None of the above.

10. A union negotiating a higher wage in a monopsonistic labour market (*element 4* in the above table)
    (a) will cause increased unemployment in the industry.
    (b) can raise the wage rate, but not employment, over the monopsonistic outcome.
    (c) can raise both the wage rate and employment over the monopsonistic outcome.
    (d) has the same effect on employment as a minimum wage set above the competitive level.
    (e) None of the above.

11. A minimum wage is said to be *binding* or *effective* if
    (a) it has been set by a union.
    (b) the minimum is below the market wage that would otherwise prevail.
    (c) it is the lowest wage that allows a level of income above the poverty line.
    (d) all workers who desire employment at that wage are in fact employed.
    (e) the minimum wage is set above the competitive wage level.

12. The "efficiency wage hypothesis" (described in *Applying Economic Concepts 14-1*) suggests that
    (a) competitive firms pay more than the competitive wage in order to induce workers to be more productive.
    (b) transfer wages are very high if workers are paid more than the competitive wage.
    (c) quit rates from jobs that pay more than the competitive wage are very high.
    (d) wages rates across industries always will be equalized.
    (e) unions always increase workers' productivity.

Labour Unions

Labour unions face an inherent conflict between the level of wages and the size of the union itself unless they face monopsonist employers or they are able to increase the demand for labour by featherbedding practices.

13. Evidence for Canada indicates that
    (a) the growth in union membership was low in the immediate post-war era (late 1940s and early 1950s).
    (b) the growth in union membership was low in the 1980s and early 1990s.
    (c) unionization rates in the public sector are lower than those in the private sector.
    (d) unions have not been able to create a union wage premium.
    (e) unions have taken no role in lobbying for legislation that applies to all workers.

14. Featherbedding practices by unions
    (a) shift the supply curve of labour to the right.
    (b) if successful will increase the demand for labour.
    (c) increase the loss in employment to union members when union wage premiums are increased.
    (d) increase the productivity of workers.
    (e) None of the above are correct.

The "Good Jobs—Bad Jobs" Debate

Good jobs are characterized by high pay and job security. It has been argued that the quantity of "good" jobs has declined as the relative importance of the manufacturing sector has diminished. It is alleged that availability of "bad" jobs has expanded in the service sector. This section discusses four reasons why the decline in the manufacturing sector may not necessarily reflect anything "wrong" with the economy.

15. Given the continuing decline in manufacturing employment, which of the following provides a possible explanation that this phenomenon is not necessarily a problem?
    (a) Despite the decline in manufacturing employment, real disposable income has continued to rise.
    (b) The decline in manufacturing employment is partly due to decreasing productivity in that sector.
    (c) Productivity increases in the service sector have been overestimated.
    (d) The income elasticity for the demand for services is falling.
    (e) All of the above are correct.

EXERCISES

1. Suppose that there is a competitive market for workers in a particular industry. The equilibrium level of employment is 200, and the wage rate (w) is $50. The labour demand and supply curves are given by $Q_D = 300 - 2w$ and $Q_S = 4w$, respectively.

    (a) A union now successfully organizes workers and obtains a wage rate of $60. Assuming that unionization does not affect the industry's demand curve, calculate the number of unionized members who are employed in this industry. How many workers lost their jobs? How many workers would like to work in this industry?

    (b) A union could have achieved the same levels of the wage rate and employment by restricting the supply of workers using required apprenticeship programs and/or reduced openings for trainees. Show that a new, restricted labour supply curve of $Q_S = -60 + 4w$ would yield the same wage and employment levels as in (a).

    (c) The reduction in employment caused by a union wage that is above the competitive level depends on the elasticity of labour demand. If the industry's demand curve for labour had been given by $Q_D = 200$, what is the implied elasticity of labour demand? How many workers would have lost their jobs due to unionization? (Assume that the labour supply curve is $Q_S = 4w$.)

2. Columns 1 and 2 represent the supply-of-labour relationship for a monopsonistic employer. Fill in the values for total cost in column 3 and then calculate the marginal cost values in column 4. This exercise should demonstrate to you that the marginal cost of labour (MC) curve lies above the supply curve of labour in a nonparallel fashion.

(1) Quantity of Labour	(2) Wage Rate	(3) Total Cost	(4) Marginal Labour Cost
8	$10.00	$80.00	_____
9	10.50	_____	_____
10	11.00	_____	_____
11	11.50	_____	_____
12	12.00	_____	_____
13	12.50	_____	_____
14	13.00	_____	_____

3. Referring to Figure 14-1, which represents the labour market in an industry, answer the following questions.

Figure 14-1

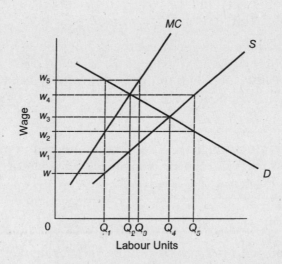

(a) If a competitive market prevailed, the equilibrium wage would be _____ and the amount of employment would be _____.

(b) If a wage-setting union enters this (competitive) market and tries to establish a higher wage at, for example, w_4, the amount of employment would be _____, and the amount of surplus labour unemployed would be _____. How would the labour supply curve look?

(c) Assume that this market consists of a single large firm hiring labour in a local market. If the firm hired Q_1 workers, it would have to pay all workers the wage _____, but the marginal labour cost of the last person hired would be _____. Because the marginal revenue product of the last person (Q_1) hired is equal to the amount, _____ there is an incentive for the firm to continue hiring up to the amount, _____ at which the wage will be _____, the marginal labour cost will be _____, and the marginal revenue product will be _____. Compare this with the result in (a).

(d) Suppose that a union now organizes in the monopsonist market and sets a wage at w_3. The amount of employment will be _____.

(e) Draw a new labour supply curve showing what happens when a union organizes this labour market but instead of setting a high wage excludes workers by stiff apprenticeship rules. Predict the effects.

4. There are two competitive labour markets in the economy of Arcadia. Market X has a labour demand function given by $w = 360 - 3Q$ and a labour supply function $w = 40 + 2Q$. The wage rate is denoted as w, and the quantity of labour is Q. Market Z has the same labour demand function as X but a labour supply function $w = 20 + 2Q$.

(a) Calculate the competitive equilibrium levels of w and Q in each labour market.

(b) Suppose that a minimum wage of 162 had been imposed in market Z. At the minimum wage, what is the quantity of labour demanded? The quantity of labour supplied? How many workers are displaced in this market?

(c) If all of the unemployed persons in (b) entered labour market X, the supply curve of labour in X becomes $w = 30 + 2Q$. How many will obtain employment in market X? What will happen to the wage in market X?

PRACTICE MULTIPLE CHOICE TEST

Questions 1 to 7 refer to Figure 14-2, which depicts a labour market for unskilled workers.

Figure 14-2

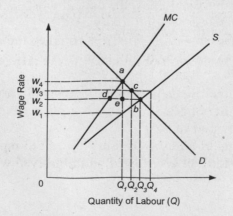

1. If perfect competition existed in this market, the wage and quantity of employment would be
   (a) w_4 and Q_1.   (b) w_3 and Q_2.
   (c) w_1 and Q_1.   (d) w_2 and Q_3.
   (e) w_2 and Q_4.

2. If this market were monopsonistic, the firm would hire
   (a) Q_1 workers.   (b) Q_3 workers.
   (c) Q_2 workers.   (d) Q_4 workers.
   (e) somewhere between Q_3 and Q_4 workers.

3. A profit-maximizing monopsony would pay a wage of
   (a) w_1.   (b) w_3.
   (c) w_2.   (d) w_4.
   (e) somewhere between zero and one-half of ($w_1 + w_4$).

4. If a minimum wage of w_2 is imposed on the monopsony, the supply curve of labour becomes
   (a) $MC - S$.   (b) acb.
   (c) w_2bS.   (d) w_2daMC.
   (e) w_2dea.

5. In this case, the minimum wage of w_2 would generate employment of
   (a) Q_1.   (b) Q_3.
   (c) Q_2.   (d) Q_4.
   (e) less than Q1.

6. If a minimum wage of w_3 were imposed on the market, the monopsonist would hire
   (a) Q_2 workers.
   (b) more than Q_3 workers since the marginal cost of labour would fall.
   (c) Q_4 workers because the demand for labour shifts to the right.
   (d) Q_1 workers.
   (e) no workers.

7. With a minimum wage of w_3, total unemployment in this market would be
   (a) $Q_3 - Q_2$.   (b) $Q_4 - Q_3$.
   (c) $Q_4 - Q_2$.   (d) $Q_4 - Q_1$.
   (e) zero.

Answer questions 8 and 9 by referring to Figure 14-3 and the information below.

An economy consists of two competitive industries, X and Y, and a total labour force of 120 workers. Industry X requires more highly skilled workers relative to industry Y. Workers, although equally productive *within* each industry, differ by the colour of their eyes. Nine of the workers in each industry have green eyes, the rest have blue eyes. Now, new owners take over industry X. They don't trust any worker with green eyes.

8. Before the new owners took possession of industry X, the differential in the wage rate between the two industries
   (a) represented "discrimination" by employers in Y, since the wage was $2 lower.
   (b) was a temporary differential of $2.
   (c) was an equilibrium differential of $2.
   (d) was $2, because employers in industry X must have been monopsonists.
   (e) was $2, because of the "mix" of green-eyed and blue-eyed workers in each industry.

Figure 14-3

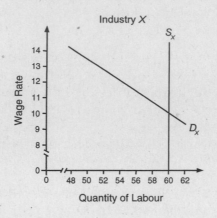

Industry X

Quantity of Labour

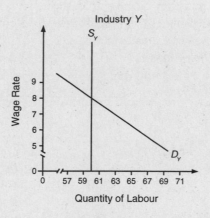

Industry Y

Quantity of Labour

9. Now, the new owners fire every green-eyed worker in X, but do not replace them with blue-eyed workers. If all green-eyed workers find jobs in Y, then
   (a) 51 workers in X are paid $13 each.
   (b) 69 workers in Y are paid $5 each.
   (c) total income of all blue-eyed workers in X increases from $510 to $663.
   (d) total income of all workers in Y falls from $480 to $345.
   (e) All of the above.

SOLUTIONS

Chapter Review

1. (d) 2. (e) 3. (e) 4. (c) 5. (c) 6. (d) 7.(c) 8. (a) 9. (d) 10. (c) 11.(e) 12. (a) 13. (b) 14. (b) 15. (a)

Exercises

1. (a) Substituting $w = 60$ into the demand equation, we obtain an employment level of 180. Twenty workers lost their jobs. At $w = 60$, 240 individuals wish to work in this industry.
   (b) Equating the new supply equation with the demand equation, we obtain $w = 60$ and employment of 180, which is the same result as in (a).
   (c) The new demand curve is perfectly inelastic; changes in the wage rate have no effect on the quantity of labour demanded. As a result, the union could increase the wage by any amount without loss of jobs.

2. Total cost: $80,00; $94.50; $110.00; $126.50; $144.00; $162.50; $182.00. Marginal cost: $14.50; $15.50; $16.50; $17.50; $18.50; $19.50

3. (a) w_3; Q_4
   (b) Q_2; $Q_5 - Q_2$; horizontal at w_4 to Q_5 on the supply curve and thereafter the supply curve for wages greater than w_4.
   (c) w; w_2, w_5; Q_2; w_1; w_4; w_4; employment is less and the amount of wages is lower than in (a).
   (d) Q_4
   (e) The supply curve shifts leftward. All wage predictions are raised, and employment levels are lowered.

4. (a) For market X, equilibrium Q is found by equating $360 - 3Q$ to $40 + 2Q$. Hence $Q = 64$ and $w = 168$. For market Z, $Q = 68$ and $w = 156$.
   (b) At the minimum wage, the quantity of labour demanded is 66 while the quantity of labour supplied is 71. Unemployment is therefore 5, and employment in market Z would be 2 fewer than under competitive conditions.
   (c) The supply curve in X now becomes $w = 30 + 2Q$ (or $Q = 0.5w - 15$ instead of $Q = 0.5w - 10$). Setting $D = S$ and solving, $Q = 66$ and $w = 162$. Thus, two of the unemployed workers from Z are now employed in X, and the wage in X falls to 162 from 168.

Practice Multiple Choice Test

1. (d) 2. (a) 3. (a) 4. (c) 5. (b) 6. (a) 7. (c) 8. (c) 9. (e)

CHAPTER 15

CAPITAL AND NATURAL RESOURCES

🌐 *LEARNING OBJECTIVES*

1 Compute the present value of an asset that delivers a stream of future benefits.

2 Explain why the demand for physical capital depends on the interest rate.

3 Understand how the equilibrium interest rate is determined.

4 Explain how competitive firms will determine the rate of extraction of a nonrenewable resource.

5 Recognize the conservation role played by free-market prices for resources.

CHAPTER OVERVIEW

This chapter discusses two types of factors of production, capital and natural resources, that share the important characteristic of being used up over time to produce output. A critical difference is that capital can be replaced while **nonrenewable resources** cannot.

The *purchase price* of an asset depends on the future earnings it is expected to generate. Using the interest rate to *discount* future net receipts to the present allows the purchase price of an asset to be calculated. A higher interest rate reduces an asset's *present value*.

An individual firm will invest in capital goods as long as the present value of the stream of future net returns that is provided by another unit of capital exceeds its purchase price. The firm's demand curve for capital is plotted against the interest rate—it is also referred to as the marginal efficiency of capital, and measures the rate of return on an additional unit of capital. The profit-maximizing size of the capital stock varies negatively with the rate of interest.

When the stock of a nonrenewable resource is known and unchanging, the *socially optimal* rate of extraction is given by **Hotelling's Rule**: the rate of increase in price should equal the interest rate. The current rate of extraction will be greater the more elastic is the demand for the resource. Controlling the price of an exhaustible resource at a constant level speeds up the rate of exploitation and removes the price incentives to react to its growing scarcity.

CHAPTER REVIEW

Capital and the Interest Rate

After studying this section, you should be able to: distinguish between the two prices of capital, the *purchase price* and the *rental price*; understand that in competitive markets the rental price is equal to capital's marginal revenue product in each period; use the concept of present value to demonstrate how the maximum purchase price of capital is related to the discounted stream of expected marginal revenue products of capital; comprehend why an individual firm will invest in capital goods as long as the present value of the stream of future net incomes provided by another unit of capital exceeds its purchase price. Make sure you fully understand the central concept in this section: present value theory.

1. The rental price of capital for a given period
   (a) is always equal to its purchase price.
   (b) will be equated with the capital's marginal revenue product in that period as a result of profit maximization.
   (c) is zero if the firm owns its capital.
   (d) is the rate of return on capital for each dollar invested in that capital.
   (e) is always equal to the interest rate.

2. If the interest rate is i, the present value of R dollars received a year from now is
   (a) Ri.   (b) $R/(1 + i)$.
   (c) R/i.   (d) $i/(1 + R)$.
   (e) i/R.

3. If the interest rate is 4%, the present value of $100 received each year forever is
   (a) $2,500.   (b) $250.
   (c) $25.   (d) $96.15.
   (e) $104.

4. If *MRP* denotes the annual stream of receipts from a machine into the indefinite future, *PP* is its purchase price, and i is the interest rate, then a capital good should be purchased if
   (a) $MRP \times i < PP$.   (b) $MRP/PP < i$.
   (c) $MRP/i > PP$.   (d) $MRP < i \times PP$.
   (e) None of the above.

5. The present value of a capital asset will increase if
   (a) the *MRP* values per period decrease.
   (b) *MRP* values are received farther into the future.
   (c) the interest rate decreases.
   (d) the purchase price of the capital asset decreases.
   (e) None of the above.

6. The cost of constructing a proposed dam is $10,000,000 and its annual maintenance costs are $100,000. The dam is expected to last forever. If the interest rate is 5%, the present value of the total cost of the dam is
   (a) $10,000,000.   (b) $12,000,000.
   (c) $2,000,00.   (d) $10,100,000.
   (e) impossible to estimate with the information provided.

7. The demand curve for capital (or the *marginal efficiency of capital* curve) shifts to the right as
   (a) capital is accumulated.
   (b) the interest rate decreases.
   (c) technology improves capital productivity.
   (d) diminishing returns to capital occur.
   (e) Both (a) and (c).

8. The higher the interest rate, *all other things equal,*
   (a) firms will find capital expansion to be more profitable.
   (b) the lower a firm's equilibrium capital stock.
   (c) the higher the present value of the income stream produced by a capital good.
   (d) the greater the shift in the firm's demand for capital curve.
   (e) None of the above.

Nonrenewable Resources

After studying this section, you will understand that the socially optimal rate of extraction for a nonrenewable resource is determined by both current and future prices of the resource, the interest rate, and the elasticity of demand for the resource. You will also be able to explain why rising resource prices serve as both a conservation device and a stimulus that encourages discovery of new supplies. Finally, this section discusses some possible failures of the price system with respect to nonrenewable resources and the role of government in dealing with them.

9. Which of the following is an example of an exhaustible resource?
   (a) Water.
   (b) Cattle.
   (c) Gold.
   (d) Labour.
   (e) Energy.

10. With perfect competition, the price of an exhaustible resource with a known stock whose cost of extraction and transportation are negligible should rise by
    (a) a constant percentage amount from year to year until the stock is depleted.
    (b) 10 percent if the rate of interest is 10 percent.
    (c) the rate at which the resource is extracted.
    (d) the rate of growth of national output.
    (e) the overall inflation rate in the economy.

11. The actual rate at which an exhaustible resource is extracted will be more even through time when
    (a) the demand curve for the resource is perfectly elastic.
    (b) there are many substitutes for this resource.
    (c) the demand curve for the resource is relatively steep.
    (d) the final products that have a high input content of this resource have a high elasticity of demand.
    (e) Both (b) and (d).

12. Which of the following would *not* be a likely consequence of an expected increase in the price of a nonrenewable resource like oil?
    (a) Substitute products (such as solar energy) would be developed.
    (b) Current rates of extraction by owners would be moderated.
    (c) Discovery of new sources of supply would be encouraged.
    (d) The necessity to conserve on oil use would be reduced.
    (e) Firms extracting would be encouraged to invest more in capital equipment required in oil extraction and refining.

13. According to *Hotelling's Rule*, the rate of extraction of any nonrenewable resource should be such that its price increases at a rate equal to the
    (a) overall rate of inflation.
    (b) growth in national income.
    (c) rate at which new supplies of the resource are found.
    (d) interest rate.
    (e) growth rate in national debt.

14. Which of the following is likely to be a consequence of a government imposed constant-price policy for a nonrenewable resource?
    (a) The resource will be exhausted much slower.
    (b) Conservation and innovation will be encouraged.
    (c) Oil companies will have less incentives to explore for new supplies.
    (d) Future users essentially receive a subsidy from current users.
    (e) All of the above.

15. Which of the following constitutes a potential failure of the price system to produce the optimal rate of resource extraction?
    (a) Private owners have better information than government agencies to determine the optimal extraction rate.
    (b) The interest rate is different from the social rate of discount.
    (c) The current extraction rate is increased when the interest rate (equal to the social rate of discount) rises.
    (d) Proper extraction management is applied by private owners of resources.
    (e) All of the above.

EXERCISES

1. (a) Just for practice, fill in the following blanks using the Table of Present Values (*PV*) at the end of this chapter, Table 15-1. (Some students may choose to use their pocket calculators that calculate present values.)

This many dollars	in *t* years	has this *PV*	at *i*
10	5	____	6%
100	50	$60.80	____
1000	____	3.00	12%
____	6	4.56	14%

(b) More practice, this time with the Annuity Table, Table 15-2.

This many dollars	in each of t years	has this PV	at i
10	5	_____	6%
100	50	$3,919.60	_____
1,000	_____	8,304.00	12%
_____	6	38.89	14%

2. The Firm's Profit-Maximizing Capital Stock

This exercise illustrates the relationships among the various components of the present value formula $(PV = MRP/(1+i)^t)$ and the desired capital stock.

The Base Case

At a current interest rate of 10 percent, *Acme Machine Shop*, maximizes profits with a capital stock of 20 machines. It is considering the purchase of another machine that costs $500. The financial manager estimates that the additional machine will generate $545 in additional net income one year from now.

(a) By making the appropriate substitutions, write the algebraic expression for the present value of this incremental capital good.

(b) Using either Table 15-1 or your calculator, calculate the magnitude of the present value to the nearest dollar. Should the financial manager recommend that *Acme* expand its capital stock (invest) by one?

The investment decision in part (b) may change if economic conditions change or if the financial manager revises her forecasts. We outline three cases below.

Case 1: Variations in the Interest Rate, *i*

(c) If the interest rate had been 8 percent rather than 10 percent, would the financial manager have made a different recommendation? Explain.

(d) What can you conclude about the effect of an interest rate decrease on the present value of a capital asset? About the relationship between interest rates and the desired capital stock?

Case 2: A Change in Expected Net Receipts, *MRP*

Suppose *Acme*'s financial manager revises her forecast of net revenues to $555 instead of $545.

(e) Assuming an interest rate of 10 percent, would the financial manager now recommend a capital stock of 21?

(f) What do you conclude about the effect of an increase in *MRP* and the present value of a capital good? About the relationship between net expected receipts and the desired capital stock?

Case 3: A Change in the Timing of Receipts, *t*

Similar to case 2, the financial manager is convinced that net revenues will be $555. However, she now forecasts that they will not be received after one year, but rather after two years! Hence, the company will receive no net receipts after one year.

(g) If the interest rate were 10 percent, would the financial manager recommend the purchase of the machine? What have you concluded about the relationship between present value and the timing of net receipts?

3. **Eddy Grant, a *Griffen*?**

This problem deals with the application of the present value concept to human capital theory that was introduced in Chapter 14. Although some readers might find it offensive to treat individuals as "capital," it is true that firms are willing to "invest" in their workers in order to increase future productivity and profits. In this case a baseball team is considering hiring a player, Eddy Grant.

Eddy Grant, an ageing catcher with the Mudville Mustangs has had a illustrious career in professional baseball. Although he has a .286 lifetime batting average and holds the all-time record for catching no-hit games, the Mustangs gave him his unconditional release at the end of the 1999 season because of his lacklustre performance during the last two baseball seasons.

Jimmy McKennett, the wily general manager of the *Grover Griffens*, believes that Grant has two good seasons left in the big leagues. With the proper coaching and sports therapy, McKennett believes that Grant can make the *Griffens* a pennant contender and increase the team's revenue through large TV royalties, fan attendance, and sales of beer, nachos, and hot dogs at home games.

Grant wants a $500,000 signing bonus at the beginning of the 2000 season, and a two-year contract that guarantees a salary of $1,000,000 at the end of the 2000 season and $1,500,000 at the end of the 2001 season. He also wants a no-trade and no-release clause during the contract.

McKennett knows that Grant will need extra therapeutic care and coaching. He estimates that these costs are $100,000 per year of the contract. Moreover, the *Griffens'* front office estimates the team's stream of additional net receipts from having Grant as a starting catcher with the current complement of players as being $1,800,000 at the end of the 2000 season and $1,7000,000 at the end of the 2001 season. The annual interest rate over the two seasons is expected to be 6 percent.

(a) Using Table 15-1, calculate the present value of the total costs associated with hiring Grant.

(b) Providing that McKennett's estimates of the stream of net receipts are based on the best possible information, should the *Griffens* offer Grant the two-year contract that he seeks? Explain.

4. Investment in Capital Stock, Again

Moosejay Printing Company is analysing a proposal to purchase equipment estimated to provide $15,000 in labour-savings annually and cost $1,000 in maintenance a year. It calculates a 10-year economic life of the equipment and $10,000 salvage at the end of the tenth year. If the purchase price of the equipment is $75,000, should it expand its current capital stock if the firm wishes a minimum rate of return of 14%? [*Hint:* If the present value of the revenue flows calculated at an interest rate of 14% is greater than the purchase price, then the rate of return on the equipment must be greater than 14%.]

5. "I'll See You in Court!"

Joseph Litigatski, a successful university professor, is involved in a tragic accident that leaves him permanently disabled and unable to hold any employment. In preparing for the personal injury trial subsequent to the accident, Litigatski's lawyer asks you to prepare an estimate of the present value of the professor's human capital. (The lawyer will come up with an independent claim for pain and suffering.)

Litigatski's current salary plus consulting income is $75,000 annually. He is 50 years old and would have worked another 20 years until his retirement. Assume that his real income would have risen 1 percent annually due to raises. As a consequence, in discounting his future income at an annual interest rate of 5 percent, the appropriate discount factor to use in Table 15-2 is 4 percent.

What is your calculation for the claim for lost human capital that Professor Litigatski should make in the trial?

6. **"They Ain't Making Anymore!"**

The mythical nonrenewable natural resource, zube oil, is produced and sold in a perfectly competitive market. The reserves of zube oil are known with certainty, and demand is constant. The entire stock is of identical quality and can be extracted and delivered to market with negligible extraction and transportation costs. Its price in 1999 is $100 per barrel. The rate of interest is 10 percent.

(a) Explain, under these assumptions, why the price of zube oil in year 2000 will be $110 per barrel.

(b) Predict the consequences of the following in the market for zube oil:

    (i)   Demand for zube oil increases as the economy grows and both population and per-capita incomes increase.

    (ii)   Additional reserves of zube oil are unexpectedly discovered.

    (iii) The government passes a law prohibiting the sale of zube oil at a price higher than the current competitive equilibrium price.

PRACTICE MULTIPLE CHOICE TEST

1. The present value of $100 received one year from now is
   (a) $100 if the interest rate is positive.
   (b) more than $107 if the interest rate is more than 7 percent.
   (c) $106 if the interest rate is 6 percent.
   (d) Both (b) and (c).
   (e) None of the above.

2. If the interest rate is 5 percent, the present value of $500 received two years from now is
   (a) $453.51.   (b) $525.
   (c) $467.19.   (d) $551.25.
   (e) $510.

3. The formula for the present value of $10 received three years from now and an interest rate of 10 percent is
   (a) $10/(.1)^3$.   (b) $10/3(1.1)$.
   (c) $(1.1)^3/$10$.   (d) $10/(1.1)^3$.
   (e) $10^3/(1.1)^3$.

4. Suppose that a capital asset whose purchase price is $10,000 is expected to produce a perpetual stream of net receipts per period of $700. It follows that
   (a) this asset should be purchased when the cost of borrowed funds is 10 percent.
   (b) this asset should be purchased irrespective of the interest rate since it generates net revenues in perpetuity.
   (c) the present value of this asset is greater than $10,000 for all interest rates above 7 percent.
   (d) the present value of this asset is greater than $10,000 for all interest rates below 9 percent.
   (e) None of the above.

Questions 5 through 9 refer to the following data concerning a machine. You will find it useful to refer to Table 15-1 at the end of this chapter.

A business can buy a machine that yields net revenue of $1,000 at the end of the first year and $2,000 at the end of the second year, after which the machine falls apart and thus has no scrap value.

5. If the rate of interest is 10 percent, the present value of the $1,000 received one year hence is equal to
   (a) $900.   (b) $990.
   (c) $909.   (d) $100.
   (e) $1,100.

6. If the rate of interest in both years is 10 percent, the *total* present value of the machine over the two-year period is
   (a) $2,562.   (b) $3,000.
   (c) $2,727.   (d) $3,520.
   (e) $3,300.

7. Assuming an interest rate of 10 percent, the firm will buy this machine if its purchase price is
   (a) less than or equal to $2,562.
   (b) greater than $2,561 but less than $2,727.
   (c) equal to $2,727.
   (d) somewhere in the range $3,000 to $3,520.
   (e) None of the above.

8. If the interest rate were 12 percent and the purchase price were $3,000, what would the first year's net revenue (before discounting) have to be to warrant purchasing this machine? Continue to assume that the net revenue in the second year remains at $2,000.
   (a) $893.   (b) $1,256.
   (c) $1,406.   (d) $1,574.
   (e) None of the above.

9. The interest rate that generates a total present value of net revenue flows for this machine of $2,487 is
   (a) 15 percent.   (b) 12 percent.
   (c) 8 percent.   (d) 14 percent.
   (e) None of the above.

10. A profit-maximizing firm will hire a unit of capital as long as its rental price is
    (a) less than the marginal revenue product.
    (b) equal to the marginal revenue product.
    (c) greater than the marginal revenue product.
    (d) less than its purchase price.
    (e) less than its present value.

11. The _____ is the rate of interest and the _____ distant the payment date, the lower will be the present value of a future payment.
    (a) higher; more.
    (b) higher; less.
    (c) lower; more.
    (d) lower; less.
    (e) None of the above.

12. The firm's demand curve for capital shows
    (a) the relationship between interest rates and present value.
    (b) an asset's present value for the current period only.
    (c) how the firm's desired stock of capital varies with changes in *MRP*.
    (d) how the firm's *MRP* changes with the interest rate.
    (e) how the firm's desired stock of capital varies with the interest rate.

13. In the very-long run, the demand for capital curve shifts to the right as
    (a) diminishing returns to capital becomes evident.
    (b) technological improvements increase the productivity of captial.
    (c) the interest rate decreases.
    (d) more capital is employed.
    (e) the present value of capital falls.

14. If the current price of oil is $2.00 per barrel and the annual interest rate is 7 percent, it pays to
    (a) produce less now if next year's price is less than $2.14.
    (b) have the same extraction rate every year regardless of what happens to oil prices in the future.
    (c) produce more now if next year's price is less than $2.14.
    (d) produce more next year if oil prices rise less than 7 percent from today's prices.
    (e) None of the above.

15. A profit-maximizing firm will leave a nonrenewable resource in the ground when its price is
    (a) uncertain in the future.
    (b) expected to rise.
    (c) expected to rise at a rate less than the rate of interest.
    (d) expected to rise at a rate greater than the rate of interest.
    (e) constant over time.

16. Suppose we have a pool of 100,000 barrels of crude oil. Currently the price of crude is $20.00 per barrel and is expected to be $21.50 per barrel in one year. With an interest rate of 8 percent, we are better off _____ the oil now, thereby earning _____ more over the year than the alternative.
    (a) extracting; $10,000.
    (b) extracting; $160,000.
    (c) not extracting; $10,000.
    (d) not extracting; $160,000.
    (e) extracting; $150,000.

17. If the current rate of interest falls, this should _____the rate of extraction of nonrenewable resources, causing their prices to _____.
    (a) increase; rise.
    (b) increase; fall.
    (c) decrease; rise.
    (d) decrease; fall.
    (e) decrease; either rise, fall or stay constant.

18. If the government were to impose a binding price ceiling on a nonrenewable resource, its rate of extraction would
    (a) be higher than socially optimal rate.
    (b) be lower than socially optimal rate.
    (c) be at the socially optimal rate.
    (d) be unaffected.
    (e) increase.

19. A "common property" nonrenewable resource
    (a) cannot be extracted.
    (b) tends to be extracted at the socially optimal rate.
    (c) tends to be extracted more slowly than is socially optimal.
    (d) tends to be extracted more rapidly than is socially-optimal.
    (e) must be shared equally among all agents with property rights.

20. Suppose that you lend me $100, and that I agree to repay you $112 in a year's time (principal plus interest). However, during the year, the average price of goods in the economy rises by 5 percent. Your real rate of return on your loan to me is therefore
    (a) 17 percent.
    (b) 12 percent.
    (c) 7 percent.
    (d) 5 percent.
    (e) none of the above.

SOLUTIONS

Chapter Review

1.(b) 2.(b) 3.(a) 4.(c) 5.(c) 6.(b) 7.(c) 8.(b) 9.(c) 10.(b) 11.(c) 12.(d) 13.(d) 14.(c) 15.(b)

Exercises

1. (a) $7.47, 1 percent, 50, $10.
   (b) $42.12, 1 percent, 50, $10.

2. (a) $PV = \$545/(1.1)$.
   (b) PV is equal to $495. Since this value is less than the machine's purchase price, the financial manager would not recommend its purchase.
   (c) Yes, the present value of the net income flows is now $504 (to the nearest dollar). Since the present value of the income stream is greater than the purchase price of $500, Acme's profits would increase if it expanded its capital stock by one machine.
   (d) There is a negative relationship between PV and i. In the example above, when the interest rate falls from 10 to 8 percent, present value increased. The decrease in the interest rate increases the desired capital stock from 20 to 21.

(e) Yes, since the *PV* of expected net revenue ($504) is greater than the machine's purchase price ($500).

(f) There is a positive relationship between *PV* and *R*. The increase in *R* makes capital expansion profitable.

(g) No, since the present value {$555/(1.1)² = $458} is less than the purchase price. Comparing the answers to part (e) and (g), we clearly see that the present value of receiving $555 one year from now is greater than the present value of receiving $555 two years from now. Thus, the more distant in time the revenue is received, the lower its present value today.

3. (a) The present value of total costs consists of the signing bonus, wages in both of the two years and the $100,000 training costs per year. Hence, *PV* = $500,000 + $1,100,000/(1.06) + $1,600,000/(1.06)², or $2,961,300.

(b) Yes, since the present value of the expected net receipts is greater than the present value of the total costs. In this case, the *PV* of receipts is given by $1,800,000/(1.06) + $1,700,000/(1.06)², or $3,205,000.

4. Yes, since the present value of the savings and the salvage value are greater than the purchase price. At 14%, *PV* of the net savings plus the salvage value is ($15,000 − $1,000) times 5.216 (according to Table 15-2) plus $10,000/(1.14)¹⁰. This sum is equal to $75,724 (i.e., $73,024 + $2,700). Since the *PV* is greater than $75,000, *Moosejay* should invest in this machine. Note also, that since the present value of net savings is greater than the purchase price, the rate of return must be *greater than* 14 percent. [In fact, the rate of return is 14.3 percent.]

5. From Table 15-2, note that the present value of $1.00 received annually for 20 years at a discount rate of 4 percent is 13.590. Multiplying this value by $75,000 gives $1,019,250 as the value of human capital Professor Litigatski lost.

6. (a) Firms with inventories must earn exactly as much per dollar of investment as they would be investing elsewhere at 10 percent. If zube oil prices were expected to rise faster than 10 percent, investors would hold more zube oil as an investment rather than release it for current consumption, driving its current price up. At the same time, the stock held for the future would increase, and future prices would fall. The same process would work in reverse if zube oil prices were rising at a rate less than 10 percent.

(b) (i) The demand curve shifts outward, causing the price to increase. Because the shift is not just a one-time increase in demand, but rather a process that continues over time, the rate of extraction of the resource will be affected: with progressively greater market demand, price will be driven up at a rate equal to the interest rate through successfully smaller increments in output.

(ii) Supply increases, causing price to fall.

(iii) If an illegal black market in zube oil does not emerge, quantity demanded will be greater and quantity supplied will be less than the free-market level. Thus, a shortage of zube oil will emerge. If the controls are believed to be permanent, the rate of extraction of zube oil will remain constant, rather than declining over time as the price rises. Thus, the deposit will be exhausted more rapidly than under a market solution, and the current generation of zube oil customers benefits at the expense of future generations where no zube oil will be available.

Table 15.1 Present value of $1.00

$$PV = \left(\frac{1}{1+i}\right)^n$$

Years hence (n)	1%	2%	4%	5%	6%	8%	10%	12%	14%	15%
1	0.990	0.980	0.962	0.952	0.943	0.926	0.909	0.893	0.877	0.870
2	0.980	0.961	0.925	0.907	0.890	0.857	0.826	0.797	0.769	0.756
3	0.971	0.942	0.889	0.864	0.840	0.794	0.751	0.712	0.675	0.658
4	0.961	0.924	0.855	0.823	0.792	0.735	0.683	0.636	0.592	0.572
5	0.951	0.906	0.822	0.784	0.747	0.681	0.621	0.567	0.519	0.497
6	0.942	0.888	0.790	0.746	0.705	0.630	0.564	0.507	0.456	0.432
7	0.933	0.871	0.760	0.711	0.665	0.583	0.513	0.452	0.400	0.376
8	0.923	0.853	0.731	0.677	0.627	0.540	0.467	0.404	0.351	0.327
9	0.914	0.837	0.703	0.645	0.592	0.500	0.424	0.361	0.308	0.284
10	0.905	0.820	0.676	0.614	0.558	0.463	0.386	0.322	0.270	0.247
11	0.896	0.804	0.650	0.585	0.527	0.429	0.350	0.287	0.237	0.215
12	0.887	0.788	0.625	0.557	0.497	0.397	0.319	0.257	0.208	0.187
13	0.879	0.773	0.601	0.530	0.469	0.368	0.290	0.229	0.182	0.163
14	0.870	0.758	0.577	0.505	0.442	0.340	0.263	0.205	0.160	0.141
15	0.861	0.743	0.555	0.481	0.417	0.315	0.239	0.183	0.140	0.123
16	0.853	0.728	0.534	0.458	0.394	0.292	0.218	0.163	0.123	0.107
17	0.844	0.714	0.513	0.436	0.371	0.270	0.198	0.146	0.108	0.093
18	0.836	0.700	0.494	0.416	0.350	0.250	0.180	0.130	0.095	0.081
19	0.828	0.686	0.475	0.396	0.331	0.232	0.164	0.116	0.083	0.070
20	0.820	0.673	0.456	0.377	0.312	0.215	0.149	0.104	0.073	0.061
21	0.811	0.660	0.439	0.359	0.294	0.199	0.135	0.093	0.064	0.053
22	0.803	0.647	0.422	0.342	0.278	0.184	0.123	0.083	0.056	0.046
23	0.795	0.634	0.406	0.326	0.262	0.170	0.112	0.074	0.049	0.040
24	0.788	0.622	0.390	0.310	0.247	0.158	0.102	0.066	0.043	0.035
25	0.780	0.610	0.375	0.295	0.233	0.146	0.092	0.059	0.038	0.030
26	0.772	0.598	0.361	0.281	0.220	0.135	0.084	0.053	0.033	0.026
27	0.764	0.586	0.347	0.268	0.207	0.125	0.076	0.047	0.029	0.023
28	0.757	0.574	0.333	0.255	0.196	0.116	0.069	0.042	0.026	0.020
29	0.749	0.563	0.321	0.243	0.185	0.107	0.063	0.037	0.022	0.017
30	0.742	0.552	0.308	0.231	0.174	0.099	0.057	0.033	0.020	0.015
40	0.672	0.453	0.208	0.142	0.097	0.046	0.022	0.011	0.005	0.004
50	0.608	0.372	0.141	0.087	0.054	0.021	0.009	0.003	0.001	0.001

Table 15.2 Present value of $1.00 received annually for n years

$$PV = (\frac{1}{1+i})^1 + (\frac{1}{1+i})^2 + \cdots (\frac{1}{1+i})^N$$

Years (n)	1%	2%	4%	5%	6%	8%	10%	12%	14%	15%
1	0.990	0.980	0.962	0.952	0.943	0.926	0.909	0.893	0.877	0.870
2	1.970	1.942	1.886	1.859	1.833	1.783	1.736	1.690	1.647	1.626
3	2.941	2.884	2.775	2.723	2.673	2.577	2.487	2.402	2.322	2.283
4	3.902	3.808	3.630	3.546	3.465	3.312	3.170	3.037	2.914	2.855
5	4.853	4.713	4.452	4.329	4.212	3.993	3.791	3.605	3.433	3.352
6	5.795	5.601	5.242	5.076	4.917	4.623	4.355	4.111	3.889	3.784
7	6.728	6.472	6.002	5.786	5.582	5.206	4.868	4.565	4.288	4.160
8	7.652	7.325	6.733	6.463	6.210	5.747	5.335	4.968	4.639	4.487
9	8.566	8.162	7.435	7.108	6.802	6.247	5.759	5.328	4.946	4.772
10	9.714	8.983	8.111	7.722	7.360	6.710	6.145	5.650	5.216	5.019
11	10.368	9.787	8.760	8.306	7.877	7.139	6.495	5.988	5.453	5.234
12	11.255	10.575	9.385	8.863	8.384	7.536	6.814	6.194	5.660	5.421
13	12.134	11.343	9.986	9.394	8.853	7.904	7.103	6.424	5.842	5.583
14	13.004	12.106	10.563	9.899	9.295	8.244	7.367	6.628	6.002	5.724
15	13.865	12.849	11.118	10.380	9.712	8.559	7.606	6.811	6.142	5.847
16	14.718	13.578	11.652	10.838	10.106	8.851	7.824	6.974	6.265	5.954
17	15.562	14.292	12.166	11.274	10.477	9.122	8.022	7.120	6.373	6.047
18	16.398	14.992	12.659	11.690	10.828	9.372	8.201	7.250	6.467	6.128
19	17.226	15.678	13.134	12.085	11.158	9.604	8.365	7.466	6.550	6.198
20	18.046	16.351	13.590	12.462	11.470	9.818	8.514	7.469	6.623	6.259
21	18.857	17.011	14.029	12.821	11.764	10.017	8.649	7.562	6.687	6.312
22	19.660	17.658	14.451	13.163	12.042	10.201	8.772	7.645	6.743	6.359
23	20.456	18.292	14.857	13.489	12.303	10.371	8.883	7.718	6.792	6.399
24	21.234	18.914	15.247	13.799	12.550	10.529	8.985	7.784	6.835	6.434
25	22.023	19.523	15.622	14.094	12.783	10.675	9.077	7.843	6.873	6.464
26	22.795	20.121	15.983	14.375	13.003	10.810	9.161	7.896	6.906	6.591
27	23.560	20.707	16.330	14.643	13.211	10.935	9.237	7.943	6.935	6.514
28	24.316	21.281	16.663	14.898	13.406	11.051	9.307	7.984	6.961	6.534
29	25.066	21.844	16.984	15.141	13.591	11.158	9.370	8.022	6.983	6.551
30	25.808	27.306	17.292	15.373	13.765	11.258	9.247	8.055	7.003	6.566
40	32.835	27.355	19.793	17.159	15.046	11.925	9.779	8.244	7.105	6.642
50	39.196	31.424	21.482	18.256	15.762	12.234	9.915	8.304	7.133	6.661

Practice Multiple Choice Test

1.(e) 2.(a) 3.(d) 4.(e) 5.(c) 6.(a) 7.(a) 8.(d) 9.(b) 10.(a) 11.(a) 12.(e) 13.(b) 14.(c) 15.(d) 16.(a) 17.(c) 18.(a) 19.(d) 20.(c)

PART SIX

GOVERNMENT IN THE MARKET ECONOMY

CHAPTER 16

MARKET FAILURES AND GOVERNMENT INTERVENTION

LO *LEARNING OBJECTIVES*

1   Recognize that two basic functions of government are the protection of individuals from others and the establishment and enforcement of property rights.

2   Understand the ability of free markets to respond to change and to promote innovation.

3   Define an externality and explain why it leads to allocative inefficiency.

4   Define public goods, and explain why they will not be provided by private markets.

5   Understand why asymmetric information can lead to market failures.

6   Understand why free markets generally will not achieve some desirable social goals.

7   Explain the direct and indirect costs of government intervention.

8   Understand some of the important causes of government failure.

CHAPTER OVERVIEW

This is the first of three chapters that consider the role of government in a market economy. This chapter reviews the case for and against the market economy. The formal defence of the market economy refers to the concept of allocative efficiency developed in Chapter 12. The informal defence is based on three attributes of free markets: flexibility and automatic coordination of decentralized decision making; stimulus for innovation and growth; and, decentralization of economic power.

Several sources of market failure that might be addressed by government policy are identified. Such failures occur when there are divergences between **private and social costs** or benefits (e.g., externalities and **public goods**), or **information asymmetries** (e.g., **moral hazard** and **adverse selection**). These sources of market failure provide an economic justification for considering remedial government action. Government intervention in free markets may also be justified when a social goal other than economic efficiency is not achieved by the market system (e.g., a more equal distribution of income).

Government policies and actions impose costs as well as benefits. There are several types of costs associated with government intervention. First, there is the direct resource cost incurred by government expenditures on goods and services. In addition, there are indirect costs that are imposed on those who are regulated as well as on third parties. These result from changes in the costs of production, costs of compliance and **rent seeking** behaviour. These costs, as well as the possibility that the government action may fail, must be balanced against the benefits of government intervention to correct market failures.

CHAPTER REVIEW

Basic Functions of Government

The "minimal" role of government is the protection of individuals from others and the establishment and enforcement of property rights. Economic prosperity has seldom been achieved without governments being able to effectively perform these functions.

1. Citizens can safely conduct their economic activities when government
   (a) plays no role in the economy.
   (b) violently competes with other organizations for economic control.
   (c) has an monopoly of violence that is exercised with a free rein.
   (d) exercise of its monopoly of violence is subject to checks and restrictions.
   (e) owns all private property.

The Case for Free Markets

This is a nontechnical section which develops a deeper appreciation for the successes of free markets. When reading this section contrast the achievements of the market with the requirements of central planning.

2. Independent decisions in a market economy are coordinated by
   (a) marketing boards.
   (b) the pursuit of profit.
   (c) allocative efficiency.
   (d) the price system.
   (e) opportunity cost.

3. Which of the following is required for a market economy to function?
   (a) Enforcement of contractual obligations.
   (b) Well-defined property rights.
   (c) Reasonable protection of private property from theft.
   (d) All of the above.
   (e) None of the above.

4. Which of the following is *not* part of the "informal defence" of free markets?
   (a) Allocative efficiency.
   (b) Decentralization of economic power.
   (c) Stimulus for growth.
   (d) Automatic coordination of decentralized decisions.
   (e) None of the above.

5. One of the most important features of the price system is
   (a) long-term stability of prices and output.
   (b) its ability to respond quickly and automatically to changing demand and supply conditions.
   (c) the assurance that government will not tax consumers and producers.
   (d) that it solves the problem of scarcity and provides abundance for all.
   (e) that it provides an equitable distribution of income.

Market Failures

This section discusses four major sources of market failure: market power, externalities, public goods and asymmetric information. After reading this section, you should be able to define each source of market failure, provide examples and discuss the implications for allocative efficiency. You should also appreciate that society's goals for the economy include issues beyond economic efficiency. Numerous definitions and new concepts are introduced in this section—it would be a good idea to keep a list of the terms and their meanings as you read.

6. The term "market failure" can refer to a market
   (a) where nothing is produced.
   (b) where there is persistent excess demand or supply.
   (c) where the allocatively efficient outcome is not achieved.
   (d) economy that results in an undesirable distribution of income.
   (e) Both (c) and (d) are correct.

7. Consider a negative externality such as cigar smoking in a room of one smoker and one non-smoker. According to the *Coarse Theorem*, if property rights to the air are given to the _____, then _____ can be obtained.
   (a) smoker; compensation.
   (b) non-smoker; tax revenue.
   (c) non-smoker; justice.
   (d) smoker; moral hazard.
   (e) smoker or non-smoker; allocative efficiency.

8. Which of the following is the *best* example of the free rider problem?
   (a) A municipal bus service with a policy of not charging senior citizens.
   (b) A local cinema that charges youths a lower price than adults.
   (c) A university professor who receives the benefits of a contract negotiated by the faculty union, but does not pay union dues.
   (d) A student who attends university for free because of a scholarship.
   (e) A person who visits the Museum of Civilization only when there is no admission fee.

9. Which of the following is the *best* example of a good that is excludable and non-rivalrous in consumption.
   (a) Pay-per-view television.
   (b) The cod fishery.
   (c) A lighthouse.
   (d) Police protection.
   (e) A radio broadcast.

10. Externalities are essentially due to
    (a) non-excludability in consumption.
    (b) non-rivalry in consumption.
    (c) a divergence between private and social costs.
    (d) the free rider problem.
    (e) the principle-agent problem.

11. Suppose my bicycle is fully insured and as a consequence, I don't bother locking it. This is an example of
    (a) adverse selection.
    (b) moral hazard.
    (c) the market for lemons.
    (d) a common property resource.
    (e) the free rider problem.

12. Winnipeg's flood control system is an example of
    (a) a negative externality.
    (b) an information asymmetry.
    (c) a common property resource.
    (d) a public good.
    (e) Okun's "leaky bucket."

13. The Government of Canada requires that all employed Canadians save for their retirement through the Canada Pension Plan. This is an example of
    (a) social responsibility.
    (b) paternalism.
    (c) allocative efficiency.
    (d) moral hazard.
    (e) adverse selection.

14. Redistribution of income conflicts with the goal of allocative efficiency because
    (a) it invariably changes incentives.
    (b) redistribution is essentially a negative externality.
    (c) recipients overstate their marginal benefits and providers overstate their marginal costs.
    (d) some recipients are not legitimately needy.
    (e) it creates a moral hazard problem.

15. Which of the following is the best example of a public good in a classroom?
    (a) A pencil.   (b) A student's notes.
    (c) A copy of the textbook.   (d) The temperature in the room.
    (e) The instructor's desk.

16. Adverse selection refers to a situation where
    (a) the managers of corporations pursue goals other than profits.
    (b) the values of consumers and producers differ.
    (c) one party to a transaction has more information about, say, the quality of the product than the other party.
    (d) the government selects the wrong form of intervention for correcting a market failure.
    (e) the management of a firm differs from its owners.

17. A positive externality would probably result from
    (a) a discharge of a toxic waste into the St. Lawrence River.
    (b) a newly painted house.
    (c) the dumping of garbage on a seldom-used country road.
    (d) cigarette smoking.
    (e) a loud radio at a public beach.

Government Intervention

Just as there are benefits to government attempts to correct market failures, there are also costs. After reading this section you should be able to explain why it is neither possible nor efficient to correct all market failures, nor is it always efficient to do nothing.

18. Efficient government intervention requires that
    (a) the costs of government enforcement be zero.
    (b) the marginal benefits of intervention be just equal to the marginal costs of intervention.
    (c) intervention should continue until all negative externalities have been eliminated.
    (d) there be no productivity losses in the private sector as a result of government intervention.
    (e) all intervention be self-financing.

19. Which of the following can the government use to correct market failure?
    (a) Taxes and/or subsidies.
    (b) Rules and regulations restricting market activity.
    (c) Public provision of goods and services.
    (d) Restructuring incentives.
    (e) All of the above.

20. In practice, assessing the benefits and costs of a proposed government program is difficult because
    (a) the effects of the program may be difficult to determine.
    (b) many benefits and costs occur in the distant future.
    (c) some costs and benefits are difficult, perhaps impossible, to quantify.
    (d) All of the above.
    (e) Both (a) and (b) are correct, but not (c).

21. Rent seeking behaviour refers to
    (a) the conversion of owner-occupied housing to rental housing.
    (b) activities by individuals seeking favourable government actions.
    (c) consumers seeking low rent housing.
    (d) actions in former socialist countries to convert public housing to private ownership.
    (e) firms that avoid the fixed costs of plant and equipment by leasing instead of buying.

EXERCISES

1. **Externalities**

   Figure 16-1 illustrates a competitive market in which the production process emits pollutants on neighbouring residences. The demand curve is D. MC_p represents the private marginal costs of production (i.e., the industry supply curve) and MC_E represents the marginal external costs to residences from emissions.

Figure 16-1

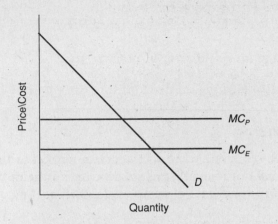

(a) Label the free market output as X.

(b) Derive the social marginal cost curve, and label it MC_S. Explain how you derived it.

(c) Indicate on the graph the society's optimal output level as Z.

(d) Explain why it would be inefficient to reduce emissions in this market to zero.

(e) Suppose this market is monopolized. Solve for the monopoly output and compare it to the optimal output Z.

2. **Public Goods**

Mr. Maple and Mr. Oak have cottages in a particular wooded retreat. Access to the cottages is by way of a 2-kilometre road that these two individuals must maintain. The individual demands for road quality on the part of Mr. Oak and Mr. Maple are shown in the graphs, where the quality of the road can be measured as the number of times the road is graded or tons of gravel added. The cost of increasing quality is shown as $S = MC$. (We assume that "zero" quality implies that the road is barely passable).

Figure 16-2

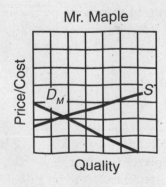

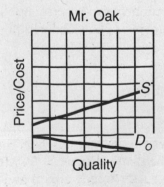

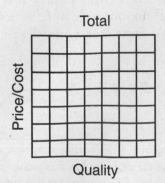

(a) What quality level will Mr. Maple maintain without any consideration for Mr. Oak? Similarly, what quality would Mr. Oak maintain without considering his neighbour?

(b) How would you illustrate the social demand for road quality? Use the graph. (*Hint:* Review the discussion of Figure 16-2 in the text).

(c) Given the costs of road improvements as shown, would the optimal quality level represent an improvement in road quality compared to the level maintained by Mr. Maple alone?

(d) If the level of road quality given by (c) were produced and the costs were shared, would Mr. Maple pay more or less than in (a)?

3. **Classification of Market Failures**

For each of the government programs or regulations cited, identify what type of market failure might be used as a rationale for government intervention. Briefly explain your choice.
(a) National defence.

(b) Pollution control regulations.

(c) Public health insurance programs.

(d) Environment Canada Weather Service.

(e) Student loan programs.

(f) Government support for scientific research.

(g) Truth-in-lending laws, requiring lenders to disclose to borrowers the true rate of interest.

(h) Minimum wage legislation.

(i) Quotas limiting the number of fish that may be caught.

(j) Municipal zoning regulations.

(k) Mandatory employment insurance policies.

4. Costly Government Intervention

The following diagram depicts a market's marginal private benefit (*MPB*) curve which gives the *incremental* private gain (*P* – *MC*) to consumers and producers as output is increased. Also shown is the marginal damage (*MD*) curve, which refers to pollution costs from incremental increases in production. These damages are external to the consumers and producers of this product; that is to say, they are third party effects.

Figure 16-3

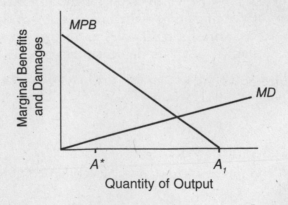

(a) With no government intervention, what level of output would obtain in this market? Why?

(b) From society's point of view, what is the optimal output level? Explain.

(c) Suppose that the government has faulty information on the precise shape of the *MD* curve, and therefore limits output to level A^*. At A^*, is society better off or worse off than in a no-intervention situation? Explain.

Extension Exercise

E-1. This exercise is an application of Arrow's Impossibility Theorem which is discussed in Extensions in Theory 16-2 (on page 399 of the text) entitled *The Problem with Democracy*.

A small community is in the process of repainting city hall. The citizens have narrowed the potential colours down to a choice of either red, white, or blue and have also agreed that combinations of the three are undesirable. To choose one colour from among the three, a committee of three individuals has been selected. Each of the committee members has a personal preference ranking of the alternatives as indicated in the following schedule (1 is most preferred, 3 is least preferred).

Individual Preference Rankings

| | Committee Member | | |
Colour	A	B	C
Red	1	3	2
White	2	1	3
Blue	3	2	1

Since a vote over the entire field of three colours results in a three-way tie (each committee member has a different most preferred colour), the committee has agreed to select the winning colour by majority voting on pairwise matches in which the loser of each match is eliminated (i.e., the colour with the most votes in the first contest between any two colours proceeds to a second contest with the remaining colour).

(a) If the agenda calls for red versus white in the first contest, what will ultimately be the colour of city hall?

(b) If the first round had pitted white against blue, what colour would have been chosen from the three?

(c) Alternatively, if the first round had matched red against blue, what colour would city hall have been painted?

PRACTICE MULTIPLE CHOICE TEST

1. The likely result in a market economy if the government taxed away all profits would be
   (a) a more rapid shift of resources to expanding industries.
   (b) the removal of the most important incentive for resource allocation.
   (c) improved market signals and responses.
   (d) improved information about temporary shortages and surpluses.
   (e) enhanced efficiency in resource allocation.

2. Which of the following is *not* an argument for increased reliance on markets for allocating resources?
   (a) The market system coordinates millions of independent economic decisions automatically.
   (b) Profits in a market economy provide a stimulus for innovation and growth.
   (c) Markets function best when external benefits are associated with consumption or production.
   (d) Market forces provide an effective means of adapting to changing economic conditions.
   (e) In a market system relative prices reflect relative costs.

3. If a ton of newspaper costs $350 to produce and in the process causes $10 worth of pollution damage to the environment,
   (a) the private cost is $360 per ton.
   (b) the social cost is $10 per ton and the private cost is $350 per ton.
   (c) the private cost is $350 per ton and the social cost is $340 per ton.
   (d) the social cost is $360 per ton and the private cost is $350 per ton.
   (e) the social cost is $10 per ton and the private cost is $360 per ton.

4. If there are costly externalities associated with an economic activity and that activity is carried out until the private marginal benefit equals the private marginal cost,
   (a) this activity should be subsidized.
   (b) the social marginal net benefit is positive.
   (c) private costs exceed social costs.
   (d) too many resources are being allocated to this activity.
   (e) output of this activity should increase.

5. The presence of external benefits associated with production implies that
   (a) private output exceeds the socially optimal output.
   (b) private output is less than the socially optimal output.
   (c) private output corresponds to the socially optimal output.
   (d) Any of the above, depending on the relative magnitude of social and private benefits.
   (e) Any of the above, depending upon whether social benefits exceeds external benefits.

6. A market economy is unlikely to provide a sufficient amount of a public good like national defence because
   (a) national defence does not benefit everyone to the same degree.
   (b) private firms produce national defence less efficiently than does the government.
   (c) consumers are poorly informed about the benefits of national defence.
   (d) it is impossible to withhold national defence from people who don't pay for it.
   (e) Both (a) and (b) are correct.

7. Which one of the following would not be a source of inefficient market outcomes?
   (a) Externalities.   (b) Public goods.
   (c) Profits and losses.   (d) Information asymmetries.
   (e) Moral hazard.

8. A Toronto resident who drives a car to work rather than taking public transportation
   (a) is reducing the free-rider problem.
   (b) is likely to be creating a negative externality.
   (c) creates a situation in which private cost is likely to exceed social cost.
   (d) is contributing to efficient resource allocation.
   (e) All of the above.

9. Competitive markets are unlikely to produce an efficient amount of a public good because
   (a) of non-excudability in consumption.
   (b) of the large costs of the public good.
   (c) these goods should be consumed until the marginal benefit is zero.
   (d) of rivalry in consumption.
   (e) Both (a) and (d) are correct.

10. Private markets will always underprovide public goods because
    (a) private markets will never provide goods at a price of zero.
    (b) of the positive externalities associated with these goods.
    (c) of the negative externalities associated with these goods.
    (d) the private marginal cost is less than the social marginal cost.
    (e) private markets will never provide goods that they know the government will provide.

11. Optimal public good provision is the level at which
    (a) the cost of providing an extra unit of the good is equal to each consumer's marginal benefit from the extra unit.
    (b) the cost of providing an extra unit of the good is equal to the sum of all consumers' marginal benefit for that unit.
    (c) the cost of providing an extra unit of the good is equal to the price of the good.
    (d) the marginal benefit of each consumer for the last unit of the good produced is zero.
    (e) voters are satisfied that an adequate amount of the good is being produced.

12. It is inefficient for the government to charge a price for consuming a good, such as weather forecasts, because
    (a) too many forecasts will be produced.
    (b) the price cannot be set to cover all research costs.
    (c) no one will be willing to pay for these forecasts.
    (d) the marginal cost of providing this information to another consumer is zero.
    (e) too few forecasts will be provided.

13. Moral hazard exists when one party to a transaction
    (a) has more information than the other party.
    (b) has the incentive and ability to shift costs onto another party.
    (c) is threatened by a hostile takeover.
    (d) purchases insurance because they know they are at high risk.
    (e) all of the above.

14. Arrow's impossibility theorem
    (a) shows that in some cases the majority-rule voting procedure results in inconsistent social decisions.
    (b) proves that efficient government intervention is impossible.
    (c) concerns the inability of governments to make sound social decisions.
    (d) suggests that it is impossible for markets to achieve efficient outcomes because of various market imperfections.
    (e) establishes that efficient resource allocation can never be obtained by governments.

15. Suppose some people derive a positive benefit from a public good but others receive a negative benefit. This public good should be produced if
    (a) the sum of everyone's marginal benefit is positive.
    (b) the sum of all the positive marginal benefits equals marginal cost.
    (c) the sum of individual valuations is maximized.
    (d) the sum of everyone's marginal benefit is at least as great as marginal cost.
    (e) those with negative benefits can be excluded from consuming the good.

16. Which of the following is *not* a cost of government intervention?
    (a) Direct resource costs.   (b) Compliance costs.
    (c) Change in production costs.   (d) Rent-seeking.
    (e) Externalities.

17. Making RRSP contributions tax deductible represents government intervention through
    (a) public provision.
    (b) redistribution.
    (c) regulation.
    (d) structuring economic incentives.
    (e) merit-goods allowances.

18. Examples of indirect costs of government intervention include all of the following except
    (a) expenditures by special interest groups to gain more preferential tax treatment.
    (b) the salaries of tax lawyers employed by many Canadian corporations.
    (c) the time spent by Canadians completing the income tax returns.
    (d) the government's administrative costs of collecting income tax revenue.
    (e) costs of complying with the Goods and Services Tax.

19. Attempts by lobbyists to influence the government's subsidy to the shipbuilding industry represents
    (a) external costs.
    (b) market power by the government.
    (c) rent seeking.
    (d) moral hazard.
    (e) a third part effect.

20. Resource allocation on the principle of one-person-one-vote will generally be _____ because the intensity of preferences is _____.
    (a) efficient, accounted for
    (b) efficient, not accounted for
    (c) inefficient, accounted for
    (d) inefficient, not accounted for

21. Which of the following best describes the reason for overfishing in Canada's offshore fisheries?
    (a) Fishing has depleted fish stocks, leading to smaller catches.
    (b) The private marginal cost incurred by fishermen is less than the social marginal cost.
    (c) The private marginal cost incurred by future generations of fishermen is greater than the private marginal cost incurred by current fishermen.
    (d) Canadian governments explicitly encourage fishing through subsidies to fishermen.
    (e) Fishing is a non-rivalrous activity.

22. The market for "lemons" is an example of market failure due to
    (a) public goods.
    (b) externalities.
    (c) monopoly power.
    (d) asymmetric information.
    (e) pursuit of social goals other than allocative efficieny..

23. Arthur Okun's comparison of the economy to a "leaky bucket" refers to the
    (a) loss of efficiency due to imperfect competition in the economy.
    (b) forgone tax revenues resulting from an inefficient tax system.
    (c) costs involved in the regulation of the economy.
    (d) the efficiency costs involved in the redistribution of income.
    (e) the reduction in tax revenues due to tax evasion.

SOLUTIONS

Chapter Review

1.(d) 2.(d) 3.(d) 4.(a) 5.(b) 6.(e) 7.(e) 8.(c) 9.(a) 10.(c) 11.(b) 12.(d) 13.(b) 14.(a) 15.(d) 16.(c) 17.(b) 18.(b) 19.(e) 20.(d) 21.(b)

Exercises

1. (a) **Figure 16-4**

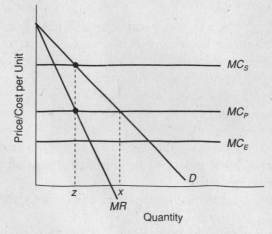

    (b) See graph: $MC_S = MC_P + MC_E$ by vertical summation.
    (c) See above.

d) The marginal benefit of consumption for all output up to Z exceeds the marginal social cost which includes both external and production costs.

(e) A monopoly maximizes profit where $MR = MC_p$. Since the monopolist faces a linear, downward sloping demand curve the MR curve is as depicted in Figure 16- 4. Note that the intersection of MR and MC_p occurs at an output that is closer to the optimal output Z than is the competitive output X. (As drawn, the intersection is right at Z, but this is not necessary).

2. (a) The point where the demand and S (= MC) curves intersect for Mr. Maple. Mr. Oak would not invest in road quality. The marginal cost of road quality is everywhere greater than the marginal benefit for Mr. Oak.

(b) Add the demand curves vertically; that is, find the total willingness to pay for each level of quality from 0 to Q^*. See Figure 16-5.

Figure 16-5

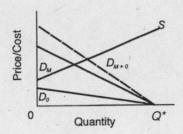

(c) Yes. The line $S = MC$ would intersect D_{M+O} to the right of the D_M intersection with S, indicating an improvement in road quality.

(d) It depends on how the costs are shared. If both Mr. Oak and Mr. Maple pay one-half, Mr. Maple would pay less than in (a). The new cost would be only slightly above what Mr. Maple paid before, but half the cost would be borne by Mr. Oak. Other cost-sharing arrangements are certainly possible.

3. (a) National defence is a public good. Adding to the population of a country does not diminish the extent to which each citizen is defended by a given size and quality of the armed forces.

(b) Pollution is an external cost.

(c) Asymmetric information. Until the advent of publicly provided health insurance, it was difficult for the elderly to purchase health insurance because insurance companies were aware of the problem of adverse selection (i.e., they feared that only those who knew themselves to be bad risks would buy health insurance).

(d) Providing weather information is a public good.

(e) Student loan programs are designed to increase the general educational level in society (a public good) and, to the extent that they reduce the immediate financial burden of going to college, should contribute to a more equitable distribution of income.

(f) It can be argued that the knowledge gained from scientific research provides a public good (e.g., cures for various diseases).

(g) Information asymmetry. Financial institutions are far more likely than the average borrower to know the true rate of interest.

(h) Minimum wage legislation is a form of price floor. Proponents usually argue that it will achieve a more equitable distribution of income. It is a means of protecting individuals from others.

(i) External cost. Fish are a common-property resource. An individual who takes more fish reduces the catch of others but does not view this as a cost, though it is to society.

(j) Externalities. Zoning laws that regulate such things as lot size, noise and certain types of activities (such as fraternities in a residential area) are meant to reduce external costs.

(k) Paternalism. Individuals may not save enough on their own to cover unexpected bouts of temporary unemployment.

4. (a) The free market would result in output A_1 since this output corresponds to $MPB = 0$, which implies that total private benefits are at a maximum. Each unit less than A_1 adds to private benefits because $MPB > 0$; similarly, each unit greater than A_1 deceases private benefits.

(b) Where the MPB and MD curves intersect at output A_0—as is shown in Figure 16-6. Beyond this, the incremental costs to society exceed the incremental benefits.

(c) Worse off. By restricting output to A^*, the net benefit forgone by society (compared to the optimal output A_0) is area ZTQ (that is, the loss in total benefits to producers, A^*TQA_0, minus the reduction in marginal damages, A^*ZQA_0).

Figure 16-6

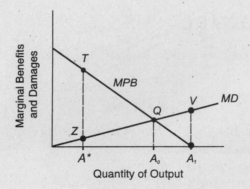

Extension Exercise

E-1. (a) Blue. Both A and C prefer red to white, so red proceeds to the second contest against blue. Both B and C prefer blue to red, so blue is the ultimate winner.

(b) Red. White wins the first round, and red wins over white in the second round.

(c) White.

Practice Multiple Choice Test

1.(b) 2.(c) 3.(d) 4.(d) 5.(b) 6.(d) 7.(c) 8.(b) 9.(a) 10.(a) 11.(b) 12.(d) 13.(b) 14.(a) 15.(d) 16.(e) 17.(d) 18.(d) 19.(c) 20.(d) 21.(b) 22.(d) 23.(d)

CHAPTER 17

ENVIRONMENTAL POLICY

(LO) LEARNING OBJECTIVES

1 Explain how an externality can be internalized, and how this can lead to allocative efficiency.

2 Understand why direct pollution controls are inefficient.

3 Explain how market-based policies, such as emissions taxes and tradeable pollution permits, can improve economic efficiency.

4 Have a general understanding of some popular arguments against market-based environmental policies.

CHAPTER OVERVIEW

The previous chapter identified several types of market failure that might be addressed by government policy. The present chapter is devoted to a discussion of environmental externalities and government attempts to address them.

Pollution problems are viewed as negative externalities. In going about their daily businesses, firms and households sometimes make decisions that harm the environment. This results in inefficiencies because decision-makers fail to take account of these external costs, thereby creating a divergence between *private* and *social* costs and benefits. Government intervention is designed to induce decision-makers to **internalize the externality**.

The allocatively efficient level of pollution is generally not zero; rather, it is the level where the marginal cost of abatement is just matched by the marginal damage of the pollution. This chapter compares the relative merits of several forms of pollution controls: *direct controls,* such as the setting of standards, and *indirect controls,* such as emissions taxes and **tradable emissions permits**.

Producers, the public and environmentalists have sometimes viewed market-based solutions to environmental problems with skepticism. The basis for their skepticism is reviewed in this chapter.

CHAPTER REVIEW

The Economics of Pollution Control

After studying this section, you should be able to explain why the economically efficient level of pollution is generally not zero. You should also be able to discuss the relative merits of standard-setting to market-based solutions as a means of controlling pollution. *Tip:* The discussion of pollution control is cast in terms of abatement instead of the level of pollution—make sure you appreciate the implications for interpretation.

1. A profit-maximizing competitive firm
   (a) always produces in excess of the output that is allocatively efficient.
   (b) always generates pollution as a by-product of production.
   (c) produces more than the allocatively efficient output when it ignores external costs associated with its production.
   (d) automatically considers external costs in making production decisions.
   (e) internalizes all external costs.

2. A commodity's allocatively efficient output is that quantity where
   (a) all marginal costs, private plus external, equal all marginal benefits, private plus external.
   (b) external costs are minimized.
   (c) the social benefit of the last unit of output is just equal to its external cost.
   (d) all externalities are eliminated.
   (e) All of the above.

3. A firm currently emitting pollutants would have an incentive to reduce emissions if
   (a) an emissions tax per unit of discharge were imposed.
   (b) private citizens were able to sue for pollution damages.
   (c) it were forced to purchase emissions permits.
   (d) a tax on output were designed to internalize the externality.
   (e) Any of the above actions were taken.

4. A common problem with the successful use of emissions taxes is that
   (a) information on external costs is not always available for setting tax rates.
   (b) they do not provide appropriate incentives for pollution reduction.
   (c) firms will generally not reduce emissions to zero.
   (d) the government must also specify the means by which firms are to abate pollution.
   (e) some firms will still pollute more than others.

5. Tradable emissions permits
   (a) are, in effect, equivalent to creating a market for "bads."
   (b) can achieve the same resource allocation as emissions taxes.
   (c) are cost-effective in that for a given amount of pollution, the total cost of abatement is minimized.
   (d) is an example in which markets themselves can be used to correct market failures.
   (e) All of the above.

6. If the production of steel generates external costs, profit maximization in steel production will result in
   (a) too much steel at too high a price.
   (b) too little steel at too low a price.
   (c) too much steel at too low a price.
   (d) too little steel at too high a price.
   (e) the socially efficient output of steel, but at too low a price.

The Politics of Pollution Control

This section presents a non-technical discussion of the arguments advanced by producers, the public and environmentalists against market-based solutions to environmental externalities.

7. The "Kyoto Protocol" is an agreement to reduce emissions of greenhouse gases by using
   (a) emissions taxes.
   (b) tradeable emissions permits.
   (c) an international system of standards.
   (d) a system of transfers from developed to developing nations.
   (e) a system of subsidies to polluting firms as a means of encouraging them to invest in abatement technology.

8. Some producers have opposed market-based solutions to externalities on the grounds that
   (a) pollution is a social responsibility.
   (b) it is immoral to buy the right to pollute.
   (c) it is unfair that some competitors may continue to pollute.
   (d) environmental protection harms society because it reduces output and employment.
   (e) Both (c) and (d) are correct.

EXERCISES

1. **Internalizing the External Cost**

   This exercise investigates the tax required to induce firms to internalize an externality. In the text, the external cost per unit of output was assumed constant (see Figure 17-1 of the text). In this problem, the marginal external cost is an increasing function of the level of output. As a result, the size of the optimal tax is not immediately obvious.

   The demand curve facing the perfectly competitive gadget industry is given by

   $$Q = 2,500 - 100P,$$

   where Q is output and P is the price per unit of output. Marginal production costs in the gadget industry are constant at $10 per unit of output. Production in the gadget industry releases pollutants into the air. These marginal external costs, EC, are estimated to be an increasing function of output according to the following equation

   $$EC = 0.005Q.$$

   (a) Graph the marginal benefit, marginal private cost and marginal external cost curves on the following grid. Label them MB, MC_p, and EC respectively. (*Hint:* See Figure 17-1 in the text for the MB curve.)

Figure 17-1

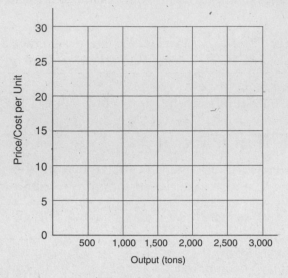

(b) What is the free market output in this industry?

(c) What is the marginal social cost curve? Graph it with the label MC_S.

(d) What is the allocatively efficient output of gadgets? Explain.

(e) What tax on gadgets would induce firms in this industry to internalize this externality? Explain.

2. This problem examines the implications for a firm's profit (or, indeed, survival) when it is required to internalize an externality.

The following schedule gives the relationship between output and total production cost for a pulp and paper firm located on a particular northern river. As the firm expands output it releases pollutants into the river which adversely affects the recreational fishing industry. The schedule also provides the cost to the fishing industry from the pulp and paper firm's different output levels.

Output (tons per week)	Total Private Cost to Pulp & Paper Industry	Cost to Fishing Industry from Pollution
1	500	100
2	550	225
3	620	365
4	710	515
5	820	675
6	1,050	845
7	1,450	1,025

(a) Complete the following table, and graph your results in the grid in Figure 17-2.

Output (tons per week)	Average Private Cost (APC)	Marginal Private Cost (MPC)	Average Social Cost (ASC)	Marginal Social Cost (MSC)
1	_____		_____	
2	_____	_____	_____	_____
3	_____	_____	_____	_____
4	_____	_____	_____	_____
5	_____	_____	_____	_____
6	_____	_____	_____	_____
7	_____	_____	_____	_____

Figure 17-2

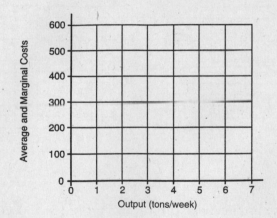

(b) If this firm were producing 4 tons of output per week, how much revenue would be required to cover its private costs? How much revenue would be required to cover the social costs?

(c) Assume that the market for this firm's product (paper) is perfectly competitive and that the firm's private costs of production are typical for the industry. Predict the long-run equilibrium price and the output for this firm in the absence of pollution controls.

(d) Assume now that firms in this industry are required either to pay compensation for the negative externalities or incur abatement costs. The industry price would be (higher/the same/lower) and the output (less/the same/greater). This firm's ability to survive would depend on the long run equilibrium price for paper being at least _____ or on its being able to keep the total of negative externalities and costs of abatement at levels as (low/high) as those of its competitors.

3. **Tradeable Emissions Permits**

The two panels in Figure 17-3 present the marginal cost curves for pollution abatement for two firms in a given industry (for simplicity, assume that there is no fixed cost associated with abatement). The regulatory agency has determined that the level of pollution emissions must decrease by a total of eight units. Assume that the type of pollution in this industry is readily measurable.

Figure 17-3

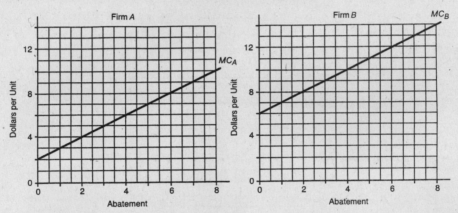

(a) Suppose that the regulatory agency directly controls these firms by ruling that each firm must decrease emissions by four units. What is the total industry cost of abating the eight units of pollution?

(b) Instead of direct controls, suppose that the regulatory agency imposes a tax on emissions of $8 per unit. What is the level of abatement by each firm?

(c) What is the total cost of abatement for the industry when the emissions tax is imposed?

(d) Now consider the effect of the introduction of a system of tradable emissions permits. Specifically, suppose that the agency rules that each firm must abate emissions by four units but that either firm can reduce this by any amount so long as it can induce the other firm to increase its abatement by an offsetting amount. What would be the resulting levels of abatement by these firms? Explain.

(e) What is the total abatement cost to the industry under the system of tradable emissions permits?

4. **Inefficiency of Standards**

Consider two firms whose production emits pollutants. Assume that each firm has access to the same abatement technology and costs. That is to say, the firms' marginal cost of abatement curves are identical. Firm R is located in a rural area whereas firm U is located in an urban area. As a consequence the marginal benefit of abatement is lower for firm R than it is for Firm U. Explain why setting of abatement standards in this industry will, in general, not be allocatively efficient. Support your discussion with a diagram.

PRACTICE MULTIPLE CHOICE TEST

1. If incremental costs of pollution abatement increase with increasing levels of abatement, the optimal
   (a) pollution level is the minimum attainable.
   (b) level of pollution reduction is the amount where the marginal benefits of prevention equal the marginal costs.
   (c) pollution level is necessarily zero
   (d) amount of abatement is zero.
   (e) pollution level is that where all external costs have been eliminated.

Questions 2 to 5 refer to Figure 17-4 which depicts the marginal benefit (MB) and marginal cost (MC) of pollution abatement.

Figure 17-4

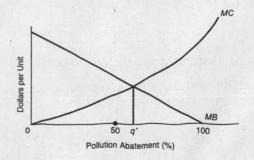

2. The marginal benefits of pollution abatement
   (a) are the value of reducing pollution damages.
   (b) increase as *MB* shifts rightward.
   (c) decline as the level of abatement increases.
   (d) are equivalent to a demand curve for pollution control.
   (e) All of the above.

3. The economically efficient amount of pollution abatement is
   (a) the output at which marginal benefits equal marginal costs.
   (b) 100 percent, since that maximizes the gains from pollution control.
   (c) zero.
   (d) dependent upon the external costs of pollution which are not given in the graph.
   (e) impossible to determine without additional information about the type of pollution.

4. New findings of adverse health effects or other damages from this pollutant will
   (a) shift the marginal cost curve rightward.
   (b) shift the marginal benefit curve rightward.
   (c) shift both the marginal benefit curve and the marginal cost curve rightward.
   (d) have no effect on either the marginal benefit curve or the marginal cost curve.
   (e) decrease the optimal abatement level.

5. Other things being equal, an improvement in pollution control technology
   (a) shifts *MC* rightward, increasing the optimal level of pollution control.
   (b) shifts *MC* leftward, decreasing the optimal level of pollution control.
   (c) shifts both the *MC* and *MB* curves rightward.
   (d) shifts *MB* rightward, increasing the optimal level of pollution control.
   (e) will not affect either of the curves in this diagram.

6. With multiple firms emitting pollutants, economic efficiency requires that
   (a) all emitters reduce pollution by the same percentage.
   (b) marginal costs of abatement be equal for all emitters.
   (c) all emitters reduce pollution by the same absolute amount.
   (d) there be zero emissions.
   (e) firms reduce emissions in proportion to their size.

7. The requirement that all pollution sources adopt a specific pollution control technique when there are many methods for controlling a certain type of pollution
   (a) is likely to be the most efficient way to achieve a certain amount of pollution abatement.
   (b) is likely to be less efficient than either emissions taxes or tradable emissions permits in achieving a given amount of abatement.
   (c) is more efficient the more divergent the abatement costs of different firms.
   (d) eliminates the need for monitoring and enforcement by the regulatory agency.
   (e) is likely to minimize total costs of achieving a given level of abatement in the industry.

8. Which of the following is *not* true of direct pollution controls?
   (a) They minimize total abatement costs for a given level of pollution.
   (b) They are slow to adopt improved abatement technology.
   (c) They are costly to monitor and enforce.
   (d) They require the government to direct firms on how to abate.
   (e) All of the above are true.

9. When we say that a firm has internalized an externality, we mean
   (a) production takes place indoors.
   (b) production occurs without any external damage.
   (c) the firm takes into account all costs associated with production.
   (d) the firm is complying with all regulatory standards.
   (e) pollution has been eliminated.

10. Complete abatement would be optimal, only if
   (a) the marginal benefit of abatement is always positive.
   (b) the marginal benefit of abatement were positive and constant.
   (c) the marginal benefit of abatement were positive and increasing.
   (d) the marginal cost of abatement were zero.
   (e) None of the above.

11. If the plastics industry has been disposing of its wastes free of charge, government regulation to ensure a more efficient use of resources would affect the industry's output and product price in which of the following ways?
   (a) Both output and price would decrease.
   (b) Output would decrease, but there would be no change in price.
   (c) Output would be unchanged, but price would increase.
   (d) Price would increase and output would decrease.
   (e) There would be no change in either price or output.

12. Internalizing a production externality will
   (a) shift the demand curve for the good to the left.
   (b) shift the supply curve (MC for a monopoly) for the good to the left.
   (c) shift both the demand and supply curves to the left.
   (d) increase the size of external costs.
   (e) have no effect on either demand or supply.

13. Which of the following groups purchased SO_2 emissions permits but did not use them?
   (a) Coal-burning electric power plants.
   (b) The Environmental Protection Agency.
   (c) Power plants with high abatement costs.
   (d) Power plants with low abatement costs.
   (e) Environmentalists.

14. Which of the following is *not* an example of a direct pollution control?
   (a) Bans on household fireplaces in some cities.
   (b) Automobile pollution controls.
   (c) A bag fee for garbage removal.
   (d) A requirement that scrubbers be installed on factory chimneys.
   (e) Laws against littering.

SOLUTIONS

Chapter Review

1.(c) 2.(a) 3.(e) 4.(a) 5.(e) 6.(c) 7.(b) 8.(e)

Exercises

1. (a) The MB curve is simply the inverse of the demand curve. That is to say, $MB = P = 25 - 0.01Q$.

Figure 17-5

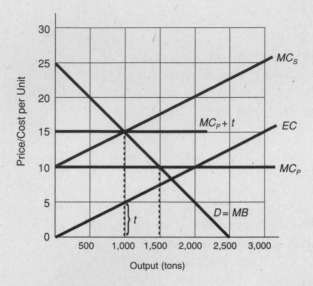

(b) 1500 units, where $MB = MC_P$.
(c) $MC_s = MC_P + EC = 10 + 0.005Q$.
(d) 1000 units, where $MC_s = MB$.
(e) The optimal emissions tax is $5 per gadget. It is calculated as the marginal external cost *measured at the efficient output*. Note that when the $5 unit tax is added to MC_P the firm's full cost per unit is $MC_P + t$ which intersects MB at the optimal output. This is slightly different than the example in the text which assumed that the marginal external cost was constant. Here marginal external cost varies with the level of output, so the tax is calculated as the marginal external cost at a specific level of output, the optimal output.

2. (a)

Output (tons per week)	Average Private Cost (APC)	Marginal Private Cost (MPC)	Average Social Cost (ASC)	Marginal Social Cost (MSC)
1	500		600	
		50		175
2	275		388	
		70		210
3	207		328	
		90		240
4	178		306	
		110		270
5	164		299	
		230		400
6	175		316	
		400		580
7	207		354	

Figure 17-6

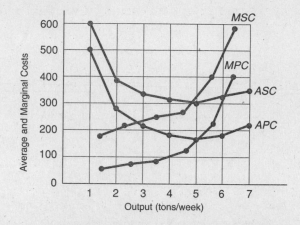

(b) $710 (per ton price of $177.50); $1,225 (per ton price of $306.25).
(c) $164; 5 tons per week (this is the output where average private costs are at a minimum).
(d) higher; less; $299 (the lowest average social cost); low.

3. (a) Each firm abates four units, so the marginal abatement costs for Firms A and B are $6 and $10, respectively. Since there are no fixed costs to abatement, total abatement cost for each firm is given by the area under its abatement marginal cost curve measured up to its level of abatement. Thus for Firm A, total abatement cost is $16 = ($2 × 4) + [($6 − $2) × 4]/2; for Firm B, it is $32 = ($6 × 4) + [($10 − $6) × 4]/2. Therefore, industry abatement cost is $48 = $16 + $32.

(b) A tax of $8 imposed on each unit of emissions represents a savings of $8 for each unit of abatement. Thus each firm abates until the savings from an additional unit of abatement equals the marginal cost of abatement. For Firm A this occurs at a level of abatement equal to six units, while for Firm B it occurs at two units of abatement.

(c) Given the levels of abatement determined in (b), abatement cost for Firm A is $30 = ($2 × 6) + [($8 − $2) × 6]/2, while for Firm B it is $14 = ($6 (2) + [($8 − $6) × 2]/2. Thus industry abatement cost is $44.

(d) Abatement of the fourth unit costs Firm A $6 but costs Firm B $10; thus the potential for gains from trade exists. For example, Firm B would pay up to $10 to avoid having to abate the fourth unit of emission, and Firm A would accept anything over $6 to induce it to increase slightly its level of abatement ($7 for the fifth unit). Thus these firms will negotiate to buy and sell emissions permits until no further gains from trade are achievable. This occurs when the firms face equal marginal abatement costs; Firm B will have reduced its level of abatement by two units to a total of two, and Firm A will have increased its level by an offsetting two units to a total of six.

(e) Since the level of abatement for each firm is the same as that under the emissions tax discussed earlier, the total abatement cost for the industry is the same at $44.

4. For simplicity, assume that marginal abatement costs are not only identical but also constant as depicted in Figure 17-7. Suppose each firm is directed to abate an equal amount A_0. Since Firm R is the low marginal benefit firm, it follows that at A_0, $MB_R < MB_U$. Society would gain if Firm U abated one unit more and Firm R one unit less. The optimal abatement levels are given as A_R and A_U, where the marginal benefit curve intersects the marginal cost curve for each firm.

Figure 17-7

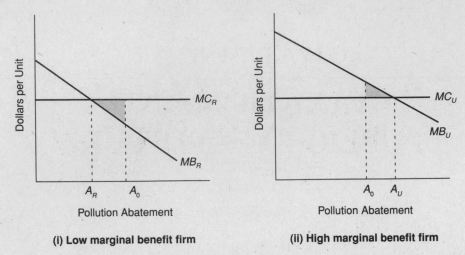

(i) Low marginal benefit firm

(ii) High marginal benefit firm

Practice Multiple Choice Test

1.(b) 2.(e) 3.(a) 4.(b) 5.(a) 6.(b) 7.(b) 8.(a) 9.(c) 10.(d) 11.(d) 12.(b) 13.(e) 14.(c)

CHAPTER 18

TAXATION AND PUBLIC EXPENDITURE

LO LEARNING OBJECTIVES

1 Explain progressive, proportional, and regressive taxes.

2 Have a general knowledge of the main taxes used in Canada.

3 Explain how a tax generates both a direct and an excess burden.

4 Understand why high income taxes may act as a disincentive to work.

5 Understand why funds are transferred between various levels of government in Canada.

6 Describe a general outline of Canada's major social programs.

7 Be aware of some common pitfalls in evaluating government's role in the economy.

CHAPTER OVERVIEW

This chapter addresses how taxation and government expenditures affect the allocation of resources and distribution of income. The importance of this discussion is underlined by the fact that government activities at the federal, provincial, and local levels represent roughly 40 percent of national output in Canada.

While the main purpose of the tax system is to raise revenue, tax policy is also a powerful device for income redistribution and restructuring of incentives. Both objectives are pursued by altering the distribution of after-tax income through **progressivity** taxes or by issuance of **tax expenditures**. Personal and corporate income taxes, excise and sales taxes as well as property taxes are the primary sources of tax revenue in Canada.

Evaluation of the tax system involves consideration of efficiency and equity for the entire system rather than individual taxes within the system. The concept of equity is discussed by assessing two principles in taxation: *ability-to-pay* and *benefits received*. Taxation involves both a **direct burden** and an **excess burden**. An efficient tax system raises a given amount of tax revenue while minimizing the resulting excess burden. For a given amount of tax revenue, efficiency and progressivity can be altered by changing the mix of the various taxes used.

Public expenditure in Canada includes the provision of goods and services, **transfer payments** to both individuals and other levels of government, and interest payments on the debt. *Fiscal federalism* refers to the the idea that the three layers of government should coordinate their spending plans and have a mechanism for **intergovernmental transfers**.

The five pillars of Canadian social policy are: education, health care, income support programs, unemployment insurance and retirement benefits. There has been increasing pressure on Canadian governments to improve their ability to deliver benefits and reduce costs.

CHAPTER REVIEW

Taxation in Canada

After reading this section, you should understand the roles of the tax system in raising revenue, redistributing income and affecting resource allocation; distinguish between progressive and regressive taxes; and, discuss the general taxes used in Canada. Make sure you understand the difference between the marginal tax rate and the average tax rate; the distinction is at the core of the definition of tax progressivity.

1. A tax expenditure involves _____ in tax revenue whereas an ordinary budget expenditure involves _____ government spending.
   (a) a reduction; a reduction.
   (b) an increase; an increase.
   (c) a reduction; an increase.
   (d) an increase; a decrease.
   (e) redistribution; an increase.

2. In 1998, total tax revenues by all levels of government in Canada represented approximately _____ of the value of GDP.
   (a) one-tenth.
   (b) a quarter.
   (c) one-third.
   (d) 40 percent.
   (e) half.

3. Tax brackets refer to the different
   (a) types of taxes an individual must pay.
   (b) taxation of individuals depending upon the number of dependents they have.
   (c) tax rates applied to different levels of income.
   (d) objectives of taxes such as redistribution, resource re-allocation or pure revenue raising.
   (e) levels of tax payments.

4. Which of the following statements concerning the GST is *false*?
   (a) It changes the relative prices of all goods and services.
   (b) It is a value added tax.
   (c) It does not discourage saving.
   (d) It is applied at 7 percent in all Canadian provinces.
   (e) Its regressivity is reduced through a system of exemptions and refundable tax credits.

5. Tax credits for tuition fees and full time studies are examples of
   (a) poll taxes.
   (b) lump-sum taxes.
   (c) regressivity.
   (d) excise taxes.
   (e) tax expenditures.

6. If the amount of tax paid increases as income rises, the tax is
   (a) proportional.   (b) progressive.
   (c) regressive.   (d) a negative income tax.
   (e) Any of the above.

7. If the income tax is progressive, the marginal tax rate must be
   (a) less than the average tax rate.
   (b) the same as the average tax rate.
   (c) greater than the average tax rate.
   (d) continuously increasing with income.
   (e) constant.

Evaluating the Tax System

This section reviews the two criteria used for evaluating the tax system: equity and efficiency. Make sure that you understand the differences between vertical and horizontal equity, and between the direct and excess burdens of taxation.

8. Horizontal equity refers to
   (a) the East-West distribution of income.
   (b) the treatment of individuals with identical incomes but different circumstances.
   (c) the treatment of households of similar composition but with different incomes.
   (d) the flat-rate tax scheme.
   (e) changes in the marginal tax rate across income levels.

9. The central idea behind the Laffer curve is that as tax rates increase,
   (a) the tax base will increase.
   (b) a tax revolt by taxpayers will be ignited.
   (c) more economic activity will go unreported so as to evade income taxation.
   (d) tax revenue will reach a maximum and then decline as tax rates continue to increase.
   (e) the size of the government increases.

10. According to the benefit principle of taxation,
    (a) the amount of taxes paid should be equal across income groups.
    (b) taxes should be paid according to the benefits that taxpayers derive from public expenditure.
    (c) there should be no user charges for government services.
    (d) the greater one's income, the greater the benefit generally received from public expenditures.
    (e) the economy benefits the most when the government maximizes its tax revenue.

11. Vertical equity in a tax system
    (a) concerns equity across income groups.
    (b) focuses on comparisons of taxes paid by taxpayers with different incomes.
    (c) is often used to support regressive taxation.
    (d) attempts to tax monopoly power by a surtax on firms that have undergone vertical mergers.
    (e) Both (a) and (b) are correct.

12. The excess burden of a tax
    (a) equals the total amount of tax paid.
    (b) refers to the amount of tax paid by consumers.
    (c) measures the inefficiency of tax cascading.
    (d) measures the administrative cost of raising tax revenue.
    (e) measures the allocative inefficiency of the tax.

Public Expenditure in Canada

After reading this section you will have a better appreciation of the extent of the public sector in the Canadian economy and be able to explain the economic logic for the distribution of government responsibilities in fiscal federalism. You will also be able to outline Canada's various social programs.

13. Which of the following in *not* treated as a broad category of government expenditure?
    (a) Transfer payments to individuals and other levels of government.
    (b) Expenditures on the purchase of goods and services.
    (c) Interest payments on government debt.
    (d) Tax rentals.
    (e) None of the above.

14. Which of the following programs was replaced by the Canada health and social transfer in 1996?
    (a) The Canada Pension Plan.
    (b) Equalization Payments.
    (c) The Canada Assistance Plan.
    (d) Established Programs Financing.
    (e) Both (c) and (d).

15. Which of the following is not considered one of the five pillars of Canadian social policy?
    (a) Retirement benefits.
    (b) Employment insurance.
    (c) Government expenditure on goods and services.
    (d) Health care.
    (e) Income support.

16. Health Maintenance Organizations (HMO's) are
    (a) paid on a capitation basis.
    (b) an alternative to the fee-for-service system of health care.
    (c) a possible means of containing costs in the Canadian system of health care.
    (d) structured so that providers of health services have an incentive to conserve.
    (e) All of the above are true.

17. The term "poverty trap" is used to refer to
    (a) low-paying jobs.
    (b) low-paying jobs with high tax rates.
    (c) low-income housing.
    (d) income-support programs that do not provide an adequate standard of living.
    (e) tax-and-transfer incentives that discourage individuals from increasing their pre-tax income.

18. Under the equalization payments program, the federal government
    (a) equalizes the tax revenue of each province.
    (b) transfers money from its general revenue to provinces with below average tax capacity.
    (c) transfers tax revenue to provinces to ensure a reasonably equal educational expenditure per student across the country.
    (d) ensures that each province taxes income at the same rate (except Quebec, which collects its own income tax).
    (e) provides equal unconditional grants to each province.

19. Which of the following is *not* a motivation for fiscal federalism in Canada?
    (a) Geographic spillover effects.
    (b) Use of the federal government's spending power.
    (c) Not all jurisdictions have access to revenue that matches the division of responsibilities.
    (d) Regional differences in preferences.
    (e) Administrative efficiency.

20. Which of the following was *not* one of the central sources of Canadian intergovernmental transfers prior to reforms in 1996?
    (a) Equalization payments.
    (b) Established Programs Financing.
    (c) Revenue sharing.
    (d) Canada Health and Social Transfer.
    (e) Canada Assistance Plan.

Evaluating the Role of Government

This section offers a brief discussion of the broad arguments for and against increasing the size of the public sector relative to the private sector. It also provides a commentary on the scope of government activity and the evolution of policy.

21. In his book *The Affluent Society*, John Kenneth Galbraith argued that
    (a) modern economies have enough wealth to provide all with an adequate standard of living.
    (b) the value of a marginal dollar spent by government is less than the marginal value spent by the private sector.
    (c) that redistribution of income generates aggregate affluence.
    (d) that the Canadian economy has sufficient resources to eliminate the poverty line as defined by Statistics Canada.
    (e) the marginal utility of public goods is higher than that for private goods.

EXERCISES

Tax Progressivity

1. (a) The table that follows shows the amount of tax paid by four individuals in four different income categories under each of three tax regimes: A, B, and C. Indicate whether each regime is proportional, regressive, or progressive.

TAX PAID BY INCOME LEVEL

Tax	$10,000	$20,000	$40,000	$60,000
A	$ 1,000	$ 2,000	$ 4,000	$ 6,000
B	800	1,400	2,600	3,600
C	400	1,200	3,000	5,600

(Income Level)

Tax A is _____.

Tax B is _____.

Tax C is _____.

(b) Taking all taxes together (A + B + C), is the tax system progressive, regressive, or proportional?

2. **Excess Burden**

This exercise is designed to illustrate the relationship between the elasticity of demand and the excess burden of a tax.

The demand curves for goods A and B are given by

$$Q_A = 40 - P_A, \text{ and}$$

$$Q_B = 60 - 2 P_B.$$

(a) Graph the demand curves on the following grid.

Figure 18-1

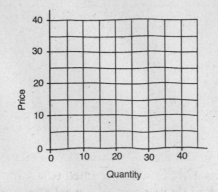

(b) Suppose the price of each good is initially $20. By inspection of the above graph, which good has the more elastic demand at a price of $20? Explain.

(c) Suppose a tax of $5 per unit is imposed on each good. Use the graph to illustrate the excess and direct burden in each market.

(d) Which commodity has the larger excess burden?

3 The Negative Income Tax

The following is an example of the Negative Income Tax that is discussed in the box entitled Applying Economic Concepts 18-1.

(a) Suppose that a negative income tax provides $5,000 guaranteed income for a family and a 50 percent marginal tax rate on earnings. Complete the table.

(A) Before-Tax Earnings	(B) Income Tax (−$5,000 + 0.5A)	(C) After-Tax Income (A − B)
$ 0	−$5,000	$5,000
2,000	−$4,000	_____
5,000	_____	7,500
7,000	_____	_____
10,000	_____	_____

(b) The following version of the negative income tax was part of a 1970 experiment. A family of five earns $90 a week in income and receives $15 a week in cash from the government (1970 dollars); if earnings fall to $50, the family will receive $43 a week from the government, and if there are no earnings, the family will receive $78 a week from the government. Calculate the implicit marginal rate of taxation.

Earnings	Change in Earnings	Cash Transfer	Change in Cash Transfer	Marginal Rate of Taxation
$ 0		$78		
50	_____	43	_____	_____
90	_____	15	_____	_____

4. Sales Taxes

This exercise compares and the Retail Sales Tax (RST), the Goods and Services Tax (GST), and the Manufacturers' Sales Tax (MST) when applied to a commodity that has four stages of production. The following schedule presents the purchases and sales at each stage.

Production Stage	Purchases from Other Firms	Sales to Other Firms/Customers
Primary	$0	$1,000
Manufacturing	1,000	4,000
Wholesale	4,000	6,000
Retail	6,000	10,000

(a) Suppose that an RST of 7 percent is introduced. At which stage in the production process is it imposed, and what is total tax revenue?

(b) Instead, suppose that a GST of 7 percent is imposed such that at each stage a 7 percent tax is paid on sales, but all taxes paid on purchases from other firms are credited. What is the net tax paid at each stage, and what is total tax revenue?

(c) Suppose that a value added tax of 7 percent is imposed. What is the tax liability at each stage, and what is total tax revenue?

(d) What is the difference between the value added tax and the GST?

(e) An alternative scheme is the MST. Suppose that this program must guarantee the same total tax yield ($700) as those in parts (a), (b), and (c), but is only applied to the manufacturing stage of production. What is the required tax rate for the MST?

PRACTICE MULTIPLE CHOICE TEST

1. The fact that there are fixed costs associated with the provision of public goods and services is the basis of justification for which of the following programs?
   (a) Tax-rental agreements.
   (b) Equalization Payments.
   (c) The CHST.
   (d) The Canada Pension Plan.
   (e) Income support programs.

2. If rich people and poor people smoke the same amount, a sales tax on cigarettes is regressive because
   (a) everyone spends the same proportion of income on cigarettes.
   (b) the demand for cigarettes is inelastic.
   (c) the tax paid per person represents a larger proportion of a poor person's income.
   (d) the rich are better informed about the health hazards of smoking.
   (e) the poor pay more taxes.

3. If a tax takes the same amount of money from everyone regardless of individual income, the tax is
   (a) a flat-rate tax.   (b) proportional.
   (c) regressive.   (d) horizontally inequitable.
   (e) All of the above.

4. If an individual's average tax rate is 30 percent and marginal tax rate is 50 percent, an additional $100 income would imply additional tax payments of
   (a) $50.   (b) $30.
   (c) $80.   (d) $20.
   (e) Indeterminable without income level.

5. Tax expenditures refer to
   (a) how the government spends its tax revenues.
   (b) an individual's annual tax payments.
   (c) tax concessions that are made to influence the behavior of taxpaying units.
   (d) intergovernmental transfers.
   (c) expenditures of future tax revenues.

6. The more elastic is demand, the greater will be the
   (a) tax revenue raised from a given excise tax.
   (b) horizontal equity of a particular tax.
   (c) progressivity of a tax.
   (d) excess burden of a tax.
   (e) direct burden of a tax.

7. The judgment concerning whether a tax is regressive, proportional, or progressive is based on a comparison of the amount of tax with the
   (a) tax base.   (b) value of the item being taxed.
   (c) taxpayer's income.   (d) distribution of income.
   (e) level of government expenditures.

8. A marginal tax rate of 58 percent on taxable income of $200,000 implies
   (a) that a person with $200,000 of taxable income pays $116,000 in taxes.
   (b) that the tax system is progressive.
   (c) that the tax system is vertically equitable.
   (d) that a dollar of income above $200,000 increases one's tax liability by $0.58.
   (e) All of the above.

9. Which of the following is an example of a tax expenditure?
   (a) Registered Retirement Savings Plans.
   (b) Old Age Security.
   (c) Canada Pension Plan.
   (d) Guaranteed Income Supplement.
   (e) Employment Insurance.

10. Which of the following is *not* an example of a government transfer payment to individuals?
    (a) Salaries of government employees.
    (b) Canada Pension Plan.
    (c) Unemployment insurance benefits.
    (d) Child tax credits.
    (e) Workers' compensation.

11. Decentralization of government economic activity can be justified by all but which of the following?
    (a) Regional preferences.
    (b) Income redistribution efforts.
    (c) Particular local needs for public expenditure.
    (d) Internalization of spillovers of services across jurisdictions.
    (e) Responsiveness to changing preferences.

12. Which of the following statements is a reasonable economic argument for some subsidization of postsecondary education?
    (a) All of the benefits of a university education accrue to the student in the form of a higher lifetime income.
    (b) It is vertically equitable that all taxpayers pay to educate individuals who will earn above average incomes.
    (c) Charging the full cost of education would deter many children from low income families from continuing their education.
    (d) There are external benefits to the entire nation from a better-educated population.
    (e) Both (c) and (d) are correct.

13. Which of the following is likely to occur if the qualification period for unemployment insurance were shortened to 10 weeks in some regions?
    (a) The scheme would tend to become a subsidy for seasonal employment.
    (b) Provincial and municipal governments would create make-work schemes that provide employment for 10 weeks.
    (c) The rate of labour turnover would increase.
    (d) Labour mobility towards occupations and locations with more stable employment prospects would be discouraged.
    (e) All of the above.

14. The next few decades promise to be a time of difficulty for retirement schemes in Canada because
    (a) private pension plans are being replaced by government plans.
    (b) a greater proportion of the population will be retired, and a smaller proportion will be working.
    (c) more people are refusing to accept mandatory retirement at age 65.
    (d) the popularity of RRSPs has meant that there is less saving for retirement years.
    (e) Both (b) and (d) are correct.

15. Which of the following is *not* true of Canadian benefit programs for the elderly?
    (a) RRSPs are a means of deferring taxes to the retirement years when one's marginal tax rate may be lower.
    (b) The Canada Pension Plan is only paid to individuals who contributed to it during their working lives.
    (c) Old Age Security is paid to all Canadians over 65 years of age with a tax clawback.
    (d) The Guaranteed Income Supplement is a demogrant paid to all Canadians over 65 years of age.
    (e) Both (c) and (d).

16. The argument that medical doctors induce patient demand for their own services is based on
    (a) a system of capitation payments.
    (b) a fee-for-service system.
    (c) the growing popularity of health maintenance organizations (HMOs).
    (d) intrinsic dishonesty on the part of many doctors.
    (e) the privatization of the health sector.

SOLUTIONS

Chapter Review

1.(c) 2.(c) 3.(c) 4.(a) 5.(e) 6.(e) 7.(c) 8.(b) 9.(d) 10.(b) 11.(e) 12.(e) 13.(d) 14.(e) 15.(c) 16.(e) 17.(e) 18.(b) 19.(b) 20.(d) 21.(e)

Exercises

1. (a) Tax A is proportional; tax B is regressive; tax C is progressive.
    (b) The tax rates are 22 percent for $10,000, 23 percent for $20,000, 24 percent for $40,000, and 25.3 percent for $60,000. The tax system is slightly progressive.

2. (a) **Figure 18-2**

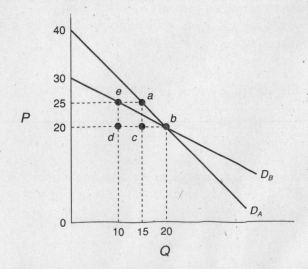

    (b) Recall from Chapter 4, $\eta = (1/\text{slope})(P/Q^D)$. Since these demand curves have the same quantity demanded at a price of $20, the difference in their elasticities is determined by their slopes. The demand curve for good A has the relatively steeper slope, so demand for it is more inelastic.

(c) As depicted in Figure 18-2, when a tax of $5 per unit is added to the $20 price of each good, quantity demanded of good A is reduced to 15 units while that for B is reduced to 10 units. The excess burden for goods A and B are area *abc* and area *bed*, respectively. The direct burdens are $75 and $50, respectively (i.e., the tax multiplied by quantity demanded).

(d) The excess burden for commodity B with the relatively more elastic demand is greater (B: (10)(5)/2 = $25, and A: (5)(5)/2 = $12.50).

3. (a) Column B: −$5,000; −$4,000; −$2,500; −$1,500; 0.
Column C: $5,000; $6,000; $7,500; $8,500; $10,000.

(b) Marginal tax rate $= \dfrac{\Delta T}{\Delta Y} = \dfrac{43 - 15}{40}$ *or* $\dfrac{35}{50} = 0.70$

4. (a) It is imposed on sales of $10,000 at the retail level. Thus total tax revenue is $700.

(b) Primary pays $70 = 0.07 × $1,000. Manufacturing pays $210 = (0.07 × $4,000) − $70. Wholesale pays $140 = (0.07 × $6,000) − $210 − $70. Finally, retail pays $280 = (0.07 × $10,000) − $140 − $210 − $70. Total tax revenue is $700 = $70 + $210 + $140 + $280.

(c) Value added at the primary stage is $1,000, so tax payments are $70. At the manufacturing stage, value added is $3,000 (= $4,000 − $1,000), so taxes here are $210. The value added of wholesalers is $2,000, implying a tax liability of $140. Finally, the value added of retailers is $4,000, so tax payments at the retail level are $280. The total is $700.

(d) There is no difference.

(e) Sales of manufactured goods are $4,000, and the government must collect $700 in tax revenue. Thus the required MST rate is 17.5 percent [($700/$4,000) × 100 percent].

Practice Multiple Choice Test

1.(b) 2.(c) 3.(c) 4.(a) 5.(c) 6.(d) 7.(c) 8.(d) 9.(a) 10.(a) 11.(b) 12.(e) 13.(e) 14.(b) 15.(d) 16.(b)

PART ELEVEN

INTERNATIONAL ECONOMICS

CHAPTER 34

THE GAINS FROM INTERNATIONAL TRADE

LEARNING OBJECTIVES

1 Understand why the gains from trade depend on comparative advantage and not on absolute advantage.

2 Explain the gains from trade due to economies of scale and learning by doing.

3 Understand how factor endowments and climate can influence a country's comparative advantage.

4 Explain the law of one price.

5 Explain why countries export some goods and import other goods.

6 Understand what is meant by a country's term of trade.

CHAPTER OVERVIEW

This chapter explains how international trade makes possible a higher average standard of living for a country. A country benefits from buying goods abroad at a lower cost. A country is said to have an **absolute advantage** in the production of a particular commodity when it can produce more of the good with a given amount of resources than can other countries. A country has a comparative advantage in producing a particular good when it has a lower opportunity cost in production than other countries. The **gains from trade** do not depend upon absolute advantage, but rather upon comparative advantage. Even if a country has an absolute advantage in the production of all goods, both trading partners can share in the gains from trade.

Comparative advantage can be attributed to differences in exogenous considerations such as factor endowments and climate. Today, there is widespread acceptance by economists that comparative advantage may also be acquired. International trade encourages countries to specialize production in the products where they have a comparative advantage as opposed to the costly product diversification associated with self-sufficiency. The gains from trade are likely to be even greater when countries can achieve economies of scale, or benefit from **learning-by-doing**.

When transportation costs are insignificant, a traded good will sell at the same price in all countries—this is the so-called *law of one price*. This price is referred to as the world price.

The division of the gains from trade between two countries depends upon the **terms of trade** which refers to the ratio of the price of exported goods to the price of imported goods. The terms of trade determine the quantity of imported goods that can be obtained per unit of exported good.

CHAPTER REVIEW

Sources of the Gains from Trade

After studying this section, you should recognize that international trade among countries involves basically the same principles of exchange that apply to trade among individuals. You will also learn that although gains from trade can occur even when production is fixed, further gains arise when nations specialize production in goods for which they have a comparative advantage. Comparative advantage arises from differences in production opportunity costs which are determined by factor endowments and climate but also by changing human skills and experience in production.

1. Country X has an absolute advantage over country Y in the production of widgets if
   (a) fewer resources are required in X to produce a given quantity of widgets than in Y.
   (b) a given amount of resources in X produces more widgets than the same amount of resources in Y.
   (c) relative to Y, more widgets can be produced in X with fewer resources.
   (d) All of the above.
   (e) None of the above.

2. If, given the same amount of inputs, Canadian farmers produce 2 tons of rice per acre while Japanese farmers produce 1 ton of rice per acre, we can be certain that
   (a) Canada should export rice to Japan.
   (b) Canada has a comparative advantage in rice production.
   (c) Canada has an absolute advantage in rice production.
   (d) Japanese rice farmers must be paid twice as much as Canadian farmers.
   (e) Both (a) and (b) are correct.

3. Comparative advantage is said to exist whenever
   (a) one country can produce a given level of output with fewer resources compared to another country.
   (b) a given amount of resources produces more output in one country compared to another.
   (c) one country has an absolute advantage over another country in the production of all goods.
   (d) different countries have different opportunity costs in production.
   (e) two countries are of different sizes.

4. If there are two countries A and B, and two goods X and Y, and if A has a comparative advantage in the production of X, it necessarily follows that
   (a) A has an absolute advantage in the production of X.
   (b) B has an absolute advantage in the production of X.
   (c) A has a comparative disadvantage in the production of Y.
   (d) B has an absolute advantage in the production of Y.
   (e) B has a comparative disadvantage in the production of Y.

5. Which of the following is *not* a source of comparative advantage?
   (a) Factor endowments.
   (b) Climate.
   (c) Country size.
   (d) Acquiring human capital.
   (e) None of the above.

6. Gains from specialization can arise when
   (a) countries have different opportunity costs in production.
   (b) there are economies of scale in production.
   (c) experience gained via specialization lowers cost through learning by doing.
   (d) trading partners have a different comparative advantage.
   (e) All of the above.

7. Free trade within the European Community led to
   (a) each member country specializing in specific products (e.g., furniture, cars, etc.).
   (b) a large increase in product differentiation, with countries tending to specialize in subproduct lines (e.g., office furniture, household furniture, etc.).
   (c) no perceptible alteration in production patterns.
   (d) less trade among EC members.
   (e) less product diversity.

8. Economies of scale and learning by doing are different because
   (a) one refers to an increase in variable costs and the other to a decrease.
   (b) economies of scale refer to a movement along the average cost curve, whereas learning by doing shifts the average cost curve.
   (c) economies of scale affect variable costs, but learning by doing affects only fixed costs.
   (d) learning by doing affects profits but not costs.
   (e) economies of scale affect costs, whereas learning by doing affects revenue.

9. According to the Hecksher-Ohlin theory,
   (a) resource-rich countries benefit the most from trade.
   (b) different opportunity costs across countries can be explained by differences in factor endowments.
   (c) different opportunity costs across countries can be explained by differences in production functions.
   (d) low wage countries gain the most from trade.
   (e) countries with similar opportunity costs can gain the most from trade.

10. The concept of dynamic comparative advantage is best characterized by
    (a) the importance of factor endowments in determining trade patterns.
    (b) changes in a country's terms of trade due to depletion of natural resources.
    (c) acquiring new areas of specialization through investment in human capital.
    (d) changes in a country's variable costs due to economies of scale.
    (e) Both (a) and (b) are correct.

The Determination of Trade Patterns

After reading this section you will understand the law of one price and its implications for a country's imports and exports. Make certain that you understand the relationship between a country's comparative advantage and its no trade price.

11. The *law of one price* refers to
    (a) the idea that international cartels will collude to charge a single price.
    (b) federal statutes that regulate firms to charge the same price domestically as internationally.
    (c) the idea that when transportation costs are insignificant, a product will tend to have the same price worldwide.
    (d) the international trade principle that export products cannot be subject to price discrimination.
    (e) None of the above.

12. A single world price of oil is likely to exist if
    (a) oil can be transported easily from one country to another.
    (b) each country produces all of its domestic consumption.
    (c) all governments restrict exports of oil.
    (d) demand is the same in all countries.
    (e) the cost of producing oil is the same in each country.

13. Canada is a major exporter of nickel because at the world price
    (a) Canadian quantity demanded exceeds Canadian quantity supplied.
    (b) Canadian quantity supplied exceeds Canadian quantity demanded.
    (c) the quantity of nickel demanded by Canadians exceeds domestic production.
    (d) Canada mines more nickel than any other country.
    (e) domestic consumption and production are the same as they would be in the "no trade" equilibrium.

The Terms of Trade

After studying this section you should be able to explain that the terms of trade, defined as the ratio of export prices to import prices, indicate how the gains from trade are divided between buyers and sellers. You will also be able to distinguish an improvement in the terms of trade from a deterioration.

14. The terms of trade
    (a) refer to the quantity of imported goods that can be obtained for each unit of an exported good.
    (b) are measured by the ratio of the price of exports to the price of imports.
    (c) determine the division of the gains from trade.
    (d) All of the above.
    (e) None of the above.

15. A rise in export prices as compared to import prices is considered a favourable change in the terms of trade since
    (a) one can export more per unit of imported goods.
    (b) employment in export industries will increase.
    (c) one can acquire more imports per unit of exports.
    (d) total exports will increase.
    (e) All of the above.

EXERCISES

1. Comparative and Absolute Advantage

This exercise provides basic production data and requires you to calculate the opportunity cost of production. It then draws out the distinction between absolute and comparative advantage and the implications for trade.

For each of the following scenarios, determine the opportunity costs of producing each good in each country, and indicate in which commodity each country should specialize its trade production.

(a) One unit of resources can produce:

The opportunity costs are:

	Radios	Cameras		1 Radio	1 Camera
Japan	2	4	Japan	_____	_____
Korea	3	1	Korea	_____	_____

Japan should specialize in the production of _____.

Korea should specialize in the production of _____.

(b) One unit of resources can produce:

The opportunity costs are:

	Radios	Cameras		1 Radio	1 Camera
Japan	2	4	Japan	_____	_____
Korea	1	3	Korea	_____	_____

Japan should specialize in the production of _____.

Korea should specialize in the production of _____.

(c) One unit of resources can produce:

The opportunity costs are:

	Radios	Cameras		1 Radio	1 Camera
Japan	2	4	Japan	_____	_____
Korea	1	2	Korea	_____	_____

Japan should specialize in the production of _____.

Korea should specialize in the production of _____.

(d) Which scenario represents reciprocal absolute advantage?

(e) Which scenario demonstrates that absolute advantage is not a sufficient condition for trade to occur? Explain.

(f) Which scenario suggests why a nation as technologically advanced as Japan can gain from trading with other countries with lower wages? Explain.

2. Countries *A* and *B* each currently produce both watches and dairy products. Assume that country *A* gives up the opportunity to produce 100 litres of dairy products for each watch it makes, and *B* could produce one watch at a cost of 200 litres of dairy products.

(a) The opportunity cost of making watches (in terms of dairy products) is lower in country _____.

(b) The opportunity cost of making dairy products (in terms of watches) is lower in country _____.

(c) Country *B* should specialize in _____ and let country *A* produce _____.

(d) The terms of trade (the price of one product in terms of the other) would be somewhere between _____ and _____ litres of dairy products for one watch.

3. **The Terms of Trade**

The following table provides (hypothetical) data on the index of merchandise export prices and the index of merchandise import prices during the 1990s in Canada.

Year	Index of Export Prices	Index of Import Prices	Terms of Trade
1990	100.6	98.6	_____
1992	103.3	102.3	_____
1994	157.1	135.6	_____
1996	176.6	157.9	_____
1998	205.4	200.7	_____

(a) Using the definition of the terms of trade that involves indexes, complete the table by calculating the terms of trade to one decimal place.

(b) What does an increase in the terms of trade signify?

(c) Would you classify the change in the terms of trade during the period 1992 to 1994 as favourable to Canada? Explain.

4. **The Production Possibility Curve and Trade**

The following table provides data on the productivity of a single unit of resource in producing wheat and microchips in both Canada and Japan.

	One Unit of Resources Produces	
	Wheat (tons)	Microchips
Canada	50	20
Japan	2	12

(a) Which country has an absolute advantage in the production of wheat? Of microchips?

(b) What is the opportunity cost of producing a ton of wheat in Canada? In Japan?

(c) Which country has a comparative advantage in the production of wheat? Of microchips?

(d) Suppose that Canada is endowed with 2 units of this all-purpose resource while Japan is endowed with 10 units. Draw each country's production possibility boundary on the following grids. (Assume constant productivity).

Figure 34-1

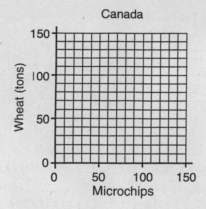

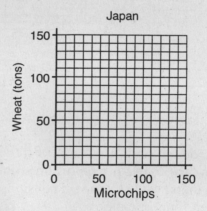

(e) Suppose that prior to trade, each country allocated half of its resource endowment to production of each good. Indicate the production and consumption points of each country in the graphs (for simplicity, assume that these are the only two countries in the world).

(f) What is world output of each good?

(g) Indicate the production points of each country after trade, and determine world production levels.

(h) Suppose that the terms of trade are one microchip for one ton of wheat and that Canada consumes as much wheat after trade as it did before trade. Indicate the post-trade consumption points of each country and each country's imports and exports.

(i) If the terms of trade changed to two microchips for one ton of wheat, which country would benefit? Explain.

5. **Imports and Exports**

Figure 34-2 depicts Canadian domestic supply and demand curves, S_c and D_c, respectively, for a commodity in a market for which Canada is assumed to face a fixed world price.

Figure 34-2

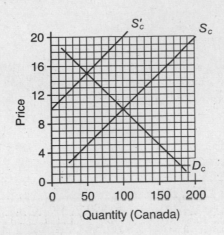

(a) At a world price of $5, Canadian producers sell _____ units, while Canadian consumers purchase _____ units. Canada therefore (imports/exports) _____ units of this commodity.

(b) Suppose a tariff of $2 per unit is imposed. Canadian production would change to _____ units, while Canadian consumption would change to _____ units. Canada would then (import/export) _____ units. The government's tariff revenue would be _____. Revenue of domestic producers would (increase/decrease) by _____, while expenditure of domestic consumers would (increase/decrease) by _____.

(c) If the world price increased from $5 to $12 per unit (assuming there were no tariff), Canadians would consume _____ units but produce _____ units. Thus Canada would (import/export) _____ units.

(d) Should domestic supply shift to S'_c while the world price remains at $12, domestic production would now be _____ units and domestic consumption _____ units. Canada would therefore be an (importer/exporter) of _____ units.

EXTENSION EXERCISES

E-1.   The following exercise examines the tendency towards specialization with trade when production is characterized by increasing opportunity costs (i.e., production possibility curve is concave). A review of Extensions in Theory 34-1 entitled *The Gains From Trade More Generally* will help you answer this exercise (see pages 828–9 of the text).

The graph in Figure 34-3 depicts a country's production possibility curve between wool and lumber. Prior to trade, the country is producing and consuming at point R, which involves 10 units of wool and 10 units of lumber. Due to large increases in construction activity in this economy, the country now decides that it wishes to consume 14 units of lumber.

Figure 34-3

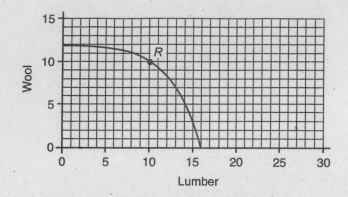

(a) How much wool must this country give up to obtain the additional four units of lumber in a no-trade environment. Explain.

(b) Suppose that the terms of trade in international markets are one unit of wool for two units of lumber. Assuming that production remains at R, how much wool would the country have to give up to obtain the additional four units of lumber if it engages in international trade? Explain.

E-2. This exercise addresses the efficiency gain from free trade by measuring the impact on consumer and producer surplus in moving from a no-trade situation to free trade for an imported good in part (a) and an exported good in part (b) (the same analysis can be applied to the removal or reduction of tariffs).

In what follows, assume that Canadian demand is a small part of world demand so that the world price P_W is independent of both Canadian demand D_C and supply S_C. Thus foreign supply is perfectly elastic at P_W. In the no-trade situation, the equilibrium price and quantity are P_E and Q_E.

(a) In Figure 34-4, P_W is less than P_E, so trade will result in imports of this good.

Figure 34-4

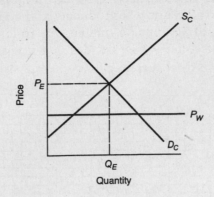

Once trade is permitted,
  (i)   label domestic consumption D_D.
  (ii) label domestic production S_D.
  (iii) What is the change in consumer surplus in Canada?

  (iv) What is the change in producer surplus of Canadian firms?

  (v)   Is the net change in total surplus for Canada positive or negative? And, how
        much is it?

(b) In Figure 34-5, P_W is greater than P_E, so trade will result in exports of this commodity.

Figure 34-5

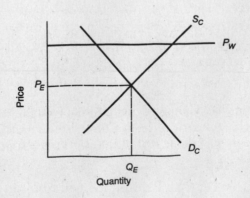

Once trade is permitted,
  (i)   label domestic consumption D_D.
  (ii) label domestic production S_D.
  (iii) What is the change in consumer surplus in Canada?

(iv) What is the change in producer surplus of Canadian firms?

(v) Is the net change in total surplus for Canada positive or negative? And, how much is it?

PRACTICE MULTIPLE-CHOICE TEST

1. In a two-country and two-good model, gains from trade would not exist if
   (a) one country had an absolute advantage in the production of both goods.
   (b) a given amount of resources produced more of both goods in one country.
   (c) one country was endowed with far more resources than the other.
   (d) the countries had the same opportunity costs in the production of both goods.
   (e) only one country had a comparative advantage in the production of one good.

2. Which of the following statements is not true about opportunity cost?
   (a) Equal opportunity costs for pairs of commodities between two countries lead to gains from trade.
   (b) Opportunity costs depend on relative production costs.
   (c) Differences in opportunity costs across countries can enhance total output of both goods through trade and specialization.
   (d) Comparative advantage can be expressed in terms of opportunity costs.
   (e) Opportunity cost can be read as the slope of a tangent to a country's production possibility curve.

3. If production of each unit of wool in country A implies that beef production must be decreased by four units, while in country B each additional unit of beef decreases wool output by four units, the gains from trade
   (a) are maximized if country A specializes in wool production and country B in beef.
   (b) are maximized if country A specializes in beef production and country B in wool.
   (c) are maximized if country A allocates 80 percent of its resources to wool and the remainder to beef, while country B does the opposite.
   (d) are maximized if country A allocates 20 percent of its resources to wool and the remainder to beef, while country B does the opposite.
   (e) cannot be realized because opportunity costs in the two countries are the same.

4. The gains from specialization and trade depend on the pattern of _____ advantage, not _____ advantage.
   (a) absolute, comparative.
   (b) monetary, nonmonetary.
   (c) absolute, reciprocal.
   (d) comparative, absolute.
   (e) size, cost.

5. By trading in international markets, countries
   (a) can consume beyond their production possibility boundary.
   (b) will always produce the same commodity bundle as before trade.
   (c) can produce outside of their production possibility boundary.
   (d) must choose one of the intercepts on the production possibility boundary, indicating complete specialization.
   (e) always produce and consume the same bundle of commodities.

Questions 6 to 9 refer to the data in the following table. You will find it useful to first calculate the opportunity costs of production for each commodity in each country.

| | One Unit of Resource Can Produce | |
Country	Lumber (bd m)	Aluminum (kg)
Australia	4	9
Canada	9	3
Brazil	3	2

6. Considering just Australia and Canada,
   (a) Australia has an absolute advantage in lumber.
   (b) Australia has an absolute advantage in aluminum.
   (c) There are no possible gains from trade.
   (d) Canada should specialize in aluminum production.
   (e) Australia has a comparative advantage in lumber.

7. Considering just Canada and Brazil,
   (a) Brazil has an absolute advantage in lumber.
   (b) Brazil has a comparative advantage in aluminum.
   (c) Canada has an absolute advantage in only one commodity.
   (d) There are no possible gains from trade.
   (e) None of the above.

8. In Australia, the opportunity cost of 1 board metre (bd m) of lumber is
   (a) 2.25 kg of aluminum.   (b) 0.44 kg of aluminum.
   (c) 0.36 kg of aluminum.   (d) 3.60 kg of aluminum.
   (e) 3.00 kg of aluminum.

9. In Canada, the opportunity cost of 1 kilogram of aluminum is
   (a) 0.33 bd m of lumber.   (b) 2.70 bd m of lumber.
   (c) 3.0 bd m of lumber.   (d) 3.33 bd m of lumber.
   (e) 1.50 bd m of lumber.

10. For a country with one important export commodity such as coffee or oil,
   (a) a rise in the commodity's price will improve the country's terms of trade.
   (b) a fall in the commodity's price is a favourable change in its terms of trade.
   (c) its terms of trade will improve only if it is able to increase the quantity of exports.
   (d) its terms of trade will improve only if world demand for its exports is inelastic.
   (e) its terms of trade improve only if the price of imports decrease.

Use the following diagram to answer questions 11 and 12.

Figure 34-6

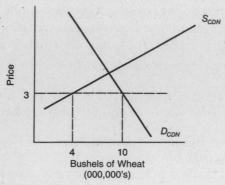

Bushels of Wheat
(000,000's)

11. At a world price of $3, Canada will
    (a) produce 4 million bushels of wheat.
    (b) consume 10 million bushels of wheat.
    (c) import 6 million bushels of wheat.
    (d) consume more wheat than it produces.
    (e) All of the above are correct.

12. If the world price remains at $3, while the Canadian demand for wheat increases, the primary result would be
    (a) an increase in Canadian production of wheat.
    (b) an increase in the price of wheat in Canada.
    (c) a decrease in wheat exports.
    (d) an increase in wheat imports.
    (e) a decrease in quantity supplied by Canadian producers.

SOLUTIONS

Chapter Review

1.(d) 2.(c) 3.(d) 4.(c) 5.(c) 6.(e) 7.(b) 8.(b) 9.(b) 10.(c) 11.(c) 12.(a) 13.(b) 14.(d) 15.(c)

Exercises

1. (a) Japan: 1 radio costs 2 cameras; 1 camera costs 1/2 radio.
        Korea: 1 radio costs 1/3 camera; 1 camera costs 3 radios.
        Japan should produce cameras. Korea should produce radios.
    (b) Japan: 1 radio costs 2 cameras; 1 camera costs 1/2 radio.
        Korea: 1 radio costs 3 cameras; 1 camera costs 1/3 radio.
        Japan should produce radios. Korea should produce cameras.
    (c) Japan: 1 radio costs 2 cameras; 1 camera costs 1/2 radio.
        Korea: 1 radio costs 2 cameras; 1 camera costs 1/2 radio.
        Japan should produce both and Korea should produce both. There would be no gains from trade.
    (d) Case (a) represents reciprocal absolute advantage; Japan has an absolute advantage in cameras, and Korea has an absolute advantage in radios.

(e) Case (c) shows that even though Japan has an absolute advantage in producing both goods, no trade will occur because relative prices (or opportunity costs of production) are identical to those in Korea.

(f) Case (b) shows that even though Japanese workers are more productive in both industries (and therefore can expect to earn more than Korean workers), mutually beneficial trade can still occur if each country exports the good for which it has a comparative advantage.

2. (a) *A.*
   (b) *B.*
   (c) dairy products, watches.
   (d) 100, 200.

3. (a) 102.0, 101.0, 115.9, 111.8, 102.3.
   (b) An increase in the terms of trade means that fewer exports are required to pay for a given amount of imports.
   (c) The terms of trade changed from 101.0 to 115.6; this was a favourable change in our terms of trade. It cost us fewer exports to buy the same imports, or for the same exports we received more imports.

4. (a) Canada has an absolute advantage in both goods.
   (b) 0.4, 6.0.
   (c) Canada, Japan.
   (d) **Figure 34-7**

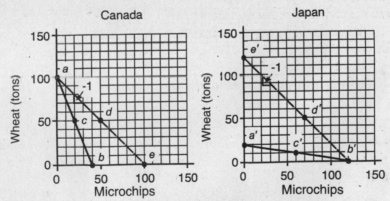

Canada's production possibility boundary is denoted *ab*, and Japan's is *a′b′*.

(e) Canada would be producing and consuming 50 tons of wheat and 20 microchips (point *c* in the diagram), and Japan would be producing and consuming 10 tons of wheat and 60 microchips (point *c′*).

(f) Assuming that these are the only countries making up the world, total output of wheat is 60 tons and world production of microchips is 80 units.

(g) Each country specializes in the commodity in which it has a comparative advantage. Thus Canada specializes completely in wheat production (see point *a*), and Japan specializes completely in microchip production (see point *b′*). World output is now 100 tons of wheat and 120 microchips.

(h) Terms of trade equal to one ton of wheat for one microchip mean that Canada can trade from its production point *a* to any point on its consumption possibility curve *ae* which has a slope of −1, representing the terms of trade. Similarly, Japan can trade from point *b′* to any point on its consumption possibility curve *b′e′*. Since it was assumed that Canada consumes the same amount of wheat both before and after trade, its consumption bundle is represented by point *d*, which contains 50 units of each good. Therefore,

Canada is exporting 50 tons of wheat in return for imports of 50 microchips. Japan, having exported 50 microchips to Canada, has 70 remaining for its own consumption. When this is combined with its 50 tons of wheat imports, Japan consumes at point d'.

(i) The terms of trade lines in the graphs would become flatter with a slope of $-1/2$. Thus Canada's consumption possibilities would increase (the dashed line rotates outward on point a), while Japan's decrease (the dashed line rotates inward on point b'). Thus Canada would get a larger share of the gains from trade.

6. (a) 50; 150; imports; 100.
    (b) 70; 130; import; 60; $120; increase; $240; increase; $160.
    (c) 80; 120; exports; 40.
    (d) 20; 80; importer; 60.

Extension Exercises

E-1.   Five units. This requires a movement along the production possibility boundary from point R to point A on the following graph.

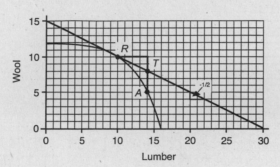

Figure 34-8

(b)   Two units. The terms of trade line has a slope of $-1/2$ and is tangent to the production possibility curve at R. Thus the economy can export two units of wool in return for imports of four units of lumber; this is represented by a movement from point R to point T on the graph.

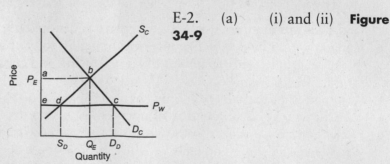

E-2.   (a)   (i) and (ii)   **Figure 34-9**

(iii)   Canadian consumer surplus increases by area $abce$.
(iv)   Canadian producer surplus decreases by area $abde$.
(v)   Positive. The increase in consumer surplus outweighs the loss in producer surplus; Canada receives a net gain in efficiency equal to area bcd.

(b) (i) and (ii) **Figure 34-10**

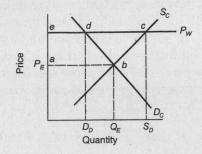

(iii) Canadian consumer surplus decreases by area *abde*.
(iv) Canadian producer surplus increases by area *abce*.
(v) Positive. The increase in producer surplus outweighs the loss in consumers surplus; Canada receives a net gain in efficiency equal to area *bcd*.

Practice Multiple Choice Test

1.(d) 2.(a) 3.(b) 4.(d) 5.(a) 6.(b) 7.(b) 8.(a) 9.(c) 10.(a) 11.(e) 12.(d)

CHAPTER 35

TRADE POLICY

LEARNING OBJECTIVES

1 Understand the various situations in which a country may rationally choose to protect some industries.

2 Recognize the most common fallacious arguments in favour of protection.

3 Explain the effects of placing a tariff or a quantity restriction on an imported good.

4 Recognize that trade-remedy laws are sometimes just thinly disguised protection.

5 Explain the difference between trade creation and trade diversion.

6 Know the main features of the North American Free Trade Agreement.

CHAPTER OVERVIEW

This chapter examines the ways in which a government may intervene in markets to restrict international trade and the resulting consequences. **Protectionist trade policy** usually takes one of two forms: **tariffs** that serve to raise import prices, and **nontariff barriers**—such as **import quotas** or **voluntary export restrictions**—that serve to reduce import quantities.

Free trade maximizes world output and living standards. Arguments for protection may rest on objectives other than maximizing living standards such as reducing fluctuations in national income or economic diversification. Protectionism may also be advanced by a large country as a means of gaining a favourable improvement in the terms of trade, and thereby increase national income. Several fallacious but widely employed arguments for protection are also discussed.

Since its inception in 1947, The General Agreement on Trade and Tariffs (GATT) has served to substantially reduce tariffs through a series of multilateral negotiations. The most recent set of negotiations, the Uruguay Round, concluded an agreement in several important areas that will serve to promote more liberal trade. It also saw the replacement of the GATT with the World Trade Organization (WTO).

Recently, there has been a sharp increase in the number and extent of regional trade-liberalizing agreements such as **free trade areas** and **common markets**. The North American Free Trade Agreement (NAFTA) is the world's largest and most successful free trade area and the European Union is the world's largest and most successful common market. These regional agreements bring about efficiency gains through **trade creation**, but may also lead to efficiency losses from **trade diversion**.

CHAPTER REVIEW

Free Trade or Protection?

After reading this section, you should be able to discuss the benefits and costs of expanding international trade; understand how tariffs and quotas influence trade patterns and affect a nation's standard of living; and, recognize fallacious arguments for protection.

1. Which of the following statements is *not* true of free trade?
   (a) Free trade leads to a maximization of world output.
   (b) Free trade maximizes world living standards.
   (c) Free trade always makes each individual better off.
   (d) Free trade can increase the average income in a country.
   (e) Free trade encourages countries to specialize in production.

2. The infant industry argument for tariffs is
   (a) only appropriate for industries where there are no economies of scale.
   (b) an example of dynamic comparative advantage.
   (c) theoretically valid if a new producer can sufficiently reduce average costs as output increases.
   (d) a proposal to earmark tariff revenues to finance day care facilities.
   (e) most applicable in developing countries because of their relative abundance of labour.

3. Protection against low-wage foreign labour is a fallacious protectionist argument because
   (a) free trade benefits everyone.
   (b) the gains from trade depend on comparative, not absolute, advantage.
   (c) when the foreign country increases its exports to us, their wages will rise.
   (d) the terms of trade will equalize for low and high-wage countries.
   (e) low-wage labourers are necessarily less productive.

4. If the objective of a government is to maximize national income, which of the following is the *least* valid reason for using tariff protection?
   (a) To protect against unfair subsidization of foreign firms by their governments.
   (b) To protect against unfair low wages paid to foreign labour.
   (c) To protect newly developing industries.
   (d) To protect against dumping of foreign produced goods.
   (e) To alter the terms of trade.

5. Strategic trade policy
   (a) involves government assistance for key growth industries by protecting domestic markets and/or providing subsidies.
   (b) involves erecting higher tariff and nontariff barriers across the board to protect domestic industry.
   (c) means that the government negotiates special trade agreements with its important defence partners.
   (d) is designed to encourage the migration of certain industries to other countries to better exploit domestic comparative advantage.
   (e) attempts to encourage investment for domestic production in those markets that a country currently imports.

6. Which of the following is *not* a fallacious protectionist argument?
   (a) Buy Canadian, and both the money and the goods stay at home.
   (b) Trade cannot be mutually advantageous if one of the trading partners is much larger than the other.
   (c) Too many imports lower Canadian living standards as our money is shipped abroad.
   (d) A foreign firm, temporarily selling in Canada at a much lower price than in its own country, threatens the Canadian industry's existence.
   (e) A high wage country such as Canada cannot effectively compete with a low wage country such as Mexico.

Methods of Protection

This section discusses protectionist trade policies that directly raise the price of imports or directly reduce the quantity of imports. It also provides a review of the various trade policy remedies and procedures available in major trading countries.

7. Countervailing duties are attempts to maintain "a level playing ground" by
   (a) retaliating against foreign tariffs.
   (b) raising or lowering tariffs multilaterally.
   (c) establishing a common tariff wall around a customs union.
   (d) assessing tariffs that will offset foreign government subsidies.
   (e) subsidizing exports.

8. Which of the following statements about nontariff barriers to trade (NTBs) is *incorrect*?
   (a) The use of NTBs has been declining worldwide for the last 50 years.
   (b) The misuse of antidumping and countervailing duties unilaterally constitutes an increasingly important NTB.
   (c) Voluntary export restraints, negotiated agreements, and quotas are examples of NTBs.
   (d) Most NTBs are ostensibly levied for trade relief purposes but end up being protectionist.
   (e) Environmental and labour standards can be used as disguised NTB's.

9. Which of the following motivations for dumping can be of permanent benefit to the buying country?
   (a) Predatory pricing.
   (b) Cyclical stabilization of sales.
   (c) Enabling foreign producers to achieve lower average costs and therefore price.
   (d) Altering the terms of trade.
   (e) All of the above.

Current Trade Policy

After reading this section you will have a better appreciation of the issues in multilateral, regional, and bilateral trade negotiations, and be able to discuss the important highlights of the NAFTA and its impact on the Canadian economy.

10. Which of the following is an example of trade diversion?
    (a) A government promotes diversification of a country's industries.
    (b) Liberalized trade encourages industries to specialize in subproduct lines.
    (c) The NAFTA encourages more trade between low and high wage countries.
    (d) The NAFTA encourages Canada to switch imports from low wage nonmember countries to Mexico.
    (e) Publicized trade disputes divert attention from the gains from trade.

11. A common market includes all but which of the following?
    (a) tariff-free trade among members.
    (b) a common trade policy with the rest of the world.
    (c) rules of origin.
    (d) free movement of labour.
    (e) free movement of capital.

12. The countries in a free trade area
    (a) impose no tariffs on each other's goods.
    (b) each have an independent tariff structure with the rest of the world.
    (c) do not permit the free movement of labour across their borders.
    (d) do not have a common monetary policy.
    (e) All of the above.

13. Which of the following was *not* one of the features of the NAFTA?
    (a) "Sunset" elimination of all tariffs within 15 years.
    (b) Elimination of countervailing duties between the two countries.
    (c) Exemption of cultural industries.
    (d) Continuance of quotas to support provincial supply management schemes.
    (e) Provision for national treatment for most service industries.

14. Which of the following was *not* an outcome of the Uruguay Round of GATT negotiations?
    (a) Major trade liberalization in agriculture.
    (b) Repacement of the GATT with the World Trade Organization (WTO).
    (c) A new dispute settlement mechanism.
    (d) Reduction in world tariffs by approximately 40 percent.
    (e) All of the above.

EXERCISES

1. **Import Quotas and Tariffs**

    (a) The three graphs in Figure 35-1 illustrate the demand and supply of an imported commodity Z in a free trade environment. Revise these graphs according to the protectionist policy outlined below each panel, and indicate the new price P^* and the new quantity as Q^*.

    Figure 35-1

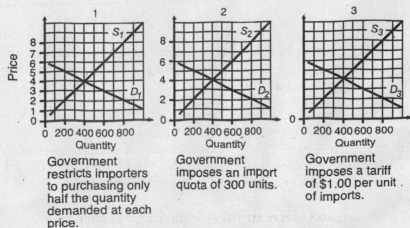

Government restricts importers to purchasing only half the quantity demanded at each price.

Government imposes an import quota of 300 units.

Government imposes a tariff of $1.00 per unit of imports.

(b) Instead of the above graphs, suppose the demand for Z were highly inelastic. Which policy would the government be least likely to choose if it wanted to minimize imports? Why?

2. Tariffs and Quotas, Again

The hypothetical market for canned tuna is described in Figure 35-2, where the foreign supply curve (S_f) is drawn as perfectly elastic (i.e., horizontal) and the domestic demand and supply curves are denoted D_C and S_C, respectively.

Figure 35-2

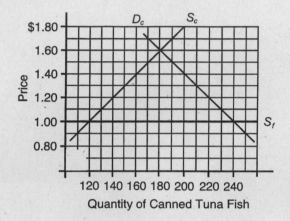

Quantity of Canned Tuna Fish

(a) Under free trade, what is the quantity of tuna consumed in Canada, the quantity supplied by Canadian producers, and the quantity supplied by foreign producers to Canadian consumers?

(b) If a 20 percent tariff is imposed, by how much does the foreign supply curve shift upward? Draw the new foreign supply curve, and calculate the consequent changes in domestic consumption, domestic production, and imports. Why is the change in imports greater than the change in domestic production?

(c) If the government wants to ensure that domestic production rises to 160, how large a quota for imported tuna should it allow? Explain.

3. Tariffs, Quotas and Revenue

The demand and supply curves for an imported good in a market where Canada does not have any domestic production are presented in Figure 35-3. D_C represents demand in Canada, and S_f represents foreign supply.

Figure 35-3

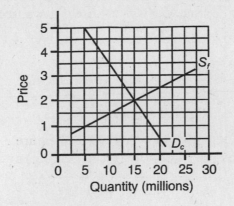

(a) What are equilibrium price and quantity and the total revenue of foreign firms?

(b) Suppose that the government imposes a specific tariff on this commodity equal to $2 per unit. What are the resulting equilibrium price Canadian consumers pay and the quantity they import? Illustrate this on the graph.

(c) What are the revenues of foreign firms and the Canadian government?

(d) Instead of the tariff, suppose that the Canadian government imposed an import quota on this good equal to 10 million units. What is the new supply curve that Canadian consumers effectively face?

(e) What would be the resulting market price and revenue of both foreign firms and the government under the quota scheme?

4. **Improving the Terms of Trade**

Suppose a country constitutes a significant proportion of world demand for widgets—for simplicity, we shall assume its represents all of world demand. Production, however, takes place by both domestic and foreign firms. The domestic supply curve of widgets is denoted S_D in Figure 35-4, and the foreign supply curve as S_F. The domestic (and, by assumption, world) demand curve is denoted D.

(a) Draw the total (i.e., world) supply curve for widgets. (*Hint:* world supply is the horizontal summation of domestic and foreign supply curves)

Figure 35-4

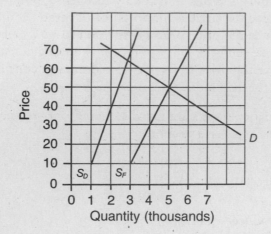

(b) Determine the world price of widgets. What is the level of domestic consumption, imports and domestic production?

(c) The domestic government seeks to improve its terms of trade by imposing a tariff on imports of widgets. Suppose it levies a tariff of $20 per imported widget. Using a broken line, draw the after-tariff supply curve for foreigner firms and the new world supply curve. What are the new price and quantity? Label them P_1 and Q_1, respectively.

(d) What effect has the tariff had on the price received by foreign firms?

(e) What effect has the tariff had on imports and domestic production?

PRACTICE MULTIPLE CHOICE TEST

1. Which of the following trade practices is *not* specifically designed as a device to promote protectionism?
   (a) Tariffs.   (b) Voluntary export restrictions.
   (c) Countervailing duties. (d) Import quotas.
   (e) Costly customs procedures.

2. Which of the following national objectives is a valid argument for some degree of protectionism?
   (a) Concentration of national resources in a few specialized products.
   (b) Increases in average incomes.
   (c) Diversification of a small economy in order to reduce the risk associated with cyclical fluctuations in price.
   (d) Ability of domestic firms to operate at minimum efficient scale.
   (e) Maximization of the national standard of living.

3. A country may favourably alter its terms of trade by restricting domestic
   (a) demand and thereby reduce the price of imports for domestic consumers.
   (b) demand and thereby reduce the price of imports received by foreign producers.
   (c) supply and thereby reduce the price of imports for domestic consumers..
   (d) supply and thereby reduce the price of imports for domestic consumers.
   (e) demand and supply and thereby reduce imports.

4. _____ serve to raise a country's standard of living only to the extent that they raise national income to permit the purchase of more _____.
   (a) Tariffs; imports.
   (b) Exports; imports.
   (c) Imports; strategic subsidies.
   (d) Imports; non-traded goods.
   (e) Exports; domestically produced goods.

5. A large country, accounting for a significant share of world demand for an imported product, can increase its national income by
   (a) encouraging domestic production.
   (b) restricting domestic demand for the product, thereby decreasing its price and improving the terms of trade.
   (c) imposing import quotas on the product.
   (d) subsidizing imports of the good and thereby monopolize world consumption.
   (e) negotiating voluntary export restrictions.

6. The problem with restricting imports as a means of reducing domestic unemployment is that
   (a) it merely redistributes unemployment from import-competing industries to our export industries when trading partners retaliate.
   (b) Canadians would rather do without than have to buy Canadian-produced goods.
   (c) Our import-competing industries are not labour-intensive.
   (d) Our import-competing industries are always fully employed.
   (e) Both (c) and (d) are correct.

7. A central difference in the effects of a tariff and a voluntary export restriction (VER)—set at the same quantity as under the tariff—is that
   (a) the VER yields a higher price for consumers than the tariff.
   (b) the tariff pushes the consumer price beyond the price associated with the VER.
   (c) government tariff revenue becomes suppliers' revenue with a VER.
   (d) as the quantity sold decreases under the VER, the revenue of producers decreases.
   (e) Both (a) and (c) are correct.

8. Opponents of strategic trade policy have argued that
   (a) it is nothing more than a modern version of old justifications for protection.
   (b) governments are not necessarily good at picking winners.
   (c) it is best to let other countries engage in export subsidization.
   (d) All of the above.
   (e) None of the above.

9. Which of the following is *not* true of the EU's Common Agricultural Policy (CAP)?
   (a) The CAP has led to agricultural surpluses in the EU.
   (b) The CAP has turned the EU from a net importer of many agricultural products to self-sufficiency.
   (c) The CAP leads the EU to heavily subsidize its agricultural exports.
   (d) The CAP benefits agricultural producers in less developed countries.
   (e) Quotas that support the CAP are being replaced with tariff equivalents.

10. The principle of national treatment that is embedded in the NAFTA means that Canada could, for example, introduce any product standards it likes, so long as
    (a) they apply only to Canadian-produced goods.
    (b) the standards are no more stringent than those existing in either Mexico or the United States.
    (c) they apply equally to Canadian-, Mexican-, and American-produced goods sold in Canada.
    (d) they apply only to Canadian exports.
    (e) they apply only to Canadian imports.

11. A major effect of a tariff is to
    (a) redistribute income from consumers to domestic producers and the government.
    (b) allow consumers to benefit at the expense of domestic producers.
    (c) discourage domestic production.
    (d) encourage consumers to buy more of the good.
    (e) reduce government revenues.

12. A free trade agreement
    (a) must include rules of origin.
    (b) eliminates the need for customs controls on the movement of goods.
    (c) allows for free cross-border movement of labour.
    (d) erects a common tariff wall against nonmember countries.
    (e) Both (a) and (d) are correct.

13. Which of the following is *not* a feature of the NAFTA?
    (a) A common regime for antidumping and countervailing duties.
    (b) The principle of national treatment.
    (c) A dispute-settlement mechanism.
    (d) Accession clause whereby other countries may join.
    (e) Reduction in the barriers to trade in both goods and services among member countries.

Questions 14 to 17 refer to Figure 35-5 which gives the domestic demand and supply curves for a commodity as well as the world price.

Figure 35-5

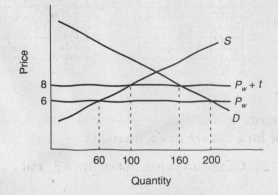

14. At a world price of $6, imports of this commodity are
    (a) 200.
    (b) 160.
    (c) 140.
    (d) 60.
    (e) 40.

15. If a tariff of $2 is levied against imports of this commodity, domestic consumption and production would be
    (a) 200 and 60, respectively.
    (b) 160 and 60, respectively.
    (c) 200 and 100, respectively.
    (d) 160 and 100, respectively.
    (e) 160 and 40, respectively.

16. Given a tariff of $2, government tariff revenue would be
    (a) $120.
    (b) $320.
    (c) $200.
    (d) $1280.
    (e) $800.

17. The tariff has _____ imports of this commodity by _____ units.
    (a) reduced; 80.
    (b) reduced; 40.
    (c) reduced; 100.
    (d) increased; 40.
    (e) increased; 60.

SOLUTIONS

Chapter Review

1.(c) 2.(c) 3.(b) 4.(b) 5.(a) 6.(d) 7.(d) 8.(a) 9.(c) 10.(d) 11.(c) 12.(e) 13.(b) 14.(a)

Exercises

1. (a) **Figure 35-6**

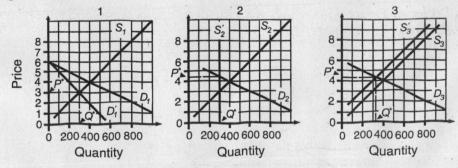

   (b) It would not choose the tariff policy. Price would rise by almost the full amount of the tariff, and there would be little change in equilibrium quantity.

2. (a) Canadian production is 120, Canadian consumption is 240, and imports are 120.

(b) The foreign supply curve shifts upward by 20 cents. Domestic production rises by 20, domestic consumption falls by 20, and imports fall by 40. Imports fall by more than domestic production rises due to the decline in total quantity demanded.

(c) At a price of $1.40, domestic production rises to 160, and domestic consumption falls to 200. The government can allow imports of 40 if this is to be an equilibrium position.

3. (a) $2, 15 million units, and $30 million, respectively.
   (b) $3.50 and 10 million units, respectively.

Figure 35-7

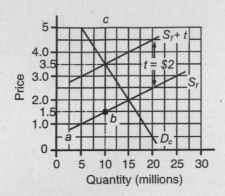

(c) Canadian consumers pay $3.50 per unit, of which $2 goes to the government. Therefore, government tariff revenue is $20 million and that of foreign firms is $15 million.

(d) The new effective supply curve is labelled *abc* in the graph.

(e) The price per unit is $3.50, revenue of foreign firms equals $35 million, and, since there is no tariff, government revenue is zero.

4. (a) and (c) **Figure 35-8**

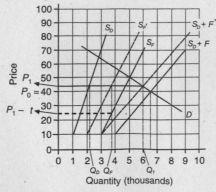

(b) The world price is $40 and denoted P_0 in the above diagram. Approximately 6,500 widgets are consumed, of which 4,500 are imported and 2,000 are produced domestically.

(c) The new price and quantity are approximately $44 and 3.75 thousand units, respectively. They are labelled P_1 and Q_1 above.

(d) The price received by foreign firms is now approximately $24 (i.e., $44 minus the $20 tariff). So the price received by foreign firms is reduced from $40 to $24 (approximately).

(e) The tariff forces a reduction in the quantity supplied by foreign producers (i.e., imports) to Q_F and an increase in the quantity supplied by domestic producers to Q_D.

Practice Multiple Choice Test

1.(c) 2.(c) 3.(b) 4.(b) 5.(b) 6.(a) 7.(c) 8.(d) 9.(d) 10.(c) 11.(a) 12.(a) 13.(a) 14.(c) 15.(d) 16.(a) 17.(a)